*scitis enim gratiam Domini nostri Iesu Christi, quoniam
propter vos egenus factus est, cum esset dives, ut illius
inopia vos divites essetis*

"For you know the grace of our Lord Jesus Christ, in that,
although he was rich, for your sakes he became poor, so
that by his poverty you might be rich."

2 Corinthians 8:9

The Eerdmans Ekklesia Series

Editors

Michael L. Budde

Stephen E. Fowl

The Eerdmans Ekklesia Series explores matters of Christianity and discipleship across a wide expanse of disciplines, church traditions, and issues of current and historical concern.

The Series is published in cooperation with the Ekklesia Project, a network of persons for whom "being a Christian" is seen to be the primary identity and allegiance for believers — superseding and ordering the claims on offer by the modern state, market, racial and ethnic groups, and other social forces. The Ekklesia Project emphasizes the importance of the church as a distinctive community in the world, called to carry into contemporary society the priorities and practices of Jesus Christ as conveyed in the Gospels.

The Ekklesia Series will draw from the broad spectrum of the Christian world — Protestantism of many traditions, Roman Catholicism, Anabaptism, Orthodoxy — in exploring critical issues in theology, history, social and political theory, biblical studies, and world affairs. The Series editors are Stephen E. Fowl, Professor and Chair, Department of Theology at Loyola College in Baltimore; and Michael L. Budde, Professor of Political Science and Catholic Studies and Chair, Department of Political Science, at DePaul University in Chicago.

Additional information about the Ekklesia Project, including submission guidelines for the Eerdmans Ekklesia book series, may be found at www.ekklesiaproject.org.

HE BECAME POOR

*The Poverty of Christ
and Aquinas's Economic Teachings*

Christopher A. Franks

WILLIAM B. EERDMANS PUBLISHING COMPANY
GRAND RAPIDS, MICHIGAN / CAMBRIDGE, U.K.

Published 2009 by

Wm. B. Eerdmans Publishing Co.

2140 Oak Industrial Drive N.E., Grand Rapids, Michigan 49505 /

P.O. Box 163, Cambridge CB3 9PU U.K.

Printed in the United States of America

14 13 12 11 10 09   7 6 5 4 3 2 1

Library of Congress Cataloging-in-Publication Data

Franks, Christopher A., 1970-

He became poor: the poverty of Christ and Aquinas's economic teachings /
Christopher A. Franks.

p.   cm.

Includes bibliographical references.

ISBN 978-0-8028-3748-6 (alk. paper)

1. Thomas, Aquinas, Saint, 1225?-1274.   2. Poverty — Religious aspects —
Christianity — History of doctrines — Middle Ages, 600-1500.
3. Aristotle.   4. Economics — Religious aspects — Christianity —
History of doctrines.   5. Jesus Christ — Person and offices.   I. Title.

BV4647.P6F73   2009

261.8′5092 — dc22

2009006928

www.eerdmans.com

Contents

Acknowledgments

In the course of this project I have been preoccupied with thoughts of material wealth and poverty. But its production has reminded me of a sort of intellectual poverty in which I stand, a salutary lack occasioning such intellectual dependencies as I could not hope to number. I take the magnitude of my indebtedness to be the measure of my wealth.

I would never have been so impassioned about the economic implications of the gospel were it not for the simple witness to the possibility of a different way in the life of Fred Herzog. He and Teresa Berger modeled for us seminarians many of the virtues I discuss in these pages long before I considered writing about them. The folks at Nueva Vida and a few other villages in Honduras surely do not realize the gift their laughter and camaraderie was to me. I might not have believed that interdependence and trust could be economic assets and could preserve joy amid the depredations of the global marketplace.

Many mentors and colleagues have helped me develop the reading of Aquinas that appears in these pages. I would not have understood Aquinas without the guidance of teachers such as David Steinmetz, Robert Sokolowski, Peter Casarella, and Michael Hoonhout. Amy Laura Hall and Reinhard Hütter encouraged my initial interest in this topic and pointed me down many fruitful paths, saving me also from many unfruitful ones. I have benefited from every conversation about my research, but I am particularly grateful for dialogue with Jana Bennett, Kate Blanchard, Jason Byassee, Richard Church, David Cloutier, Holly Taylor Coolman, Clint Corcoran, Berry Crawford, Dana Dillon, Beth Felker Jones, David Stubbs, and Scott Williams. J. Kameron Carter and Thomas Hibbs read the dissertation from which this book developed, and made very useful commentary. John Bowlin and William George gave me some good leads and important cautions. A number of colleagues have read at least partial drafts of this work: Fritz Bauerschmidt, David Burrell, Kelly Johnson, Matt Levering, D. Stephen Long, Doug Meeks, and Charles Pinches. Stanley Hauerwas read everything I threw at him before I could forget what I wrote — often, it seemed, before I had finished printing it out. Meanwhile, he was helping me see our need to name the distorted ways of life that possess us and to imagine alternative ways that might enable us to hear the gospel by showing us how to live it. Of course, these debts do not excuse me from responsibility for whatever deficiencies remain in the succeeding arguments.

Most of all, I thank my wife, Sandy, my most frequent and practically minded dialogue partner. She and my sons, Isaac and Noah, and my daughters, Sophia and Rebekah, have made this work possible.

Abbreviations

CI	*Contra Impugnantes Dei Cultum et Religionem*
CR	*Contra Doctrinam Retrahentium a Religione*
De Malo	*Questiones Disputatae de Malo*
De Regno	*De Regno ad Regem Cypri*
DP	*De Perfectione Spiritualis Vitae*
In I ad Cor.	*Super Primam ad Corinthios*
In Roman.	*Super Epistolam ad Romanos*
In Sent.	*Scriptum super Libros Sententiarum*
NE	Aristotle's *Nichomachean Ethics*
ScG	*Summa contra Gentiles*
Sent. Eth.	*Sententia Libri Ethicorum*
Sent. Pol.	*Sententia Libri Politicorum*
ST	*Summa Theologiae*

Mendicancy as a Key to Thomas's Economic Teaching

Thomas Aquinas's economic teachings are not dead. No one should try to count the modern writers who have pronounced the scholastic discussion of usury and just price a relic from a bygone era that we neither can nor should retrieve.[1] However, just as some critics of modernity have turned to Aquinas looking for alternative ways of conceiving other areas of knowledge, so a persistent chorus of voices continues to speak economic wisdom inspired by Aquinas to the modern (or postmodern) age.[2]

1. The dismissers range from the expected, such as Ludwig von Mises, to the surprising, such as Martin Rhonheimer. See Ludwig von Mises, *The Theory of Money and Credit,* trans. H. E. Batson (New Haven: Yale University Press, 1953), pp. 88-89; see also Martin Rhonheimer, "Sins Against Justice (IIa IIae, qq. 59-78)," trans. Frederick G. Lawrence, in *The Ethics of Aquinas,* ed. Stephen J. Pope (Washington, DC: Georgetown University Press, 2002), pp. 287-303, here p. 291.

2. Of course, Leo XIII's interest in renewing the study of Thomas for its modern relevance already extended to economic questions, as in his encyclical *Rerum Novarum.* Similar — though less explicitly Thomistic — appeals to medieval economic wisdom were made by G. K. Chesterton and Peter Maurin. Jesuit economist Bernard Dempsey tried to give an account of economy congenial to Aquinas. Bernard W. Dempsey, *The Functional Economy: The Bases of Economic Organization* (Englewood Cliffs, NJ: Prentice-Hall, 1958). More recently, a rather different kind of Thomistic criticism of modernity has been associated with the work of Alasdair MacIntyre. Economic ethics has not been MacIntyre's primary concern, but he would rightly point out the error of isolating a distinct area of human action that can be abstracted from the rest and called "economics." And his criticism of modernity does come with a trenchant indictment of contemporary capitalism. Also, the Aquinas to whom he so frequently appeals was among those medieval theologians who MacIntyre tells us "understood, as later theologians have failed to do, the close connection between devel-

Despite much great work that is being done on Thomas's economic teachings, we remain uncertain how to understand them and to grasp their ongoing implications. Surely, Thomas is not merely a medieval way station en route to the modern discovery of the "laws" of economic life. But how can we get outside our assumption of those laws enough to grasp his arguments as something else — as potential reorientations that challenge the practices that make those laws seem plausible? That task has been achieved to some extent, but a more comprehensive study of Thomas's economic teachings can deepen our grasp of the persistent logic that undergirds them and its difference from modern assumptions. Further, shall we understand Thomas's economic teachings as presupposing Christian charity and rooted in it — and thus fully intelligible only on the basis of Christian revelation? If so, what are we to make of Thomas's significant agreements with Aristotle on these issues? Though many authors note Aquinas's agreements with Aristotle, they rarely discuss why it makes sense that Aquinas should recognize these particular Aristotelian positions as fitting into the divine pedagogy by which God leads human beings into the life of holiness.

In this book I contend that a helpful way of approaching such questions is to study Thomas's economic teachings with an eye toward his devotion to the poor Christ. This approach has the great advantage of highlighting the importance of the virtues of humility, patient receptivity, and hopeful trust, virtues that involve embracing a lowliness that unsettles modern sensibilities. Emphasizing such lowly virtues helps us appreciate the character of the challenge Thomas's economic teachings offer us and clarifies the trajectory that connects his Aristotelian-sounding discussions of justice in exchange with his evangelical encomia on following the cross of Christ.

---

oping capitalism and the sin of usury." Alasdair MacIntyre, *Marxism and Christianity*, 2nd ed. (London: Duckworth, 1995), p. xiii. Cf. D. Stephen Long, *Divine Economy: Theology and the Market* (New York: Routledge, 2000), in the Radical Orthodoxy series edited by John Milbank, Catherine Pickstock, and Graham Ward. From yet another perspective, but one still critical of modernity, Joan Lockwood O'Donovan has sought to rehabilitate medieval economic wisdom, although her account favors medieval writers other than Aquinas. See her chapters on Franciscan notions of property and on medieval usury theory in Oliver O'Donovan and Joan Lockwood O'Donovan, *Bonds of Imperfection: Christian Politics, Past and Present* (Grand Rapids: Eerdmans, 2004).

Created Lowliness and Deferent Dependence

If there is a lowliness set forth in Aquinas's economic teachings, those of us shaped by the modern market society are not disposed to heed it, or perhaps even to recognize it. Whenever I walk through a Wal-Mart, I find myself lured by an exuberant sense of my entitlement to be the potential owner of so many useful things. After studying Aquinas for a while, I began to wonder what a just price would be at Wal-Mart. The problem is not only discerning what prices can support a living wage, but also what prices might reflect the true usefulness of things rather than the relative strengths of untutored human wants. Apart from a virtuous community to estimate such prices, just price can probably not be determined. But even if I could discover the just price for the bath mat in Aisle 10, to whom would I pay it? I doubt that the cashier would know what to make of my offer to pay double the asking price. Furthermore, I suspect that my fellow customers would be baffled by my refusal to accept the common wisdom that I should purchase a commodity for the cheapest price I can get someone to sell it for. Our economic practices condition us to consider ourselves entitled to whatever we can get in the struggle of the marketplace. The lowliness that would let go such claims and yield to the communal and ecological factors that shape a truly just price is hard to come by. Of course, the problem is not simply Wal-Mart, but our underlying market-driven assumptions about wealth and exchange. The economic practices that pattern our lives form in us habits of imagining ourselves as proprietors, as primordial owners, whose claims to the goods we can buy and the security they often represent are sovereign and unconditioned.

Aquinas's economic teachings challenge us by inviting us to accept a lowliness quite opposed to our typical proprietorship. This lowliness is partly an aspect of our status as creatures, of our ontological poverty before God. Accepting our created lowliness empties us of all pretense to self-possession and prompts us to respect the limits on our claims to security. It fits us for our membership in a wider network of relationships (with God, with other people, and with other animal and vegetative beings) on which we depend. In such lowliness we can acknowledge how the conditions of our membership shape the possibilities for our flourishing before we act. This lowliness invites us to entrust ourselves to God's provision for us, seeking our sustenance in deference to the workings of the natural networks of growth through which God's provision comes.

This contrast between Thomas's created lowliness and modern proprietorship is crucial to understanding Thomas's agreements with Aristotle. Aristotle does not share a notion of our created lowliness, but he does situate the human agent within a membership of a larger natural order that conditions and limits human activity involving wealth. Good human action defers to the workings of this order, acknowledging human dependence and even entrusting human flourishing to the sustenance this order can be counted on to provide. So Aristotle and Aquinas both reject economic practices that threaten to promote an unconditioned claim to security from nature's goods. Thomas's arguments that sound Aristotelian reflect this common interest. Aquinas defends a lowliness and receptivity that echoes Aristotle's concern to foster a deferent acknowledgment of dependence.

It is worth pausing at this point to note that some contemporary writers are helping us imagine a recovery of the kind of deferent dependence that Thomas appreciated in Aristotle. An instructive example is found in Wendell Berry's essay "Two Economies."[3] The burden of this essay is to develop an encompassing account of economy. Berry recognizes that whatever is reckoned as part of the industrial economy or the money economy or the national economy or even the global economy still leaves out of account the significance of many unseen interrelationships among all kinds of creatures across both space and time. The entirety of those interrelationships constitutes a pattern or order we cannot fully comprehend. Although a full accounting of it remains beyond our grasp, it is the presupposition of every economy, and that order lays in store for us "severe penalties . . . if we presume upon it or violate it."[4] To identify this comprehensive economy and distinguish it from the human economies, or "little economies" that depend on it, Berry suggests the name "Kingdom of God"; but then he substitutes the more culturally neutral "Great Economy." It is the contrast between the Great Economy and any little human economy that prompts Berry to speak of "two economies."

According to Berry, in modernity we very often pretend that our human economy is exhaustive, assuming that there are not two economies,

3. Wendell Berry, "Two Economies," in *Home Economics* (New York: North Point Press, 1987), pp. 54-75. I do not mean to suggest that Berry is following Aristotle or Aquinas. I do not know whether Berry has read them, but his thought bears affinities with theirs.

4. Berry, "Two Economies," p. 55.

but only one. In this case we have a human economy that thinks it is the Great Economy, and thus it never notices how it transgresses the Great Economy's order. Berry attempts to evoke the kinds of virtues and forms of knowledge involved in acknowledging the limitations of our human economies and our dependence on the Great Economy. "We participate in our little human economy to a considerable extent . . . by factual knowledge, calculation, and manipulation; our participation in the Great Economy also requires those things, but requires as well humility, sympathy, forbearance, generosity, imagination."[5] Berry emphasizes the need for knowing when to yield, for cultivating a patient sympathy that trusts the workings of the Great Economy enough to learn what it has to teach. In short, he calls for deferent and trusting virtues that acknowledge our dependence on what is beyond our comprehension. Absent those virtues, we end up destroying what we do not know as we rationalize the mysterious in our effort to secure the future.

I invoke Berry's argument simply to suggest the resonance found in some contemporary writers with the project of imagining the kind of deferent dependence prized by both Aristotle and Aquinas, a deferent dependence against which modernity has largely rebelled. I also find Berry's distinction between the Great Economy and the little human economy very helpful for understanding why Aristotle and Aquinas thought a monetized economy should be subject to the particular kinds of limits for which they both argued.

The lowliness we must imagine in order to grasp the logic of Thomas's economic teachings was once more common than it is today. I suspect that has much to do with the increasing subjection of human activity to the organizing influence of markets. Berry's argument implies that an Aristotelian or Thomistic concern for situating, limiting, and conditioning economic claims might be found among many premodern and/ or non-market-based societies.[6] Whereas a deferent dependence like Aristotle's (if not Aquinas's ontological poverty) was at one time almost a matter of course, modernity finds acceptance of any kind of lowliness or poverty repugnant. Ben Quash evokes modern assumptions about human

5. Berry, "Two Economies," p. 60.

6. Consider also Karl Polanyi's claim that only with the Industrial Revolution was the idea of disembedding the economy from its sustaining presuppositions conceivable. Karl Polanyi, *The Great Transformation: The Political and Economic Origins of Our Time,* 2nd ed. (Boston: Beacon, 2001).

nature this way: "The human being belongs to himself . . . he is a center of self-governing rationality and will, and no one and nothing else governs him."[7] He is characterized by this self-belonging; I call him the "proprietary self." Any poverty becomes a kind of violence.[8] Human claims to secure welfare from raw materials appear to be self-justifying and prior to any external order.

I do not need to venture a historical narrative explaining "what went wrong." But one of the ways to get outside our modern assumptions and recover Aquinas's lowliness is to consider how the older view's decline occurred partly through the gradual rejection of Thomas's economic teachings and the corresponding economic changes. Scholars have recognized numerous factors contributing to the emergence of what I am calling the proprietary self — from the medieval juridicizing of the papacy to the rise of nominalism to Renaissance naturalism to Cartesian philosophy.[9] I believe that there is some truth to all these suggestions, but here I highlight a factor of particular relevance to my inquiry, namely, the changing experience of the world and humanity's place in it that corresponded to the growing dominance of monetary exchange in a set of markets that increasingly seemed to demand respect for their own auton-

7. Ben Quash, "Offering: Treasuring the Creation," in *The Blackwell Companion to Christian Ethics,* ed. Stanley Hauerwas and Samuel Wells (Oxford: Blackwell, 2004), pp. 305-18, esp. p. 306.

8. William James called the fear of poverty among the educated classes "the worst moral disease from which our civilization suffers." William James, *The Varieties of Religious Experience: A Study in Human Nature* (New York: Penguin, 1985), p. 369. In an interesting engagement with James's valorization of voluntary poverty, Lee Yearley ("The Ascetic Grounds of Goodness: William James's Case for the Virtue of Voluntary Poverty," *Journal of Religious Ethics* 26 [1998]: 105-35) elaborates on this comment: the poverty we fear is in many ways a prerequisite of moral virtue, since it secures "indifference to many occurrences, willingness to sacrifice, and immunity to bribery . . . [as well as] ability to conceive of alternative states" (p. 122). But Yearley points out that James's celebration of heroic poverty is undermined by his skepticism about the theological convictions that could sustain it and by his neglect of the role of a social body in reproducing it.

9. Some of the most perceptive interpretations of this history with which I am familiar are in Amos Funkenstein, *Theology and the Scientific Imagination from the Middle Ages to the Seventeenth Century* (Princeton, NJ: Princeton University Press, 1986); Charles Taylor, *Sources of the Self: The Making of Modern Identity* (Cambridge, MA: Harvard University Press, 1989); John Milbank, *Theology and Social Theory* (Oxford: Blackwell, 1990); and William C. Placher, *The Domestication of Transcendence: How Modern Thinking about God Went Wrong* (Louisville: Westminster John Knox, 1996).

omous logic.[10] Those changes gave birth to our modern notions of "economics" and of the "economy" as an isolatable system or arena of human action.[11] Thomas seems to have sensed that changing economic practices could affect one's approach to nature. His economic prescriptions, which were ignored or refused in the march toward modern economy, were in some measure structured to defend the necessity of acknowledging our created lowliness and the corresponding trusting receptivity.

Created Lowliness and the Lowliness of the Cross

By this point, the reader may concur about the importance of reimagining this lowliness, but still wonder why I insist on reading Thomas's economic teachings with an eye to his devotion to the poor Christ. In short, Aquinas's evangelical fervor for following Christ makes clear the full depth of this lowliness. For Thomas, the character of our ontological poverty as creatures is disclosed in Christ. Our sense of the depths of our created lowliness is a function of our grasp of the distance across which Christ raises us to the heights of divinity. Furthermore, this ontological poverty is a sign of our neediness — that we are created for communion. And it is the self-abandoning depths of charity revealed in Christ's naked cross that anticipate and invite us to that communion. As the cross summons us to an ever-deeper humility and vulnerability for the sake of charity, we learn the true character of the humility and receptive trust our created lowliness demands.

So there is a kind of correspondence between our created lowliness and the lowliness of the cross.[12] Aristotelian deference bears important

10. The role of economic change in these developments is not a new idea. See Polanyi, *The Great Transformation,* and C. B. Macpherson, *The Political Theory of Possessive Individualism: Hobbes to Locke* (Oxford: Oxford University Press, 1962).

11. The very notion of "Thomas's economic teachings" is thus a modern notion. But I use the term in a quite nonmodern sense. In this book, that notion does not single out teachings relating to the "laws of economics"; rather, it refers to any teaching related to human action involving external goods. Although the phrase "Thomas's economic teachings" could be misleading, I have found it convenient to use it in place of the more cumbersome phrase "Thomas's teachings about human action involving external goods."

12. This created lowliness has much in common with the dependence and vulnerability MacIntyre explores in his *Dependent Rational Animals,* a commonality I discuss further in the concluding chapter of this study. But while MacIntyre wants to specify this lowliness

analogies to Thomas's created lowliness, but moving from the former to the latter sets human action within the movement of Christian life toward ever-greater charity. Embracing our created lowliness in Christ reflects and expresses a self-offering charity, and the cross of the poor Christ summons that charity to a beatitude of ever-greater self-offering. Thomas not only transforms Aristotelian deference, but he also sets it on a trajectory that deepens it. Deferent dependence demands acknowledging limitation and embracing a certain threshold of insecurity. In Aquinas, acknowledged limitation deepens into humility, and the threshold of insecurity lowers into a vulnerability that Aristotle frankly would find shameful. Aristotle can affirm that action that accords with nature reflects deference, but he cannot see in such action what Aquinas can, that is, a hint of the poverty that points human action to its perfection.

Since we have a hard time imagining our created lowliness, we often fail to grasp the correspondence between our nature and the lowliness of the cross. As a result, we have difficulty grasping the call of the poor Christ as good news. Apart from this lowliness, it seems that to defend nature it must be contrasted with the evangelical. Aquinas's agreements with Aristotle are sometimes understood to counterbalance his evangelical fervor. Instead, the charity revealed in the cross of Christ marks a sort of *telos* toward which all of Thomas's moral teachings are directed.

If we can imagine a recovery of this created lowliness and its fulfillment in the lowliness of the cross, we can learn to see the proprietary self's drive for security and self-sufficiency as both uncharitable and incommensurate with natural order. Failing to imagine such a recovery could leave us assuming the naturalness of the proprietary self. In that case, we will mistakenly suppose that Thomas's concern for the integrity of the natural translates in our day into affirming the goodness of a "reasonable" economic practice that neglects the lowliness called for by Aquinas's teachings on justice in exchange and marginalizes the more radical extremes that Jesus sometimes articulates in the Gospels.

---

in simply natural terms, I suggest that a fuller account of this lowliness invites theological contemplation. Alasdair MacIntyre, *Dependent Rational Animals: Why Human Beings Need the Virtues* (Chicago: Open Court, 1999).

The Lowliness of the Cross and Mendicancy

We will understand Aquinas's economic teachings better if we read them in light of his devotion to the cross of the poor Christ. To explore that devotion, we must turn to his writings on mendicancy. Scholars can be forgiven for neglecting Thomas's mendicancy. He has a reputation as a rather moderate devotee of poverty, particularly compared with some of his Franciscan contemporaries and their successors. Also, the culture of many of our churches perpetuates a sense that evangelical counsels such as voluntary poverty are spiritual disciplines that are supplemental, if not irrelevant, to more properly ethical concerns such as those relating to economic activity. What could the devotional habits of nuns and friars have to do with the great questions of human economic organization?

But Thomas was passionate about Christ's poverty, and he knew no wall separating spiritual-devotional practices from properly ethical questions.[13] Throughout this book I suggest that the best way to study Thomas's economic teachings is to study *all* of Thomas's economic teachings. The goal of human action is to be perfected in the charity of Christ.[14] It is in Aquinas's discussions of mendicancy that he considers the practices and virtues that embody that charity for action involving external goods.

As we will see, Thomas's discussions of mendicancy are quite moving, for Christ's poverty entranced him. As Marie-Dominique Chenu contends, "The refusal of Monte Cassino is, for Thomas, the same gesture made by Francis of Assisi."[15] Of course, Thomas was also attracted to the Dominican penchant for study. But we should not underestimate the role of evangelical poverty, particularly in light of Thomas's impassioned defenses of the poverty of Dominican life in his polemical treatises, which

---

13. The argument of this book bears out these claims, but here it is fitting to note the important work of Servais Pinckaers in breaking down the modern division between the "spiritual" and the "moral" in Aquinas. See Servais Pinckaers, *The Sources of Christian Ethics*, trans. Sr. Mary Thomas Noble, O.P. (Washington, DC: The Catholic University of America Press, 1995), and the collection of essays in *The Pinckaers Reader*, ed. John Berkman and Craig Steven Titus (Washington, DC: The Catholic University of America Press, 2005).

14. On Thomas's perfectionism, see A. N. Williams, *The Ground of Union: Deification in Aquinas and Palamas* (New York: Oxford University Press, 1999).

15. Marie-Dominique Chenu, O.P., *Saint Thomas d'Aquin et la théologie*, Maître spirituels, 17 (Paris, 1959), p. 11, cited in Jean-Pierre Torrell, O.P., *Saint Thomas Aquinas*, vol. 1, *The Person and His Work*, trans. Robert Royal (Washington, DC: The Catholic University of America Press, 1996), pp. 15-16.

display what Jean-Pierre Torrell calls his "personal mysticism of attachment to the poor Christ."[16]

Despite growing appreciation for Thomas Aquinas as a theologian, and despite broad recognition of his perfectionism, his works on religious life remain largely unremarked on in scholarship on his ethics.[17] Perhaps this is a reflection of the modern "de-natured" self and its fragmentation of "morality" from "spirituality."[18] In the modern period, *morality* has been understood, in lawlike fashion, as dealing with obligations that constrain our freedom and apply universally. The particular vows that mark the religious life, then, do not seem to relate to morality directly. Instead, they appear perhaps as *devotional* practices that provide motivation or a special transcendent orientation for one's moral acts.[19]

On the other hand, many scholars since Chenu have worked to undermine any strict separation of spirituality from morality or from speculative theology in Thomas.[20] Perhaps interpreters neglect the importance of religious life for Aquinas's ethics because of how he works to show the possibility of perfection apart from religious life. One of the most important features of his treatment of poverty is his contention, against the tendencies of certain Franciscans, that poverty is only an instrument of per-

16. Torrell, *Saint Thomas Aquinas,* 1: 89.

17. This despite some excellent treatments of Thomas's thought about religious life. For evangelical poverty specifically, see the fine study by Jan G. J. van den Eijnden, O.F.M., *Poverty on the Way to God: Thomas Aquinas on Evangelical Poverty* (Leuven: Peeters, 1994). Other recent work includes Ulrich Horst, O.P., *Evangelische Armut und Kirche: Thomas von Aquin und die Armutskontroversen des 13. und beginnenden 14. Jahrhunderts* (Berlin: Akademie, 1992), and G. d'Urso, "S. Tommaso d'Aquino e la povertà religiosa," *Rivista di Ascetica e Mistica* 54 (1985): 283-95.

18. Pinckaers has emphasized the connection between the moral-spiritual division and the teachings of the nominalists. Pinckaers, *The Sources of Christian Ethics.*

19. James Keenan seeks to overcome the stalemate between proportionalists and absolutists by pointing in the direction of a conception of virtue that encompasses both inner intentions and external objects of action. Thus he pushes beyond the atomistic conceptions of human action prevalent in late twentieth-century interpretations of Thomas. But he fails to recover the full integration of Thomas's treatment of human action insofar as he still sees evaluation on the supernatural plane as having to do with "motivation" rather than with the specification of an act. James Keenan, *Goodness and Rightness in Thomas Aquinas's* Summa Theologiae (Washington, DC: Georgetown University Press, 1992).

20. See Marie-Dominique Chenu, O.P., *Toward Understanding St. Thomas,* trans. A. M. Landry, O.P., and D. Hughes, O.P. (Chicago: Henry Regnery, 1964). More recently, prominent work in this area has been done especially by Torrell.

fection and not the thing itself.[21] Yet some of Thomas's own claims alert us that the optional character of the counsels does not disqualify them from teleological priority. For "the observance of the precepts apart from the counsels is directed to the observance of the precepts together with the counsels; as an imperfect to a perfect species."[22]

A third plausible factor is changing theological sensibilities after Vatican II. Those in religious orders who are most likely to study the material on voluntary poverty seem unwilling to emphasize the broader significance of the counsels. Such hesitation likely relates to a post–Vatican II insistence on affirming the world of the laity and the world beyond the walls of the church. There seems to be a fear that if the "autonomy" of the created order is hedged in any way, it will mark a return to an otherworldly and hierarchically top-heavy church.[23]

Whatever the cause of neglect, we begin to see reasons why it should be overcome if we attend to the structural significance of the discussion of states of life at the end of the second part of the *ST*. Leonard Boyle has pointed out the importance of attending to structure to grasp what Thomas is doing in the *ST*.[24] Just as Boyle shows how the investigation of Christ and the sacraments is the culmination of the whole work, so we can see the treatise on gifts, forms, and states of life as the culmination of the second part. Thomas Hibbs has argued that the discussion of the active and contemplative lives recalls "the treatise on the ultimate end, in which the contemplation of God is identified as the goal of human life."[25] Hibbs details how the paradoxes of Thomas's anthropology and the dialectical el-

---

21. For a thorough study of Thomas's place in the controversy over the precise role of poverty in perfection, see Horst, *Evangelische Armut und Kirche*.

22. *ST* II-II 189.1. (Translations from the *Summa Theologiae* are from the Fathers of the English Dominican Province, unless otherwise noted.)

23. These sentiments are even evident in Torrell, *Saint Thomas Aquinas,* vol. 2, *Spiritual Master,* trans. Robert Royal (Washington, DC: The Catholic University of America Press, 2003), pp. 245-51.

24. Boyle helps us see that the second part points back to God, its source and goal, and ahead to Christ, the means to the goal, proposing that Thomas sought to keep ethics from getting bogged down in the practical and casuistical by shaping it into a treatment of human action in general and by situating it in the midst of speculative theology. Leonard Boyle, O.P., *The Setting of the Summa Theologiae of Saint Thomas* (Toronto: Pontifical Institute of Medieval Studies, 1982).

25. Thomas S. Hibbs, "*Imitatio Christi* and the foundation of Aquinas's ethics," *Communio* 18 (1991): 556-73, here p. 570.

evation of nature by grace reveal the *ST*'s Christocentricity. The centrality of Christ for Thomas's ethics culminates with the description of the Dominican life as a fitting *imitatio Christi*, because, when preachers pour forth the fruits of their contemplation for others, they reflect the self-diffusing goodness evident in the Incarnation. In this way, "the rhetorical structure and doctrinal content of the second part mirrors and points to the Dominican way of life."[26]

Recognizing the structural role of the account of religious life helps us account for the unity of the *ST*. Fergus Kerr wistfully proposes that, if there is a theme that ties the doctrine of God, the moral theology, and the Christology together, beatitude would be a strong candidate.[27] Kerr evocatively summarizes this proposed unity by pointing out where beatitude is most prominently treated: "In short: the beatitude which is God (at ST 1.26) is the beatitude which is the ultimate fulfilment of the human heart and mind (ST 1.12.1); it is the beatitude which motivates the moral life (ST 1-2.1-5); it is the beatitude made accessible to human beings by Christ's humanity (ST 3.prologue); it is the beatitude enjoyed by Christ himself (ST 3.10)."[28] Kerr's sketchy proposal could, I believe, be filled out in interesting ways, especially if that beatitude is understood as the blissful self-donation of the life of the Trinity. Here I wish simply to note that one locus Kerr's summary leaves out is the end of the second part. There, this "beatitude which is God" is the beatitude that is inchoately available in this life through contemplation.[29] Contemplation, in turn, is most excellent in those who contemplate in order to pass on the fruits of contemplation, as in an order of preachers.[30] And imitating the poverty of the poor Christ is important for this contemplation, not only to cast away solicitude, but also to aid participation in the self-surrendering charity of God that is the object of contemplation.

By showing how the Dominican life, and the counsel of poverty in

---

26. Hibbs, "*Imitatio Christi*," p. 571.

27. Fergus Kerr, O.P., *After Aquinas: Versions of Thomism* (Oxford: Blackwell, 2002), pp. 128-32. Cf. Pinckaers, for whom the treatise on beatitude at the start of the second part "is the centerpiece in the construction of the *Summa theologiae*, to such an extent that the *secunda pars* may accurately be described as the morality of beatitude." Pinckaers, *The Pinckaers Reader*, p. 117.

28. Kerr, *After Aquinas*, p. 131.

29. *ST* II-II 180.4, 5.

30. *ST* II-II 188.6.

particular, illuminates the rest of Aquinas's economic teachings, this study will point in the direction of a larger argument, namely, that the evangelical life of the counsels is pivotal to Aquinas's discussion of the Christian life. That is, although the commands prescribe all the acts of the virtues, and the counsels are not required for perfection, we see better how the virtues are to be embodied if we understand what the counsels teach about the obstacles to a fuller realization of the virtues. The sense of the commands is clarified in light of the counsels. A full-blown argument supporting this more general claim is beyond the scope of this book, but here I provide a step toward such an argument by suggesting how the counsel of voluntary poverty, rooted in devotion to the poor Christ, illuminates the commands of justice, hope, and charity that relate to external goods.[31]

Poverty is an uncomfortable subject for us. It denotes lack and insufficiency, and, as I have suggested above, it seems to us a kind of violence. Surely, what human action should aim for is not poverty but a modest sufficiency.

What Thomas means by voluntary poverty is not willed destitution.[32] Poverty does involve lack and insufficiency, but one embraces poverty not in order to go hungry but in order to receive what one needs from

---

31. A rather obvious questioning of my thesis arises at this point, namely, can the same argument be made for the other counsels? Can the counsel of continence illumine the commands of virtue that relate to sexual conduct? Can the counsel of obedience illumine the commands of virtue that concern social relations in general? More pointedly, as "unnatural" as these counsels seem, do they nevertheless have something to teach us about nature? Although I have done no detailed study of those counsels, I suspect that the same argument can be made. Just as poverty reminds us of the lowliness and receptivity that is part of the exercise of economic justice, so continence reminds us of the subordination of the use of the body to the good of the soul that is part of proper sexual conduct. Similarly, obedience reminds us of the discipline of the will that is part of the exercise of civic virtues. What is more, all three counsels highlight the aspect of renunciation, of self-abandonment in imitation of Christ, that is part of the movement of all virtues toward the perfection of charity.

32. Raniero Cantalamessa helpfully distinguishes different kinds of poverty. What he calls negative material poverty is the poverty against which Scripture preaches when, for example, the Law says that there shall "be no one in need among you" (Deut. 15:4). Cf. Leslie J. Hoppe, O.F.M., *There Shall Be No Poor Among You: Poverty in the Bible* (Nashville: Abingdon, 2004). The poverty of Christ that Thomas commends means rather to remind us how riches so easily lead to a sort of negative spiritual poverty and how the positive spiritual poverty toward which Christians are called is signified by and conducive to a kind of positive material poverty. Raniero Cantalamessa, O.F.M. Cap., *Poverty*, trans. Charles Serignat (New York: Alba House, 1997).

others. Voluntary poverty is a matter of refusing the impetus to try to establish oneself as independent and self-sufficient; it is a matter of refusing the drive to secure oneself against humiliation and against dependence. Ultimately, it is a matter of refusing to secure oneself against the giving and receiving that bind persons together in bonds of charity. One of Aquinas's biblical examples is Jesus' command to the disciples in Matthew 10:9 to take no provisions for their missionary journey, but to depend on the hospitality of others.

But the notion of embracing poverty in order to receive is filled with ambiguity. In *The Fear of Beggars: Stewardship and Poverty in Christian Ethics,* Kelly Johnson recalls for us the multifaceted theological rationales that have underwritten the practice of voluntary poverty in Christian tradition.[33] She then narrates how this practice, having reached its peak in the Franciscans just as the money economy they opposed was picking up steam, unraveled into hypocrisy and scandal. The order that praised poverty most highly became the order that Langland could caricature as a band of cynical manipulators. In attempting to renounce rights completely, the order severed the connection between rights and duties, undermining the basis of justice, and the order eventually "collapsed into the very world it arose to challenge."[34]

However, Johnson does not leave us with the idea that voluntary poverty is incoherent. She tells how attempts to reconstrue the Christian practice of material humility through the rhetoric of stewardship have led to their own problems, especially the ordering of Christian economic teaching around assumptions that the model disciple "has disposable wealth and that existing property rights are underwritten by God."[35] Rather than abandoning the ideal of voluntary poverty, Johnson suggests that what is needed is a Christian vision of economic life in which voluntary beggars might appear as witnesses to an eschatological fulfillment in which both poverty and property right will be no more.

Such reflections remind us that poverty is not itself the end and that voluntary poverty makes sense only as witness to eschatological plenitude. A supplement I would offer, however, highlights an important aspect of

33. Kelly S. Johnson, *The Fear of Beggars: Stewardship and Poverty in Christian Ethics,* Eerdmans Ekklesia Series, ed. Michael L. Budde and Stephen E. Fowl (Grand Rapids: Eerdmans, 2007).
34. Johnson, *Fear of Beggars,* p. 69.
35. Johnson, *Fear of Beggars,* p. 98.

my argument. My study of Aquinas suggests that evangelical poverty can have a further intelligibility in addition to its eschatological witness. Not only does renunciation now anticipate fulfillment later, but also present renunciation is already a kind of participation in the divine charity that is our ultimate beatitude. In other words, eschatological plenitude does not simply cancel poverty, for a sort of self-abandoning poverty is partially constitutive of that plenitude.[36] The lowliness of the cross corresponds not only to our created lowliness, but also to the lowliness of self-offering in Trinitarian communion.

In the epigraph of this book, St. Paul appeals to the recalcitrant Christians of Corinth to participate in the collection he is coordinating among the gentile churches for the Jerusalem community. He couches the appeal as an opportunity to participate in God's grace, a grace that is already filling the Macedonians, making them liberal givers. When Paul turns to Jesus' example, he raises the stakes. This is not merely a chance to overflow with grace like the Macedonians. Paul challenges the Corinthians to be what they are, to act in grace according to the grace they have already received. And that grace goes beyond the liberality of the Macedonians into that ultimate generosity manifested in Christ: the basis, the motivation, and the example for all Christian giving. As Sondra Ely Wheeler points out, the gift of Christ "can only be the basis of an uncalculating and sacrificial generosity."[37] But giving such a sacrificial gift involves a paradox, just as Christ delivered riches through poverty. The magnitude of their generosity and self-sacrifice is simultaneously the measure of their wealth.

In Thomas's account of divine charity, this paradox derives from the very nature of love. A lover offers herself to the beloved, seeking union. But this self-offering becomes the occasion of reception as mutual self-offering

---

36. Such self-abandonment within the mutual give and take of charity is to be distinguished from any pure self-sacrifice, as John Milbank rightly contends in his "Can Morality Be Christian?" and elsewhere. However, the interpretation that I am offering here does put more emphasis than I think Milbank would on the kenotic aspect of divine charity. In my view, this is not to qualify the divine plenitude but to recognize that, the greater our grasp of the magnitude of Trinitarian mutual self-offering, revealed to us most fully in Christ's self-emptying, the deeper our appreciation of the depths of the divine charity that constitutes divine plenitude. John Milbank, "Can Morality Be Christian?" in *The Word Made Strange: Theology, Language, Culture* (Oxford: Blackwell, 1997), pp. 219-32.

37. Sondra Ely Wheeler, *Wealth as Peril and Obligation: The New Testament on Possessions* (Grand Rapids: Eerdmans, 1995), p. 143.

culminates in mutual indwelling.[38] That the most immense charity has been revealed through the cross of the poor Christ shows us how pouring ourselves out into the most humble vulnerability can both signify and occasion the deepest reception of the riches of divine grace.[39]

If the God who is such love is the exemplar of creation, we should not be surprised to find that some intimation of this humble vulnerability (perhaps experienced as the deferent dependence assumed by Aristotle) is natural to us. In other words, we are made for giving and receiving. Our ontological poverty before God, partially expressed in our dependence on what Berry calls the Great Economy, reflects our created orientation toward the give and take of the divine charity, an orientation excessively and gratuitously fulfilled through our elevation to the possibility of friendship with God through Christ.

Nature, Grace, and Mendicancy

Before I take up the argument that follows, which will draw us into a rather detailed consideration of many of the pertinent texts of Aquinas, it will be useful to consider where to locate this argument with respect to some broader but still germane topics in the study of Aquinas. Two areas are especially relevant: first, nature and grace, and second, developing a theological economics. I do not propose to settle the issues these topics raise in this introduction, nor is my argument chiefly concerned with settling them. But my reading of Aquinas's economic teachings does bear on those issues and produces conclusions that speak to them. Here I only go far enough into the issues so that during the subsequent argument the reader can keep these broader concerns in mind, and so that I can begin to suggest how my conclusions will illuminate these concerns.

Aquinas's created lowliness transforms Aristotle's deferent receptivity. But the analogies are extensive enough that they can both use similar arguments about proper action with external goods, and they can call such

38. *ST* I-II 28.1-3.

39. My argument claims that this most immense charity revealed on the cross offers a pattern for human action. For an extended argument that charity specifies good action rather than being a mere motivating factor, see Michael S. Sherwin, O.P., *By Knowledge and By Love: Charity and Knowledge in the Moral Theology of St. Thomas Aquinas* (Washington, DC: The Catholic University of America Press, 2005).

action "natural." For Aquinas, though, created lowliness is correlative to the lowliness of the cross that points human action to its perfection by grace. So Thomas's economic teachings touch on the question of the relationship between nature and grace, or, more specifically, between the teleological directionality appropriate to the human animal by virtue of its innate capacities and the one and only beatitude that truly fulfills it, available only on account of Christ and by the gratuitous action of God.

Questions concerning nature and grace have become acute in modernity. Three areas of debate will suffice to evoke the kinds of issues involved. First, in the middle of the twentieth century, Henri de Lubac became the flashpoint for a controversy among Thomists over whether there is, as de Lubac claimed, a natural desire for the vision of God, and whether such a desire would preclude imagining a "pure nature," in which humans would have only an end proportionate to their nature.[40] Here the texts of Aquinas became the battlefield for struggles over the legitimacy of natural philosophy, the origins of modern Deism and atheism, and the relationships Catholics would have with Protestants and with the modern world.

Second, in the wake of Vatican II, positions have proliferated among Catholic moral theologians attempting the renewal that the council called for. Nature and grace are also at issue here, because much of the maneuvering has taken place among those who downplay the specifically Christian contribution to moral theology's content. Proportionalists, new natural-law theorists, and others who fit neither camp (such as Jean Porter) all make arguments that imply the weightiness of features of human action that should in principle be discernible in common cause with non-Christians, and they often claim to be articulating an attention to the "natural" that is broadly within the spirit of Aquinas. In contrast, Servais Pinckaers has sought renewal not by attending to what our contemporaries could agree is "natural," but by extending the return to sources begun earlier by representatives of the so-called *nouvelle theologie,* and by affirming that the heart of Catholic moral theology explores the way the Christian gospel answers to the human desire for happiness.

Third, the Catholic magisterium's continued appeals to natural law

40. Henri de Lubac, S.J., *Surnaturel: Etudes historiques* (Paris: Aubier, 1946); cf. his *The Mystery of the Supernatural,* trans. Rosemary Sheed (London: Geoffrey Chapman, 1967). For another helpful commentary on this debate, see Fergus Kerr, O.P., *Immortal Longings: Versions of Transcending Humanity* (Notre Dame, IN: University of Notre Dame Press, 1997), esp. pp. 164-84. Cf. *Revue Thomiste* 101 (2001): 5-315, the special issue devoted to de Lubac.

to support controversial moral positions have met with ridicule among some who find any notion of objective and unchanging moral truth to be philosophically and culturally obsolete. In response, some Catholic thinkers (such as Martin Rhonheimer) have sought to recover the philosophical intelligibility of appeals to natural law.

I cannot sort through all these debates here, but I can suggest what my thesis contributes. My examination of Thomas's economic teachings suggests three pertinent lessons, two about relating Aristotle to the gospel, or non-Christian to Christian thought, and a further lesson about the importance of the pattern of the cross of Christ within Christian thought.

The first implication about relating Aristotle to the gospel is that Aquinas does not assimilate Aristotle's thought unchanged.[41] The Aristotelian economic teachings, which reflect Aristotle's deferent wonder before an encompassing natural order, Thomas rearticulates in novel ways and sets them within an account of Christian virtues and gifts such that this deferent wonder gets repeated as an ontological-poverty-ordered-toward-charity that Aristotle would not have recognized.

This transformation is consistent with Thomas's assimilation of Aristotelian material more broadly. The natural-supernatural distinction was invented in the medieval schools to assimilate Aristotle into theology. With that distinction, theologians could, for example, use Aristotle's account of form and substance to organize their account of created things while still distinguishing what Aristotle implies about the proper acts of things from what Christian theology must say about those acts — that is, that there is a difference between natural capacities and supernaturally infused capacities. But particularly in Aquinas's case, he assimilated Aristotle piecemeal, not entire, and transformed him in the process. For example, from Thomas's perspective, there is an *aporia* in Aristotle's account of being insofar as he cannot identify what makes things exist. Thomas transcends

---

41. This implication is in line with much recent scholarship on Thomas that has moved away from an older paradigm that saw Thomas as a basically Aristotelian philosopher whose theological convictions were incidental. The trend in scholarship since Chenu has been increasingly to recover Thomas the theologian. Although Aquinas appreciated Aristotle's philosophy, he shared Paul's contempt for "human wisdom" whenever such wisdom "judged it inappropriate that a man would suffer the Cross, out of scorn for disgrace" (*In I ad Cor.*, I, 19, n. 50, cited in Torrell, *Saint Thomas Aquinas*, 2: 246). Mark Jordan rightly highlights that critical perspective in *The Alleged Aristotelianism of Thomas Aquinas*, The Etienne Gilson Series, 15 (Toronto: Pontifical Institute of Mediaeval Studies, 1992).

this *aporia* in his own development of the metaphysics of creation, which is not inconsequential for his account of human activity.[42] Within Aquinas's account of the God-world relationship, there can be no full account of "nature," let alone human nature, intelligible apart from God's activity, even God's gracious activity.

Within the modern debate over the natural desire for the vision of God, scholars defending the traditional Neo-Thomist position against de Lubac would remind us that some account of an end proportionate to natural human capacities is implied by Thomas's metaphysics and is required in order to respect God's freedom not to elevate humanity to union with the divine through the Incarnation. Although de Lubac argued compellingly that Thomas envisioned only one end that could fulfill human longings, namely the beatific vision, a long tradition of Thomist interpretation has viewed that desire not as an innate appetite but as an elicited desire, contingent on God's decision to elevate humanity to a supernatural end, a decision not necessitated by the structure of human nature. In this line of interpretation, humans are *capax Dei*, but that capability is not a potency of the kind that must be fulfilled for humans to be humans. Rather, it is an obediential potency, a susceptibility to be raised by divine power, which is fitting to humans because of their intellectual nature, but by no means binding God to bestow a supernatural end.[43]

I have no stake in defending all the details of de Lubac's exegesis of Aquinas or the terminology he uses to express it, but my inquiry into Thomas's economic teachings suggests that there is more to the de Lubac position than this traditional Neo-Thomist line admits. In short, it is too simple to accept the Neo-Thomist assumption that there must be "some

42. David Burrell, C.S.C., "Analogy, Creation, and Theological Language," in *The Theology of Thomas Aquinas,* ed. Rik Van Nieuwenhove and Joseph Wawrykow (Notre Dame, IN: University of Notre Dame Press, 2005), pp. 77-98, esp. pp. 81-82.

43. This line of interpretation goes back at least to Cajetan. For the fascinating history of the rise and disintegration of the Neo-Scholasticism against which de Lubac rebelled, see Gerald A. McCool, S.J., *Catholic Theology in the Nineteenth Century: The Quest for a Unitary Method* (New York: Seabury Press, 1977), and *From Unity to Pluralism: The Internal Evolution of Thomism* (New York: Fordham University Press, 1989). The generally Neo-Thomist line still has its defenders. See the impressive contemporary formulation by Lawrence Feingold, *The Natural Desire to See God According to St. Thomas Aquinas and His Interpreters* (Rome: Apollinare studi, 2001); cf. Steven A. Long, "On the Possibility of a Purely Natural End for Man," *The Thomist* 64 (2000): 211-37. Feingold receives extensive discussion in *Nova et Vetera* 5, no. 1 (2007).

content for the term 'natural' which is not conceptually dependent upon the notion of 'elevation.'"[44] True, Thomas says that God need not have bestowed the grace of humanity's union with divinity through Christ, and that "it suffices for the perfection of the universe that the creature be ordained in a natural manner to God as to an end."[45] This is a completely hypothetical scenario, imagining the possibility of no sin and no Incarnation; but Thomas finds it important to maintain that possibility lest we think the Incarnation was not an act of God's freedom. But it is not clear that for Aquinas this hypothetical humanity could be ordained to God in a natural manner *apart from grace.* Consider Aquinas's discussion of Adam's abilities before sin. Although Adam could do all the divinely commanded acts by his natural powers, he could not fulfill the commandments in the *way* they are meant to be fulfilled apart from grace.[46] Similarly, Aquinas argues that Adam's original virtue was due to the subjection of his reason to God, a subjection only possible by grace.[47] It seems that, though the distinct activities of human rectitude are in theory doable by Adam without grace, the integral condition of human rectitude is unintelligible apart from grace. This is, I take it, another example of how Aquinas used the natural/supernatural distinction to assimilate Aristotelian insights, while transforming them in light of Christian revelation.[48]

My account of Thomas's economic teachings lends some support to de Lubac by displaying an ontological poverty to the human being corresponding to the longing of the human heart for spiritual fellowship with God.[49] The most fundamental concern of de Lubac, I think, was to place Aquinas within a biblical and patristic tradition of reflection holding that when God graciously interacts with human beings, empowering them and

44. Kevin Staley, "Happiness: The Natural End of Man?" *The Thomist* 53 (1989): 215-34, here 227-28.

45. *ST* III 1.3 ad 2.

46. *ST* I-II 109.4.

47. *ST* I 95.1.

48. The denial of the need for grace, of course, suggests Pelagianism, which Aquinas was always keen to avoid. It is striking how the Neo-Thomist assertion that natural beatitude must be attainable apart from grace echoes the Pelagian complaint that surely God could not command what is beyond our own power. In response, Thomas puts Aristotle's notion of friendship to Augustinian use. See *ST* I-II 109.4 ad 2.

49. On Thomas's transformation of Aristotle's notion of beatitude, see Denis J. M. Bradley, *Aquinas on the Twofold Human Good: Reason and Human Happiness in Aquinas's Moral Science* (Washington, DC: The Catholic University of America Press, 1997).

illuminating them above and beyond God's activity as source of being and motion, that gracious activity answers to the needs of the human soul in such a way that humans would be lost without that gracious presence. The reading of Thomas's economic teachings offered here underscores that fundamental neediness. This is not to say that God owes humanity the Incarnation. Rather, while our natural constitution cries out for something that in the light of revelation we can identify as community with God, the specific grace of union with God through Christ offers such community in an unexpectedly personal and complete way.[50] But the grace of Christ comes as good news, as a fulfillment, because of that original neediness. "Far from coming only as an unwelcome and disorientating shock, the Christian dispensation turns out to offer the beginnings of a fulfillment of dimly apprehended longings."[51]

The second implication of my thesis for relating Aristotle to the gospel is that Aquinas's agreements with Aristotle do not constitute a model for assimilating to the gospel modern accounts of nature. Rather, the deferent dependence Thomas appreciated in Aristotle, a posture that, while common among premodern peoples and wherever the weight of ancient local custom persists, is specifically alien to most modern assumptions about what is "natural." Today human nature is often construed in proprietary, rights-bearing terms, leaving the rest of creation to constitute "nature" as a collection of inert materials, even "raw materials," for the exercise of human proprietorship. But Thomas's account of nature, while assimilating significant insights from Aristotle, resists being the model for assimilating a proprietary account of nature to the gospel.

In some of the modern nature-grace debates, there remains the specter of an autonomous or self-sufficient nature. That is no wonder when one considers the passion within the project of modernity, deriving most obviously from political and scientific concerns (but also, I think, from philosophical and economic ones), to identify a "nature" that could specify the real world supposed to exist beneath the contingencies of religious conviction — nature, as it were, "on its own." But such a nature is both devoid of the mystery implied by the deferent posture of Aristotle and characterized by the same "self-belonging" that distinguishes the proprietary

---

50. I am indebted to Servais Pinckaers for this way of formulating the point. See Pinckaers, *The Pinckaers Reader*, p. 99.

51. Kerr, *After Aquinas*, p. 135.

self. Such a nature is diametrically opposed to the notion of a constitutional lack, an ontological poverty of the kind my thesis will unfold in Aquinas, and of which Aquinas saw at least hints in Aristotle.

Pinckaers has traced the roots of such modern assumptions about human nature at least as far back as the nominalist revolution associated with William of Ockham. As I have indicated, I think those roots go further back and are more complex (though I do not think Pinckaers believes that Ockham single-handedly invented what I am calling the "proprietary self"); but Pinckaers's account of this revolution helps us grasp the significance of the shift toward a modern view of human nature. According to Pinckaers, in Aquinas human freedom is an expression of the collaboration of reason and will, such that nature as ordered by the eternal reason of God is a kind of condition for the possibility of human reasoning and willing and thus choosing. In Ockham human freedom precedes reasoning and willing as a neutral faculty, not necessarily inclined one way or another; Pinckaers calls this the "freedom of indifference." Such a view of humanity disconnects freedom from nature such that the subject stands over against nature, which is "relegated to a lower level, to the physical, biological, or sensitive plane."[52] Morality is no longer "natural" to the human subject, but only arises through externally imposed obligation.[53]

The present inquiry into Thomas's economic teachings highlights the difference between modernity's "de-natured" or "self-belonging" sub-

---

52. Pinckaers, *The Pinckaers Reader,* p. 365.

53. Addressing the philosophical inadequacy of such a de-natured self has been the purpose of sustained work by Martin Rhonheimer, though without the historical interest of Pinckaers. Rhonheimer applauds proportionalists for rejecting a view of natural law as a set of norms derived from natural order and imposed on free subjects. But he faults proportionalists for reproducing the same dichotomy between external natural order and de-natured free subjects. They simply want to reverse the order of dominion. The proportionalists, Rhonheimer claims, still have a "biologistic" view of nature, but the harmony between nature and reason must be reclaimed if Aquinas, or the doctrine of natural law, is to be understood. Rhonheimer is on the right track here, I think, except that his concern for "the ought" shows that perhaps he himself has not fully escaped the de-natured self. See esp. Martin Rhonheimer, *Natural Law and Practical Reason: A Thomist View of Moral Autonomy,* trans. Gerald Malsbary (New York: Fordham University Press, 2000). For arguments that more fully undo the de-natured self and its alienation from "morality," see Bernard Williams, *Ethics and the Limits of Philosophy* (Cambridge, MA: Harvard University Press, 1985), and Charles Pinches, *Theology and Action: After Theory in Christian Ethics* (Grand Rapids: Eerdmans, 2002).

ject and Thomas's account of our ontological poverty and our member-ship in an encompassing order whose rationality is inscribed in our agency. By focusing on economic teachings, this reading of Aquinas adds to Pinckaers's diagnosis by pointing to the role of economic change in pav-ing the way for modern assumptions about human nature.

In addition to the two implications of my thesis about relating Aris-totle to the gospel, a further implication centers on the importance of the pattern of the cross of Christ within Christian thought. Specifically, my reading of Thomas's economic teachings affirms that the perfection Thomas associates with the pattern of the cross, a pattern specified partic-ularly well by the evangelical counsels, is the goal in light of which Thomas's whole account of Christian life is best understood. In other words, Aquinas's ethics does not find its center of gravity in naturally good actions to which infused virtues and gifts add little. Rather, Christian life is always summoned deeper, so that its center of gravity is its goal, the charity revealed on the cross.

Readings of Aquinas's ethics that suggest the autonomous integrity of the natural tend to downplay or neglect evangelical perfection. Such readings make it easy to miss the way Thomas draws the reader, at every level of moral discourse, to enter further into the life of charity in order to be united with God and brought into conformity with Christ.[54] It is tempting today to downplay the weight Aquinas places on the evangelical life, not only for the reasons offered above but also for fear that an account of human action focused on Jesus Christ will be insufficiently universal. Jean Porter, in her book *Nature as Reason: A Thomistic Theory of the Natu-ral Law*, suggests that the nature-grace issue has in fact become an issue of the universal and the particular in terms of our awareness of "diverse cul-tures and ways of life."[55] Porter undertakes to bridge this transmogrified nature-grace gap. To do so, she attempts a naturalistic account of what is universal in human action that at the same time shows how particular Christian convictions both legitimate the account of human nature and specify a more determinate vision of human happiness that would still presuppose her naturalistic account of human well-being.

---

54. These themes have been brought out nicely in Luc-Thomas Somme, *Fils adoptifs de Dieu par Jésus Christ: La filiation divine par adoption dans la théologie de saint Thomas d'Aquin* (Paris: Vrin, 1997).

55. Jean Porter, *Nature as Reason: A Thomistic Theory of the Natural Law* (Grand Rapids: Eerdmans, 2005), p. 324.

Porter's proposal for resolving the contemporary version of the nature-grace problematic is to follow in the spirit of the medieval scholastics by taking nature as seriously as Scripture does. But since, for her, the "natural" is always haunted by the "universal," which means "not tied to particularistic convictions,"[56] taking nature seriously means downplaying the significance of specifically Christian content, such as the gracious perfection offered through Jesus Christ.[57] Porter seems to suggest that a kind of harmony between nature and grace, between the universal and the particular, is achieved by seeing Christianity's message of grace as a specific vision of happiness rooted in a more general notion of well-being construed from a more "universal" perspective (even if Christians have theological reasons to appreciate that perspective).[58]

But my argument suggests that Thomas's focus on the cross of Jesus Christ is no cause for concern about the universality of his teachings. Rather, for Aquinas it is through Christ that we know best the divine love at the heart of God's creative activity, and hence it is in following Christ that Christians have the best grounds for expecting that their account of human action will find resonance with others, such as Aristotle, who have sought the truth.[59] I hope my argument displays that Christians' turning

56. Porter, *Nature as Reason,* pp. 125-26, 135.

57. So Porter's novel distinction between naturalistic "well-being" and a more specific "happiness" functions to preserve the centrality of a notion of well-being derived not from a theological account of human nature but from an account that is supposedly abstracted from theological convictions. In this regard, it is interesting that her sketch of the terrestrially happy life (even as a life of infused virtue!) does not mention the knowledge or worship of God (*Nature as Reason,* pp. 221-24). But, as in much modern theology, concern for such a "universal" account is justified theologically because of the doctrine of creation: "We have theological reasons for valuing those distinctive forms of social life proper to us as a species, even prior to considering how these are to be specified in accordance with our overall theological beliefs and commitments" (p. 135). This strategy isolates creation from redemption as though creation were not already an eschatological claim.

58. Thus does Porter provide a version of the "Thomist axiom" (grace does not destroy, but perfects nature) that offers assurances for the human goodness known apart from faith: "We can have confidence that God's call and judgment of us will not be wholly at odds with our best ideals for ourselves — which is not to say that we judge God by human standards, but rather that we acknowledge that our own standards are themselves reflections (however fragmentary and distorted) of God's creative wisdom" (*Nature as Reason,* p. 328). This assurance is quite opposed to the use of the axiom found in Thomas (see chap. 4 below); cf. Pinckaers, *The Pinckaers Reader,* pp. 366-67.

59. My argument suggests, then, that Thomas's recognition of our ontological pov-

their eyes toward Jesus offers a terrific source of renewal that is precisely relevant to the "wider world," and very likely so in ways that will have more in *common* with many non-Christians than approaches that downplay Christian particularity.[60]

Helena Norberg-Hodge tells of her experience working and living among the Ladakhis, a relatively isolated people living on the Tibetan Plateau high in the Himalayas.[61] She describes their traditional life of making shoes from yak skins, building houses from mud and stone, and engineering complex irrigation systems to bring glacial meltwater to their fields. Ladakhis include both Buddhists and Muslims, but Norberg-Hodge suggests that traditionally they have been united both in their sense of belonging to an interdependent membership and in their patience and accommodation to the contours of the natural order of which they are a part. Norberg-Hodge laments how the expansion of Western-style markets into Ladakh has brought proprietary attitudes that foster struggle and competition. The pressures of the global economy have begun to create a cultural inferiority complex, a sense of consumerism, the loss of traditional skills, and the breakdown of traditional interdependence. Western globalization has also introduced ecological exploitation and ethnic discrimination. My argument suggests that pursuing the lowliness of the cross may give Christians a kind of common cause with traditional Ladakhis and many other peoples.

To sum up my discussion of nature and grace, I hope to move be-

---

erty is a much more plausible candidate than the idea of natural rights for a Christian contribution to our understanding of human nature that might find resonances in many times and cultures. Cf. Porter, *Nature as Reason*, pp. 342-57. Modern subjective rights, after all, correspond to the rise of the proprietary self. To the extent that they find wide acceptance, I suspect it is because the forms of social and economic organization that reproduce and discipline the proprietary self, which have now extended their reach nearly all around the world, also reproduce the language of subjective rights as the most recognizable and effective form of protest. For a theological critique of rights language, see Joan Lockwood O'Donovan, "Historical Prolegomena to a Theological Review of 'Human Rights,'" *Studies in Christian Ethics* 9 (1996): 52-65.

60. Pinckaers similarly suggests that the more faithful Christian moral theology is to the New Law inscribed through the Holy Spirit, the more resonance it will have with the universal aspirations of humanity. Pinckaers, *The Pinckaers Reader*, p. 175.

61. Helena Norberg-Hodge, "The Pressure to Modernize and Globalize," in *The Case Against the Global Economy and For a Turn Toward the Local*, ed. Jerry Mander and Edward Goldsmith (San Francisco: Sierra Club, 1992), pp. 33-46.

yond the question of whether Thomas is more Aristotelian, with more appreciation for the integrity of nature, or more evangelical, with more of an Augustinian emphasis on the waywardness of nature apart from God's help. I believe that this question is often addressed in too abstract and formal a manner. I hope to display how the life of the evangelical counsels points the direction toward which all of Christian living is summoned. Aristotle is sometimes helpful in discussing particular features of Christian living largely because he presupposes the kind of account of what is natural in human action that is particularly suited to showing how grace perfects it without destroying it.

Aquinas's Theological Economics

I hope readers of this book gain a deepened understanding of Thomas's economic teachings. But I also hope readers begin to recognize the richness of those teachings as sources for renewing how Christians today think and act with respect to property and exchange. Therefore, this inquiry contributes to theologians' attempts to develop a theological economics.

Not long ago it was easy enough to assume that theology had little to say about economics directly. The modern discipline of economics was born through a process of differentiation. As money increasingly became the medium of people's livelihoods, and as investors and merchants gradually freed their practices from many of the strictures of prior custom, the study of these phenomena gradually emancipated itself from the orbit of theology or philosophy. In modernity it has frequently been assumed that "the economy" is a fully differentiated sphere of human life, with its own autonomous logic.[62]

Recently there has been increasing interest among theologians in developing a theological account of economic life. Markets and the particular kinds of analysis of human action associated with them now dominate the lives of much of the world's populace. But many theologians have rec-

---

62. Some theologians still celebrate this development as an achievement. Max Stackhouse, for example, praises the great insight of modern economics, the recognition that rather than economic life's being an aspect of political and household life, governments and families "depend on flourishing economies." Max Stackhouse, "Business, economics, and Christian ethics," in *The Cambridge Companion to Christian Ethics,* ed. Robin Gill (Cambridge, UK: Cambridge University Press, 2001), pp. 228-42, here p. 233.

ognized that capitalist approaches to human action, rather than marking a straightforward acceptance of "hard realities," presupposed their own, often skewed, philosophical and/or theological accounts of the human being. One strand of such scholarship draws from Karl Marx to emphasize the material significance of biblical themes of justice and redemption in contrast to capitalism's marginalization or spiritualization of them.[63] Another strand builds on the philosophy of Alfred North Whitehead to challenge the "misplaced concreteness" within modern economic analysis that falsely keeps philosophical and theological issues at bay.[64] A further strand seeks to show the heretical character of capitalism by explicating Christian doctrine in conversation with notions of "gift" that undermine the autonomous will enshrined in modern economic practice.[65] Other approaches could be named.

These developments help us recognize the philosophical and theological mistakes that have become, through a complicated history, presuppositions that possess us. My reading of Aquinas's economic teachings shares a great deal with these theological trends. The main contribution my reading makes to these concerns is twofold. First, I suggest that the Aristotelian distinction between use value and exchange value, which Aquinas presupposes, is crucial for understanding our predicament. Second, I defend the usefulness of such Aristotelian-Thomistic considerations for Christians by showing that they do not counterbalance an evangelical concern to foster charity. On the contrary, the charity revealed in the cross of Christ defines the trajectory of those Aristotelian-Thomistic considerations and completes their tendency to resist any proprietary stance.

Aristotle's distinction between use value and exchange value helps us understand our bondage to mistaken philosophical and theological assumptions. I suggest that an important role in the development of these questionable presuppositions was played by the rise to dominance of monetary exchange within particular kinds of markets: that is, the power of

---

63. Gustavo Gutiérrez, *A Theology of Liberation*, 15th anniversary ed., trans. Caridad Inda and John Eagleson (Maryknoll, NY: Orbis Press, 1988), will stand for the vast amount of literature here.

64. John B. Cobb, Jr., is a prominent figure here. See his joint venture with Herman E. Daly, *For the Common Good: Redirecting the Economy toward Community, the Environment, and a Sustainable Future*, 2nd ed. (Boston: Beacon, 1994).

65. For a seminal essay in this direction, see John Milbank, "Can a Gift Be Given?" *Modern Theology* 11 (1995): 119-61.

markets expanded to the point that exchange values lost their inherent connection to use values. As that transition was being achieved, being lost was the habit of deferent wonder at human membership in a trustworthy whole that surpasses us, and as a result Thomas's economic teachings gradually came to seem inapplicable. Now questionable presuppositions, such as the "proprietary" construction of the self, reinforce corresponding assumptions about nature, reproducing market dominance and thus keeping us from grasping the full significance of Thomas's teachings on usury and just price or from appreciating the call of the poor Christ.

From a Christian perspective, what this analysis of our predicament suggests is that we are caught in social and economic patterns that keep reproducing sin. Not that sin is new with capitalism; nor is the social reproduction of sin new.[66] But the triumph of exchange value organizes patterns of human activity that are particularly relentless and intractable in their reproduction of sin.[67] These patterns dictate a proprietary drive for security, permanence, and protection against risk. Action in accordance with these patterns regularly results in injustice and exploitation. It is important for us to recognize these tendencies in order to resist them; but to get any traction, we must pair that recognition with alternative social patterns, patterns in which exchange value is subservient to other human goods.[68]

66. This is one reason natural law is not equivalent to "what everyone knows." For an interesting argument that knowledge of the natural law is historical and socially mediated and that social practices sometimes actually hinder knowledge of the natural law, see Pamela M. Hall, *Narrative and the Natural Law: An Interpretation of Thomistic Ethics* (Notre Dame, IN: University of Notre Dame Press, 1994).

67. Daly and Cobb suggest an interesting analogy between "the market" and a language: both are ad hoc but rationally ordered community conventions. They use the analogy to extol the market's ability to convey information, but the analogy is also useful to point out, on the one hand, how the market in a sense "speaks us," as our cultural-linguistic system does, and, on the other hand, how market conventions, like linguistic ones, can be spoken in new ways to recover elements of an older language that have been lost. See Daly and Cobb, *For the Common Good,* p. 44.

68. One of the most important books we have relating theology to the market society is M. Douglas Meeks, *God the Economist: The Doctrine of God and Political Economy* (Minneapolis: Fortress Press, 1989). Meeks seeks to demystify the dominance of exchange value by reinscribing exchange value practices within a broader notion of care for a household, as Aristotle situates *chrēmatistikē* within *oikonomia.* Meeks differs from Aristotle in that the household in question is the entire household of God, centered on Israel and the church but ultimately extending to all creation. Meeks is especially concerned to replace God concepts

Thomas's teachings about economic justice can help us imagine what might be involved in such alternative practices. The key to understanding these teachings is to see how the priority of use values corresponds to a receptivity, a yielding to the contours of an antecedent order, that refuses the drive for security and nobility so common among all sinful humans and so seemingly inescapable in market societies. Thomas calls into question many of our basic assumptions about titles to interest on money because they seek to secure an increase in wealth merely from the conventions of exchange value. He equally questions our assumption that prevailing prices in a competitive market are necessarily just. Both assumptions turn out to be complicit with our temptation to secure ourselves by claiming too much.[69]

In addition to displaying the importance of the distinction between use value and exchange value for navigating these issues, my reading of Thomas's economic teachings points out how Thomas's Aristotelian-sounding explorations of these issues in terms of justice do not limit or qualify the role of charity or of the imitation of Christ. It is often supposed that when Thomas seems the most Aristotelian, his evangelical fervor necessarily recedes into the background.[70] For example, Joan Lockwood

---

that reify the modern economic actor writ large and thereby sanctify the status quo with a biblical account of God the householder as a communion of persons: Father, Son, and Holy Spirit. Meeks has helped us imagine alternative practices that would resist the tyranny of exchange value. Nevertheless, I wonder whether the social conception of the Trinity can do all the work Meeks wants it to do. Indeed, I wonder if the work he wants it to do ends up determining his account of the Trinity. For an account of how attempts to use the Trinity as a social model can actually hinder the contemplative ascent toward the Trinity that would produce the transformation these attempts seek, see Matthew Levering, *Scripture and Metaphysics: Aquinas and the Renewal of Trinitarian Theology* (Oxford: Blackwell, 2004), Challenges in Contemporary Theology series, edited by Gareth Jones and Lewis Ayres.

69. A recent recovery of some of these same teachings of Thomas can be found in Long, *Divine Economy*. Long offers a more astute engagement with the writings of economists than I attempt here. Although we differ over a few details, I take our readings of Thomas to move in largely the same direction, except that I put more emphasis on the embedding of economic activity in the workings of nature, and I offer a somewhat more positive account of Christian theology's dialectical engagement with certain forms of non-Christian thought. For another discussion of theology's dialectical engagement with the natural order that is similar to my view, see Thomas S. Hibbs, *Virtue's Splendor: Wisdom, Prudence, and the Human Good* (New York: Fordham University Press, 2001), esp. p. 185.

70. But see Eugene Rogers's intriguing argument that, when it comes to Aquinas's teaching on the role of revelation in our knowledge of God, the more Aristotelian Thomas

O'Donovan has sought to recover the economic perspective of an evangelical Christian Platonism centered on an Augustinian notion of nonproprietary community, bound by common participation in shared goods and loves.[71] Such a notion, she suggests, was the communal vision animating much medieval economic thought. While Thomas by no means overturns that tradition, O'Donovan tells us that he does stand in some tension with it insofar as he allows greater natural validity to the institution of individual ownership, following Aristotle in giving "a larger communal role to the just distribution and exchange of property."[72]

O'Donovan is right to note differences between Thomas and some of his contemporaries, but my reading of Aquinas suggests that the fundamentally antiproprietary ideal that she lauds still characterizes Thomas's overall economic teaching. Thomas allowed more room for practices that assume the institution of *proprietas,* not as some hedge against a too-radical ideal but in order to defend the significance of the virtue of justice against certain mendicants who seemed to claim that Jesus' practice points only to a complete renunciation of all legal rights, a sort of pretense of total self-abnegation. But Thomas takes even those claims about justice and orders them toward the form of charity, specified most completely in the cross of the poor Christ, which is anything but proprietary. Furthermore, apart from something like Aquinas's quasi-Aristotelian defense of recep-

---

is, the more evangelical he is. Eugene F. Rogers, Jr., *Thomas Aquinas and Karl Barth: Sacred Knowledge and the Natural Knowledge of God* (Notre Dame, IN: University of Notre Dame Press, 1995).

71. Joan Lockwood O'Donovan, "The Theological Economics of Medieval Usury Theory," in O'Donovan and O'Donovan, *Bonds of Imperfection,* pp. 97-120. Kathryn Tanner's proposal for a theological economics based on principles of noncompetitive mutual benefit bears some similarities to O'Donovan's notion. But for Tanner, unconditioned giving and mutual benefit become principles abstracted from a socially embodied account of God's work in the world. This abstraction leads to two unfortunate results. First, Tanner too easily makes the leap from the plenitude of the Word, even amid the suffering with which it is united in Jesus, to the absence of cost or risk within gracious human giving: "[O]ne isn't giving by a giving away that might leave one bereft" (p. 84). Second, having no socially embodied alternative practices to pose against the market, she is left applying these abstract principles wherever they can find purchase within the market as it is. And the most obvious way the market seems to promise something that looks like noncompetitive mutual benefit is by intensifying current trade patterns while seeking to level the bargaining field. She ends up being much less radical than she at first appeared. Kathryn Tanner, *Economy of Grace* (Minneapolis: Fortress, 2005).

72. O'Donovan, "Theological Economics," p. 99.

tive wonder before an encompassing order, our imaginations remain captive to the modern proprietary subject. Then nonproprietary community remains an abstract ideal, and we have difficulty hearing the summons of the poor Christ with joy.

In summary, the basic trajectory that characterizes Thomas's economic teachings is toward a lowly and trusting receptivity that interrupts our impulse to secure our future and our nobility. This impulse is natural when moderate. But in a market society we receive habits that press us toward an unconditioned and unlimited pursuit of it. Further, in the cross of Christ we learn that the self-concern at the root of this impulse finds its fulfillment in a self-abandoning charity that interrupts this impulse to a surprising degree. The lowly and trusting receptivity that moderates this impulse in accord with nature is summoned toward deeper lowliness and receptivity in which nature is perfected. This lowly receptivity corresponds to our fundamental ontological poverty, which is best understood and is brought to its completion in the charity of the poor Christ on the cross. My reading of Aquinas's economic teachings highlights a feature that is often neglected: the importance of this ultimately Christological embrace of poverty.

Overview

We are now in position to preview the structure of the argument that follows. In order to grasp the character of Thomas's economic teachings, we must take it as our first task to distinguish them from modern approaches typified by the assumption of what I am calling the "proprietary self." Chapter 1 seeks to display this distinction by portraying the fundamental difference between an Aristotelian-Thomistic approach to external goods and John Locke's approach. I explicate this difference via Aristotle's distinction between use value and exchange value: this helps me describe the difference between nonmarket societies, with their corresponding kinds of approaches to nature, and modern market society, with its distinctive kinds of understanding of nature. Locke is a useful foil for Thomas here because he offers a superficially similar account of nature and property that we can contrast with Thomas's in light of the "proprietary" character of Locke's assumed subject. What we are able to see is that Aquinas shares Aristotle's deferent and receptive posture in contrast to Locke's proprietary stance, which from Thomas's perspective can perhaps best be labeled "presumptive."

Chapter 2 offers an interpretation of Thomas's teachings on usury and just price in light of the distinction I explore in chapter 1. The qualities of a non-market-society approach to nature that I investigate in chapter 1 bring a new intelligibility to these teachings. I suggest that a misguided search for awareness of the "realities of the market" has derailed most contemporary interpretations of these arguments, and that Thomas's positions on both issues are best understood as attempts to defend Aristotelian deference toward the antecedent natural order and to resist the presumption that would overreach in its attempts to secure the future.

Even in Thomas's discussions of economic justice, he transforms Aristotle's positions to some degree. But the full extent of that transformation can only be seen when Thomas's interest in Aristotelian deference is set within the context of Christian convictions about creation and the movement of Christian life toward greater participation in divine charity. In order to evoke that wider vision, I explore in chapter 3 the economic implications of selected theological virtues and gifts to show how, for Thomas, Christian life at its best acknowledges ontological poverty and is oriented toward self-abandonment. Then I investigate Aquinas's account of the relationship between the commands and counsels to confirm the teleological movement of Christian life toward cruciform charity. In short, the counsels help to specify more concretely the direction toward which the commands point.

Having gotten that far, my argument that following the cross of the poor Christ is the *telos* that illuminates all of Thomas's economic teachings could still fail. Some have claimed that the evangelical character of Thomas's account of voluntary poverty is doubtful at best. In chapter 4, therefore, I offer an interpretation of Thomas's account of voluntary poverty, drawing on the polemical treatises he produced for the mendicancy debates to clarify his views articulated elsewhere. This approach lays bare how Thomas sees the goal of human action with external goods in a humble vulnerability that only makes sense in light of the charity revealed in Christ.

Because that humble vulnerability constitutes an exposure that is so receptive, so unsecured, one might wonder whether this is the same Thomas who had such agreements with Aristotle. Indeed, from Aristotle's perspective, Thomas's humble vulnerability would seem to move toward a self-abnegation and self-destruction that cannot be natural. I address these concerns in chapter 5 by showing that poverty itself, a simple lack, is not the perfection at which Thomas's economic teachings aim. To that end, I discuss poverty's instrumentality, revealing what it is instrumental to, ultimately the bliss of self-surrendering participation in the communion of divine charity. Since this communion is the pattern of all nature, Aristotelian deference and trusting receptivity appear as a pale groping toward the lowly and receptive grace revealed in Christ, which is finally supremely natural.

In my concluding chapter I gesture toward the possibilities of recovering something like Aquinas's lowliness in our contemporary economic practice. Thomas's teachings, I suggest, could be an important pointer not only toward economic justice but also toward a reacknowledging of our membership in a trustworthy order pervaded with divine intelligibility. However remote such possibilities may seem, the fact that we are always already depending on such an order means that the basis for resisting distorted and distorting practices is constantly being renewed. These possibilities hold promise for putting us on the road to recovering a posture from which we could hear the summons of the poor Christ as the offer of the fulfillment of our nature.

I must conclude this introduction with an exhortation. The recovery of Aquinas's economic teachings confronts us with a renewed evangelical call for the embrace of certain kinds of poverty. There is no need to belabor the tyranny of material goods that is continually gaining strength within our market economies. I dare say that people who want to become good generally recognize the need to reject a crass consumerism.[73] But we often do not recognize how we are also diminished simply by adopting some of the more elemental assumptions and practices of modern economic arrangements, such as the notion that money makes money or that everything has its price or that the value-preferences that determine price are sovereign and self-justifying. We perhaps unwittingly become participants in injustice and in the pillaging of creation. Imagining the cruciformity of the poor Christ as the goal of our economic action may

---

73. For a now classic account of how consumerism in both its crass and subtle forms afflicts us and how it can be challenged by the gospel, see John F. Kavanaugh, *Following Christ in a Consumer Society: The Spirituality of Cultural Resistance*, 25th anniversary ed. (Maryknoll, NY: Orbis Press, 2006).

help us escape being possessed by the drive to assert our preferences and to secure the future. I hope to help us develop such imagination by portraying the beauty of Christ's call to relinquish that drive as the key to encountering the significance of Thomas's economic teachings.

CHAPTER 1

Aristotelian Deference
and Nonmarket Society

In the march to market-based social organization, some things have been lost. Most important for our understanding of Thomas's economic teachings, this march has eroded the sense of a constitutional human lack or neediness corresponding to human dependence on and membership within an encompassing and trustworthy order. This sense is, I think, common to many nonmarket societies. Because Thomas's appreciation of it accounts for many of his sympathies with Aristotle, we can usefully refer to it as "Aristotelian deference."

We cannot understand Thomas's economic teachings without paying attention to the role of this Aristotelian deference. Interpreters of Thomas frequently read his comments on traditional economic teaching as moments in the rationalization of economic inquiry, part of a set of shifts in the thirteenth and fourteenth centuries that marked a breakthrough to new insights about the realities of how "economy" works; thus Thomas easily becomes a sort of proto-Locke. But reading Thomas that way fails properly to historicize modern assumptions about economy and nature. The proprietary self was always there, it seems, waiting to be discovered.[1] Thomas's economic teachings, however, were not an advance on

---

1. John Milbank recognizes the same tendency in Weber's sociology: "It takes an *a priori* principle of sociological investigation for what should be the *subject* of a genuine historical enquiry: namely the emergence of a secular polity, the modern *imagining* of incommensurable value spheres and the possibility of a formal regulation of society." John Milbank, *Theology and Social Theory: Beyond Secular Reason* (Oxford: Blackwell, 1990), p. 89.

the road to understanding "economy." They were, in part, an attempt to preserve the kind of Aristotelian deference that acknowledges how economic relationships are embedded in social and organic relationships, undermining the notion of an "economy."

In later chapters I will explore the differences between Aristotelian deference and the ontological poverty we can find in Thomas. But first we must grasp the similarities, particularly in contrast to modern assumptions. The key to understanding this Aristotelian deference and how it differs from modern assumptions is Aristotle's distinction between use value and exchange value. I suggest that nonmarket societies are generally arranged so that any exchange value assigned to things serves the ends of use value, at least for the most part. The predominance of use values gives priority in human economic activity to the antecedent shape of the natural order, of which humans find themselves members. On account of this membership, humans appropriately assume not a self-justifying or presumptive posture but an awe-filled deference and a receptive, even trusting, conformity to nature's provision.

On the other hand, in societies where the circulation of exchange value has become the dominant organizing force, exchange value is to some extent freed from its traditional subordination to use value. In such societies, the self-justifying claims of the proprietary self are right at home. Indeed, market economy fosters a construal of nature in which human claims to secure welfare from raw materials seem to be prior to any external order. This is the "self-belonging" individual familiar to us from many contexts. The proprietary claims of this individual are assumed to be supremely natural: "The prevailing form of idealistic naturalism today is the political language of subjective 'rights' which has universalized a proprietary concept (property right) into a legalistic and individualistic ethic of self-possession."[2] If we assume that Thomas's thought represents a moment in the realization of the naturalness of such an approach, we cannot help but misunderstand him.

By flagging the distance between market economy and the thought of Aristotle and Thomas, I do not mean to suggest that they knew nothing of markets. But the presence of markets does not suffice for a market economy. Markets, understood as meeting places for barter or buying and sell-

---

2. Oliver O'Donovan and Joan Lockwood O'Donovan, *Bonds of Imperfection: Christian Politics, Past and Present* (Grand Rapids: Eerdmans, 2004), p. 7.

ing, are widely known throughout history. On the other hand, a market economy "is an economic system controlled, regulated, and directed by market prices; order in the production and distribution of goods is entrusted to this self-regulating mechanism."[3] Market economy is a phenomenon that has developed for the most part since Thomas's day. In thirteenth-century Europe, markets had a notable function, but they remained marginal to the bulk of economic activity.[4] Social organization, including the regulation of production, distribution, and consumption, was of a very different sort, both in Thomas's time and in Aristotle's, from what characterizes market economy.

Just as markets were not invented after Thomas's day, neither were self-justifying claims by human beings. I do not argue that nonmarket societies are devoid of such claims or the vices Thomas would associate with them. The contrast I wish to draw is between societies where such a posture could appear vicious despite its prevalence and societies where the proprietary self appears as a necessary feature of human existence, partly because a general struggle for wealth based on exchange value is diffused throughout society.[5]

This chapter will unfold the distinction between use value and exchange value, and the corresponding distinction between nonmarket and market society, in order to establish the character of Aristotelian deference. To clarify the difference it makes for our understanding of Thomas, I will compare Thomas's discussion of property with the less deferent account of John Locke. Locke will serve as a convenient point of comparison with Thomas because he shares many of our significant market-based assumptions, while still discussing issues of natural order, property, and exchange in a way that compares readily with Thomas. In this chapter I highlight the distance between the deference and trusting dependence of the Aristotelian posture and the presumptive and thus homeless character of the Lockean self.

3. Karl Polanyi, *The Great Transformation: The Political and Economic Origins of Our Time,* 2nd ed. (Boston: Beacon, 2001), p. 71.

4. N. J. G. Pounds, *An Economic History of Medieval Europe,* 2nd ed. (New York: Longman, 1994).

5. Robert L. Heilbroner, *The Worldly Philosophers: The Lives, Times, and Ideas of the Great Economic Thinkers,* 6th ed. (New York: Touchstone, 1986), p. 25.

Two Types of Economy

The best place to begin for understanding the difference between Aristotelian economic views and the assumptions of market economy is Aristotle's distinction between use value and exchange value.[6] He draws this distinction most succinctly in the *Politics*. "With every article of property there is a double way of using it; both uses are related to the article itself, but not related to it in the same manner — one is peculiar to the thing and the other is not peculiar to it. Take for example a shoe — there is its wear as a shoe and there is its use as an article of exchange; for both are ways of using a shoe, inasmuch as even he that barters a shoe for money or food with the customer that wants a shoe uses it as a shoe, though not for the use peculiar to a shoe, since shoes have not come into existence for the purpose of barter."[7] Aristotle makes this rather commonsense distinction do a lot of work. That a shoe can be either worn (use value) or exchanged (exchange value) seems to be a rather pedestrian observation (no pun intended). But if we maintain the distinction consistently and rigorously, it is of momentous import. Indeed, it provides the tools for marking the primary difference between market and nonmarket economy.

Use value is not particularly mysterious in itself. It simply arises from the fact that human artifacts are made to serve specific human purposes. As Aristotle says in the *Nichomachean Ethics*, "whoever produces something produces it for an end."[8] The use value of a product, therefore, derives from the natural properties it has as, say, a shoe or a loaf of bread. And as the qualities of these artifacts that fit them for a certain use differ, so are the use values of various commodities incommensurable with one another.

Exchange value is a quite different kind of thing. It depends on finding a way to bring these incommensurable artifacts together and to compare them according to a common quantitative measure. Money is often the medium, though it need not be. The logic of the comparison remains the same either way. Aristotle gives the following example.[9] According to

6. On the importance of this distinction in Aristotle's thought, I follow the reading of Scott Meikle, *Aristotle's Economic Thought* (Oxford: Clarendon Press, 1995).

7. Aristotle, *Politics*, I, 1257a6-13. (Quotations from the *Politics* are drawn from the translation by H. Rackham, Loeb Classical Library [London: William Heinemann, 1932].)

8. Aristotle, *NE*, VI.2, 1139b1-2. (Quotations from the *Nichomachean Ethics* are taken from the translation by Martin Ostwald [New York: Macmillan, 1962].)

9. Aristotle, *NE*, V.5, 1133b24-28.

their exchange value, we may say that 1 house = 5 minae = 5 beds. Whether the minae mediate between the house and the beds makes little difference, at least for the purposes of determining exchange value. But what sort of thing can exchange value be? According to their natural qualities, a house and a bed are incommensurable. And according to Aristotle's metaphysics, only objects that share some quality can be placed in an equation that compares them quantitatively in the context of qualitative similarity.[10] In *NE* V.5, in the midst of his discussion of justice, Aristotle tries to determine what kind of quantity exchange value could be.

This question is important for understanding what would count as just exchange. Aristotle considers money as the possible basis of commensurability, but barter shows that commensurability does not depend on money. He considers need *(chreia)*, but it has no unit of measure. He considers money reckoned as the conventional representation of need: need divided into measurable units, as it were. Here he seems to have hit on the answer. He says: "Of course it is impossible that things differing so greatly from one another should in reality become commensurable. But it can be done adequately by relating them to need. Accordingly, there must be some unit, and it must be established by arbitrary usage — hence the name 'currency.'"[11] The problem is that the effort of the chapter is bent, not on commensurating things "adequately," but on finding what property of commodities makes it possible that in exchange a bed does not differ in quality from a house.[12] As Meikle proposes, Aristotle's comment that commensurability is "in reality" impossible must be taken as his admission that he can find "no acceptable solution" for the problem he has formulated.[13] There remains a metaphysical gap between use value and exchange value.

In the *Politics*, Aristotle explores this gap further. The two kinds of value an artifact may have correspond to two different kinds of acquisitive action. Household management *(oikonomikē)* requires the art of wealth-getting *(chrēmatistikē)* to provide the useful things it needs. But wealth-getting can fall into either of "two quite different patterns of acquisition and exchange."[14] The one, which Aristotle calls natural *chrēmatistikē*, seeks

---

10. Meikle, *Aristotle's Economic Thought*, pp. 13-17.
11. Aristotle, *NE*, V.5, 1133b19-23.
12. Meikle, *Aristotle's Economic Thought*, p. 38.
13. Meikle, *Aristotle's Economic Thought*, p. 27.
14. Meikle, *Aristotle's Economic Thought*, p. 47.

those things that are "necessary for life and useful for the community of city or household."[15] It is ordered, in other words, to the pursuit of use values. The other, which Aristotle says is especially called *chrēmatistikē*, but is actually unnatural and unnecessary, takes unlimited acquisition to be its end. It is easy to confuse the two, for they use the same tools and they both seek acquisition, but they go about it in different ways: "One has another end in view, the aim of the other is the increase of the property."[16]

Of course, for Aristotle, the end determines the nature of the activity. The end of natural *chrēmatistikē* is use value. Although it seeks this end most straightforwardly through direct appropriation from the land, Aristotle does not eschew exchange value here, for often the needs of the household can only be met through exchange. One exchanges a commodity that one has in excess in the hopes of acquiring a commodity one lacks. Here Aristotle introduces exchange value as a means to the end of pursuing use values. This kind of wealth-getting is limited by the requirements of "natural self-sufficiency."[17] In unnatural *chrēmatistikē*, on the other hand, exchange value is introduced as an end in itself. Since means are limited by the ends they serve, but ends are sought without limit, if exchange value is pursued as an end, the accumulation sought is necessarily unlimited.[18]

As Meikle points out, the gap between use value and exchange value is required by Aristotle's metaphysics, and Aristotle maintains it throughout his economic thought. The gap allows Aristotle to distinguish not only between two different kinds of value, and two different kinds of acquisitive activity, but also between two different definitions of wealth. True wealth is the use values that are necessary for flourishing. But wealth can also be

15. Aristotle, *Politics*, I, 1256b27-28.

16. Aristotle, *Politics*, I, 1257b37-38.

17. Aristotle, *Politics*, I, 1257a30-31.

18. We could characterize the distinction as between *chrēmatistikē* at the service of *oikonomia* and *chrēmatistikē* as an end. As Herman E. Daly and John B. Cobb, Jr., point out, the modern discipline of economics often functions as a study of *chrēmatistikē* as an end. Daly and Cobb, *For the Common Good: Redirecting the Economy toward Community, the Environment, and a Sustainable Future,* 2nd ed. (Boston: Beacon, 1994), pp. 138-39. In this respect, it is interesting that Mary Hirschfeld has found a corrective to some of the assumptions of modern economics in the work of Hazel Kyrk, whose work on the importance of household management for economic theory had little influence among economists, who considered her work mere "home economics." Mary Hirschfeld, "Standard of Living and Economic Virtue: Forging a Link between St. Thomas Aquinas and the Twenty-First Century," *Journal of the Society of Christian Ethics* 26 (2006): 61-78.

considered as the accumulation of exchange values, for many erroneously assume that riches "consist of a quantity of money."[19]

Aristotle did not go so far as to use this distinction to identify two different types of economy. Of course, Aristotle had no notion of "the economy" in our modern sense, perhaps precisely because his society was not regulated by markets as ours is. But once this idea of "economy" arises, we can use it to refer to any more or less systematic arrangement of production, distribution, and consumption. Therefore, we are perhaps not completely in error when we identify an "economy" in ancient Greece or in medieval Europe.[20] But in doing so, we must be careful to make clear how qualitatively different those economies were from what we today call "the economy."

It is Aristotle's own distinction between use value and exchange value that most aids us in doing just that.[21] In nonmarket societies, because markets are peripheral, exchange value itself remains marginal to the organization of economic activity; use values — and the incommensurable diversity they reflect — predominate. In such societies, human decisions operate primarily over the realm of irreducible and incommensurable natural kinds, with little or no reference to any exchange value that may be associated with those kinds. The constraints on decision-making are not primarily fluctuations or regularities in the movement of exchange value; rather, they are natural necessities and social mores. In a market society, on the other hand, human decisions operate primarily over exchange values, for economic activity is for the most part regulated by the circulation of exchange values. Here the most immediate constraints on decision-making are the apparent inevitabilities, the regularities and the cycles, arising from the circulation of exchange value itself. These regularities impose constraints that even seem to override custom and ethics.

Nonmarket Economy and Natural Order

In the context of nonmarket society, we see reflected in Aristotle's economic thought how fitting it is for humans to have a sense of the priority of their membership in a natural order that exceeds them. The order of

---

19. Aristotle, *Politics*, I, 1257b8.

20. On the appropriateness of this label, see M. I. Finley, *The Ancient Economy* (Berkeley: University of California Press, 1973).

21. Meikle, *Aristotle's Economic Thought*, pp. 171-72.

which they are members is a benevolent one, at least in the sense that its arrangement conduces to human welfare. At the same time, their dependence on this order requires a kind of yielding, a willingness to conform to its contours.

A nonmarket society, as I have said, is one in which market patterns are marginal to the bulk of economic activity. If markets are marginal, so is exchange value. Most acquisition is unmediated by exchange value. The marginality of exchange value does not mean that acquisition must be a kind of direct appropriation from nature, as in subsistence farming, though in such a society much acquisition will likely be of that kind. In addition, there may be complex arrangements of give and take that still do not depend on exchange value. As Karl Polanyi points out, many societies prior to or only minimally affected by the encompassing market economy have been characterized by intricate patterns of economic organization based on reciprocity or redistribution.[22] Such patterns are governed by social customs that shape a sense of social recognition, commonality, and membership. Instead of economic activity being constrained by the laws and cycles of exchange value, then, it is constrained primarily by the contingencies and necessities of the natural world and by the shape of the antecedent social fabric that is woven together with the fabric of natural order.

This sense of a benevolent antecedent natural order comes to the fore in Aristotle's discussion of the origins of wealth in Book 1 of the *Politics*. Humans seeking acquisition find themselves encompassed by a natural order appropriate to their needs. Just as nature provides a variety of food sources for the many wild animals, so there are a number of ways humans find sustenance from nature, such as agriculture, herding, hunting, or brigandage.[23] All of these ways of life are to be understood as ways

22. Polanyi, *Great Transformation*, p. 49.

23. Aristotle, *Politics*, I, 1256a19-1256b7. Aristotle apparently includes brigandage to cover the acquisition of natural slaves. Its inclusion here gives G. E. R. Lloyd concern that the normative use of "nature" stands in tension with the descriptive use. Lloyd, "The idea of nature in the *Politics*," in *Aristotelian Explorations* (Cambridge, UK: Cambridge University Press, 1996), pp. 184-204. What this concern fails to recognize is that Aristotle thought the naturalness of slavery to be empirically verifiable in slaves' servility of character. His assumption of slavery's naturalness reflects not a gap between descriptive and normative appeals to "nature," but an empirical mistake of taking the effects of domination for their cause. See Alasdair MacIntyre, *Whose Justice? Which Rationality?* (Notre Dame, IN: University of Notre Dame Press, 1988), pp. 104-5.

that nature nourishes what nature generates, analogous to the way nature provides mother's milk to nourish the young. We see, Aristotle says, that when nature brings forth new life, it provides for the sustenance of that new life, whether in the form of the nourishing egg or of the milk generated within the mother. As nature so obviously provides for the nourishment of the immature, we can be certain that the animal will not be abandoned by nature as it moves toward its developmental *telos*. Humans can thus expect that nature will provide their sustenance, and any of these diverse ways of acquiring it are modes of acquisition according to "the order of nature."[24]

This order not only promises nourishment; it also requires that human acquisitive practices be fitted to it. While nature sustains what nature generates, only the acquisition that is limited by what is required for human sustenance is natural. Not that acquisition must end with bare subsistence, for nature intends more than subsistence; indeed, nature intends human flourishing, and this is the reason for the *polis*. Isolated households may be able to maintain their subsistence, but the isolated household is only a stage in the development of the *polis*, which comes into being for the sake of fostering the good life.[25] But even if the limit on acquisition is beyond mere subsistence, it is nevertheless a limit, requiring that human acquisitive activity yield to what nature provides.[26]

There are two sides to this yielding. First, the origin of all wealth in natural processes must be respected. There are those who find an origin of wealth in making exchange value breed more exchange value, but such practices in truth involve "men's taking things from one another."[27] If nature's provision matches human need, then seeking wealth apart from nature's provision — through the conventions of exchange value — is necessarily excessive. Real wealth is derived from the work nature does in

24. Aristotle, *Politics*, I, 1256b26.

25. Aristotle, *Politics*, I, 1252b28-31.

26. Hirschfeld points out that the modern concern for upward mobility and technological advance has erased any sense of an upper limit on consumption and that local agreements about what constitutes human flourishing can provide a corrective. Hirschfeld, "Standard of Living and Economic Virtue," pp. 73-75. Cf. Christine Firer Hinze, "What Is Enough? Catholic Social Thought, Consumption, and Material Sufficiency," in *Having: Property and Possession in Religious and Social Life*, ed. William Schweiker and Charles Mathews (Grand Rapids: Eerdmans, 2004), pp. 162-88.

27. Aristotle, *Politics*, I, 1258b2-3.

offering sustenance to its offspring.[28] Nothing is more natural than "drawing provision from the fruits of the soil and from animals."[29] Thus we conform ourselves to nature by drawing our acquisition from the wellspring of nature's provision.

Second, we must recognize the limits of acquisition in what is "enough." Aristotle's references to the "natural limit" on acquisition must be understood in terms of what is enough for flourishing. In Book 7 of the *Politics*, he suggests that acquisition ought to be limited because *eudaimonia* is found in larger measure in those with moderate goods but high character than in those with excessive goods but deficient character.[30] This stands to reason, since the usefulness of external goods is limited by their instrumentality, while the goods of the soul can never be in too great a supply. Furthermore, in Book 1 he says that there must be a limit to wealth if it is to deserve the name. For no one is rich whose desires do not find rest in what they obtain, but are constantly agitated to get more.[31]

Sometimes Aristotle characterizes this "enough" as what is required in order to be self-sufficient *(autarkēs)*.[32] The translation of *autarkēs* as "self-sufficient" can be misleading insofar as it suggests that independence of others is integral to it.[33] Just as often — and most certainly here — Aristotle uses the term to mean simply "lacking nothing," as he does in the *NE*, where he defines it as "that which taken by itself makes life something desirable and deficient in nothing."[34] Thomas's commentary on the *Politics* similarly affirms that true riches are able "to take away *indigentia* [lack, need] and to make a sufficiency for those who have them, as namely a man has enough unto himself to live well."[35] This is what nature provides for

---

28. Modern economics tends to suppose that the traditional distinction between "real wealth" and "money wealth" no longer applies, if it ever did. Daly and Cobb have suggested, on the contrary, that recovering this distinction is long overdue. Daly and Cobb, *For the Common Good*, pp. 418-42.

29. Aristotle, *Politics*, I, 1258a37-38.

30. Aristotle, *Politics*, VII, 1323b1-7.

31. Aristotle, *Politics*, I, 1256b30-40.

32. Aristotle, *Politics*, I, 1256b1-7.

33. Meikle, *Aristotle's Economic Thought*, pp. 44-45.

34. Aristotle, *NE*, I.7, 1097b14-15.

35. "[T]ollere indigentiam et facere sufficientiam habenti eas, ut scilicet homo sit sibi sufficiens ad bene vivendum." *Sent. Pol.*, I.6, to Aristotle, I, 1256b30-40. (Translations from Thomas's Aristotelian commentaries are my own, unless otherwise noted; cf. the translation by Richard J. Regan [Indianapolis: Hackett, 2007], p. 48.)

her members, a "natural self-sufficiency."[36] To respect that provision and conform to it, humans must seek those use values that are necessary for the operation of virtue, and they must have the virtue to let go of the drive to grasp at more than this.[37]

Aristotelian Deference and Dependent Trust

The dependence on this natural order, the trust in its workings, and the importance of yielding to its contours that we have been exploring cohere with the deferent sense of membership in natural order seen elsewhere in Aristotle's writings. A sense of wonder at nature and trust in its workings is evident in Aristotle's natural philosophy. In the *Metaphysics,* he locates the very origin of philosophy in such wonder: "It is because of wonderment that men, both now and at first, start to study philosophy."[38] And the natural order that prompts such awe exhibits a striking rationality in its organization and purposiveness. Aristotle often uses anthropomorphic images of nature's activity: "Nature like a good householder throws away nothing of which anything useful can be made." "Nature behaves as if it foresaw the future."[39] It is doubtful that Aristotle actually imagined any kind of conscious agency at work here.[40] But modern commentators, eager to exonerate Aristotle of any kinship with notions of intelligent design, often underestimate the work such images do for him. It is true that he rarely invokes divine purpose, and even those invocations seem undermined by the aloofness of deity in the *Metaphysics.*

36. Aristotle, *Politics,* I, 1257a30-31.

37. In his determination to find insights that anticipate modern economic science in Aristotle, S. Todd Lowry neglects entirely the role of virtue in defining this limit, reading it as a naturally functioning equilibrating process determined by diminishing marginal utility. S. Todd Lowry, "Economic and Jurisprudential Ideas of the Greeks," in *Ancient and Medieval Economic Ideas and Concepts of Social Justice,* ed. S. Todd Lowry and Barry Gordon (Leiden: Brill, 1998), pp. 11-37, esp. pp. 31-33.

38. Aristotle, *Metaphysics,* I, 982b12-3, cited in Jonathan Barnes, *Aristotle* (Oxford: Oxford University Press, 1982), p. 65.

39. Aristotle, *De Generatione Animalium,* 2.6, 744b16-17; *De Partibus Animalium,* 686a22, cited in W. D. Ross, *Aristotle,* 5th ed. (London: Methuen & Co., reprint 1953), pp. 78-79.

40. Abraham Edel, *Aristotle and his Philosophy,* with new intro. (New Brunswick, NJ: Transaction Publishers, 1996), p. 65; see also Ross, *Aristotle,* p. 79.

Yet, regardless of the role of any divine agent, what is striking is the sense of membership in an orderly and well-managed household, tweaked to the benefit of its members. Consider Aristotle's wonder at the notion that the size of teeth, the speed of their growth, and the rate of their wearing down conspire to fit an animal's lifespan: "That is why here too nature has produced an excellent contrivance to fit the case; for she makes loss of the teeth coincide with old age and death."[41] Furthermore, in the *Nichomachean Ethics*, Aristotle appeals to nature's skillful ordering as the reason why flourishing depends on virtue, and is not left completely to chance. Virtue opens the possibility of flourishing to a wider constituency than chance would and thus is better, and if better, then it is what nature does. For "in the realm of nature, things are naturally arranged in the best way possible."[42] Aristotle's profound sense of the benevolent and orderly membership that connects and provides for all things is well captured in the following passage from the *Metaphysics:*

> In what way does the nature of the world contain what is good and what is best — as something separate and independent, or as its own orderliness? Rather, in both ways, as an army does. For the excellence of an army resides both in its orderliness and in its general, and especially in the latter. For he does not depend on the orderliness but it does depend on him. And all things — fish and birds and plants — are ordered in a way, yet not in the same way; and it is not the case that there is no connection between one thing and another. There is a connection.[43]

The connection is not something one could see or measure. One can only glimpse intimations of it simultaneously with the wonder that never ceases to stimulate inquiry. Such glimpses are one with the awe and trusting dependence of membership so poignantly captured in the image of nature's nourishment as mother's milk. This membership precedes and encompasses us, calling forth our deference and trusting receptivity.

---

41. *De Gen. Anim.*, 2.6, 745a27-b3, cited in Barnes, *Aristotle*, pp. 73-74.
42. Aristotle, *NE,* I.9, 1099b21-22.
43. Aristotle, *Metaphysics*, XII, 1075a11-18, cited in Barnes, *Aristotle*, p. 65.

The Promise and Threat of Money

Money plays a crucial role in accounting for the difference between nonmarket and market society, for it introduces the possibility of loosening exchange value from its subordination to use value, a possibility without which a market society would be unthinkable. Yet money plays an important role even in the society Aristotle discusses. It is important to look at what Aristotle says about money, because while money is in one sense "natural," it also provides the occasion for economic activity that does not yield to the contours of the natural order.

The fact that nature provides for what nature generates does not suggest that everything a community needs will always be ready to hand without recourse to exchange. In fact, fairly early in the course of the development of the *polis*, the practice of barter arose in order to get nature's goods to where they were needed. Sometimes a community has an excess of something and a deficiency of something else, and a neighboring community has a complementary excess and deficiency.[44] In that case, exchange itself becomes a means of getting nature's provision to those it is meant to sustain, a part of nature's care for nature's membership.

Aristotle supposes that money was devised as such exchanges became more prevalent, and especially as the distances between trading communities increased, for one of money's main advantages is its portability. Aristotle's appraisal of money is for the most part positive. Its invention was a matter of course in the development of the *polis*, for it was "an outcome of the necessary interchange of goods."[45] In the *NE*, Aristotle elaborates on the virtues of money: in addition to its portability, it aids in attaining equality in exchange by providing a common measure, and it irons out discrepancies in the timing of people's needs by functioning as a store of value until need arises.[46] By facilitating exchange in these ways, it helps to hold the *polis* together.

At the same time, however, money poses a serious danger. It is with the invention of money that people have an apparently compelling reason to take the accumulation of wealth as an end in itself. Once money was invented, unnatural *chrēmatistikē* followed in its wake.[47] Without money, ex-

---

44. Aristotle, *Politics*, I, 1257a19-25.
45. Aristotle, *Politics*, I, 1257a41-42.
46. Aristotle, *NE*, V.5; 1133a18-1133b18.
47. Aristotle, *Politics*, I, 1257a41-b5.

change value attaches only to objects that also have some separate use value, as a shoe can be either exchanged or worn. In fact, the very material configuration of the shoe, its natural kind, conveys a reminder of its use value; the fact that some other end besides exchange value is involved is hard to forget. But money is the conventional abstraction of exchange value from the shoe: once it is invented, its abstractive capabilities attach the luster of "real" (use value) wealth to a piece of leather, paper, or what have you. Then money, which provides no reminder of any further end but exchange value, seems to be wealth. Money thus changes from a means to acquire useful things and becomes a goal of acquisition that supervenes on the desire for useful things. This is the source of the illusion that wealth consists of piles of money, as Midas erroneously supposed.[48]

The distortions that money can introduce threaten the harmony between human economic activity and the natural order. First, when people take exchange value as an end, they lose sight of the pursuit of virtue and the "natural limits" on acquisition that go with it. Aristotle says that, true, there is a rationale to seeking property for its own sake. People desire life unreservedly, and that unbounded desire gets transferred to the means of sustaining life.[49] But this transfer shows that they do not realize that a few things suffice for the good life.[50] Seeking such excessive property consumes all their energies, and they neglect the cultivation of virtue. Second, nature's sustenance of human beings requires human industry in tilling the soil, working at crafts, and so on. The use values humans need for their flourishing depend on the quality of human work. But use values themselves are compromised when production is subordinated to the end of exchange value. Aristotle condemns the maker of the Delphian knife, which was apparently a kind of ancient-world Swiss Army knife: it was usable as a knife, a file, and a hammer, packing all those uses into one tool for the sake of being cheap.[51] What

48. Aristotle, *Politics*, I, 1257b13-17.

49. Robert Heilbroner sees an analogous insatiability endemic to capitalism. First, he says, the abstraction of wealth from use values makes calculations of relative wealth a reason for envy. Second, the human desire for self-preservation drives the capitalist imperative, for even the wealthy are made to feel vulnerable since the movement and growth of capital depends on relinquishing and recapturing it. Robert L. Heilbroner, *The Nature and Logic of Capitalism* (New York: W. W. Norton, 1985), pp. 54-57.

50. Aristotle, *Politics*, I, 1257b40-1258a2. For the limited role of property in the good life, see *NE*, X.8, 1178a24-1178b7.

51. Aristotle, *Politics*, I, 1252b1-5.

was wrong with the Delphian knife, according to Aristotle, was that "it is made to be exchanged and is bad at its job for that reason."[52] In other words, use value was diminished for the sake of exchange value. This can happen with any commodity or service that can be exchanged. Neither philosophy nor medicine, for example, is immune from corruption through being subordinated to exchange value. It makes all the difference whether a teacher maintains his or her true end while receiving remuneration for teaching, or becomes like the Sophist, "who makes money from an apparent but unreal wisdom."[53] Further, medical or military arts can be perverted by being turned into means for obtaining ever-increasing amounts of exchange value.[54] Third, as we have seen, money introduces the possibility of acquiring wealth solely through manipulating the conventions of exchange value. Since such manipulations cannot in reality be productive of wealth, this kind of acquisition becomes a mask for injustice, an obstacle to nature's sustenance reaching the human need for which it was intended. The priority of exchange value made possible by money jeopardizes the flourishing that the natural order intends for human beings.

Market Society and the Priority of Exchange Value

I have claimed that, in contrast to Aristotle's presentation of human membership in an antecedent natural order calling forth deference and receptivity, market society produces a construal of nature in which human claims to secure welfare from raw materials are self-justifying and prior to any external order. I cannot claim that Aristotle, or Thomas for that matter, envisioned such a development. But clearly Aristotle's economic thought (and Thomas follows him quite closely in these matters) aims at fostering the yielding involved in acknowledging membership in an antecedent natural order. Further, Aristotle certainly recognizes that taking exchange value as an end is a threat to that yielding.

What neither Aristotle nor Thomas imagined was a society in which most or all economic activity would be regulated by markets. Such a shift

---

52. Meikle, *Aristotle's Economic Thought*, p. 56.

53. Aristotle, *De Sophisticis Elenchis*, 165a23, cited in Meikle, *Aristotle's Economic Thought*, p. 70.

54. Aristotle, *Politics*, I, 1258a11-14.

involves a fundamental reorientation in the understanding of nature. When markets systematically regulate a society, all acquisition must have an eye to exchange value. Even direct acquisition from nature comes under the constraints and pressures imposed by the potential of the acquired goods to enter circulation as exchangeables. And most acquisition occurs only by the mediation of exchange value. This arrangement is radically different from a society in which the gravitational center of economic activity is in direct appropriations that can neglect exchange value and in social customs of reciprocity and redistribution that shape a sense of social recognition, commonality, and membership. The mediation of exchange value displaces the sense that welfare depends first of all on membership in an antecedent natural and social order.

Market society evokes the sense that welfare depends first of all on securing exchange value for oneself. This sense is at the root of the assumption common in modern economics that all economic activity begins in self-interest. In one sense, this assumption is true: everyone does what is required for survival, for what Roger E. Backhouse calls "the ordinary business of life."[55] But there is a fundamental difference here between nonmarket and market societies. In a nonmarket society, what is required is to take one's place within an antecedent membership. Karl Polanyi has challenged the notion that economic activity, even in nonmarket societies, must begin in a drive to secure and to safeguard one's own possessions. On the contrary, nonmarket society exerts pressure to act "so as to safeguard [one's] social standing, his social claims, his social assets. . . . The maintenance of social ties . . . is crucial. First, because by disregarding the accepted code of honor, or generosity, the individual cuts himself off from the community and becomes an outcast; second, because, in the long run, all social obligations are reciprocal, and their fulfillment serves also the individual's give-and-take interests best."[56] The drive to secure one's own possessions first and foremost is more characteristic of a market society, because in it economic activity is regulated by exchange value; what is incumbent in the "ordinary business of life" is to secure exchange value. Without a steady cache of exchange value, one cannot join that anonymous coterie of exchangers that mediates everyone's livelihood.

55. Roger E. Backhouse, *The Ordinary Business of Life: A History of Economics from the Ancient World to the Twenty-First Century* (Princeton, NJ: Princeton University Press, 2002).
56. Polanyi, *Great Transformation*, p. 48.

This displacement of natural and social membership by the priority of exchange value does not mean that a market society eclipses all sense of belonging or of social interdependence. Indeed, the circulatory system of exchange value itself is a kind of social glue that in some ways heightens the dependence of each individual on a wider system. But in the non-market style of reflection that we see in Aristotle, an immediate natural and social membership is prior to all particular claims to sustenance. In a market society, on the other hand, one's place within the network of exchange depends on the prior securing of exchange value. Without exchange value, one has no place in the system. One's claim to exchange value must be prior to economic interdependence, prior to one's belonging. And if such claims are prior to one's entrance into a wider order, they are for that reason primordial, unconditioned by the shaping of an antecedent order, undisciplined by the kind of yielding that Aristotle evoked.

The undisciplined — even self-justifying — character of these individual claims is further bolstered by the unquestionability conferred on exchange value itself. Aristotle notes in the *NE* that exchange value is a sort of metaphysical oddity: it attributes to things a substantive, measurable quantity that cannot be derived from the thing's essence. We wish we knew what it was; yet, even though we do not, it performs an important function, so we will keep it. This treatment of exchange value pays it respect, but finds its arbitrariness to be somewhat question-begging. In a society regulated by exchange value, the possibility of exchange value's existence is taken more for granted. Instead, exchange value is understood as a condition of the possibility of other things, a starting point for thought rather than a curious oddity to be investigated. The arbitrariness of it, instead of rendering it potentially dubious, guarantees that the perhaps equally arbitrary human appraisals on which it is based will share in its unquestionability. One does not ask whether exchange values reflect human desires that yield to the shape of nature's provision; rather, one accepts human desires as givens of economic life. If exchange value is basic, then the individual desires that work together to determine it must be basic, primordial.

The dominance of exchange value is a large part of the reason that use values, rooted in qualities of things that are antecedent to human desires, have gotten eclipsed in modern economic thought. Whereas Aristotle carefully maintained the distinction between use value and exchange value, economists since the mid-nineteenth century have tended to reduce the concept of economic value to a unity, one definable in terms of exchangeability. Hence, in contrast to Aristotle's two definitions of wealth, John Stuart Mill offers but one: "all useful or agreeable things, which possess exchangeable value."[57] In 1890, Alfred Marshall could recall Adam Smith's mention of the distinction between use value and exchange value only to dismiss use value without argument and conclude that "the term value is relative, and expresses the relation between two things at a particular time and place."[58] Here exchange value, and the relative "agreeableness" associated with it, stands supreme and unassailable.

If individual claims are prior to external order and self-justifying in this way, if they are not patient of Aristotle's yielding, then it stands to reason that the claims of diverse individuals, all of whom have their own self-justifying interests, will tend to compete. It is important to remember that individual greed is not at fault. The exigency of securing exchange value, dictated by the shape of the system, produces this result. The market configuration constrains economic activity to take this shape, to be rooted in the individual's need to secure exchange value. Hence, exchangers face one another, not primarily as fellow members in a network of common recognition, but as strangers whose competing self-interests can never be "got behind" — because they are construed as primordial by this system. Aristotle's fabric of social and natural co-membership can no longer be primordial, can no longer be the canopy of commonality and recognition that encompasses and governs economic activity. Instead, the imperative that identifies me first of all with my exchange value, and hence with my property, becomes inescapable. It is no wonder that, in such a society, social agreement comes to be understood as a byproduct of the interactions of these antecedent individuals.[59]

Market society produces a construal of nature in which what is archaic is the individual's claim for security rather than the fabric of a natu-

57. John Stuart Mill, *Principles of Political Economy* (New York, 1969), p. 9, cited in Meikle, *Aristotle's Economic Thought*, p. 49.

58. Alfred Marshall, *Principles of Economics*, 4th ed. (London, 1898), p. 8, cited in Meikle, *Aristotle's Economic Thought*, p. 192.

59. C. B. Macpherson has argued that modern market society provides the basis for the understanding of political society assumed by classical liberal political theory. His argument converges with mine in some ways, although he does not make much of the Aristotelian distinction between use value and exchange value in accounting for the peculiar character of market society. Consequently, his account of nonmarket society focuses almost entirely on the constraints of custom and status, with little reflection on how such traditional mores reflect deference to a natural order. C. B. Macpherson, *The Political Theory of Possessive Individualism: Hobbes to Locke* (Oxford: Oxford University Press, 1962).

ral and social membership. What Aristotle's analysis helps us see is that the priority of this individual claim is not a necessary anthropological phenomenon but is linked with the ascendancy of exchange value.

Thomas and Locke on Natural Order and Property

The foregoing account of the primacy of use values and the corresponding deference to natural order in Aristotle's economic thought forms the necessary background for understanding Thomas's comments on property and on justice in exchange. As we shall see in later chapters, this background also helps us grasp why Thomas's account of just and charitable use of external goods exhibits an orientation ordered to its *telos* in the humble vulnerability of the cross of the poor Christ. Human action that is properly located within an encompassing order that exceeds us is human action that can culminate in the self-surrendering receptivity of the cross, which is a participation in the encompassing ecstasy of the divine charity. On the other hand, human action that begins in unconditioned individual claims set against a world of raw materials cannot but stand in unremitting tension with the pattern of the cross.

In the remainder of this chapter I will underscore the difference between Thomas Aquinas's rather Aristotelian view and the understanding of nature typical of modern market society by contrasting Aquinas with John Locke. Such a comparison may be particularly helpful to us as we try to overcome our tendency to read a modern view of nature back onto Thomas, especially because Thomas is often understood to stand in some significant degree of continuity with Locke, particularly on issues of nature and property.[60] The comparison will show that Locke's view of nature is populated by the kinds of unconditioned and antecedent individuals associated with the ascendancy of exchange value.[61] Thomas's view, on the other hand, reflects the priority of the fabric of natural and social membership that we have investigated in Aristotle.

60. See, for example, B. Andrew Lustig's argument for a "tradition of property in common" shared by Thomas and Locke in his "Natural Law, Property, and Justice: The General Justification of Property in John Locke," *Journal of Religious Ethics* 19 (1991): 119-48.

61. Locke, of course, is one of the prime exhibits in Macpherson's explication of classical liberal political theory in terms of "possessive individualism." Macpherson, *The Political Theory of Possessive Individualism.*

John Locke is a fitting interlocutor with Thomas on issues of wealth. Indeed, many of their interests in discussing nature and property appear to be quite similar. Like Thomas, Locke sees an order to nature that is orchestrated by God. Within that order, humans occupy a rather high place in the hierarchy of natures, of "ranks of creatures," as he calls them.[62] Humans are especially honored as God's "workmanship."[63] Like Thomas, Locke affirms that within this order, humans have a sort of dominion, for the "inferior creatures" are made for human use.[64] And both Thomas and Locke affirm that, according to nature, the goods of the earth are meant for human beings *in common*. Furthermore, Locke affirms that because of the way in which humans belong to this order, their appropriation of what they need is natural. This seems to be an echo of Thomas's affirmation that "when someone acquires that which nature has made for his own sake, the acquisition is natural."[65] They even seem to share some agreement on the importance of external goods succoring the poor. Such goods are given to humans in common, and although property is legitimate, those in dire need are due relief from the surplus of the rich.[66]

Despite these similarities, we can see how, in comparison to Thomas, Locke's views bear witness to the shift I have described that takes as primordial the individual's claim for security, rather than the fabric of natural and social membership.[67] It may be argued that Locke is a pre-market-society thinker on the grounds that the notion of a fully market-regulated society was yet to have a referent.[68] But it must be noted that the confluence of market patterns that would reach a definitive stage in nineteenth-

62. John Locke, *The Second Treatise of Government,* ed. Thomas P. Peardon (New York: Macmillan, 1986), chap. 2, § 6.

63. Locke, *Second Treatise,* chap. 2, § 6.

64. Locke, *Second Treatise,* chap. 2, § 6; chap. 5, §§ 25-27. Cf. *ST* II-II 66.1.

65. "[Q]uando aliquis acquirit id quod natura propter ipsum fecit, est naturalis acquisitio." *Sent. Pol.,* I.6, to Aristotle I, 1256b7-26.

66. *ST* II-II 66.7; John Locke, *First Treatise of Government,* in *Two Treatises of Government,* ed. Peter Laslett (New York: Cambridge University Press, 1963), pp. 205-6.

67. Macpherson claims that in seventeenth-century English possessive individualism, "the individual is essentially the proprietor of his own person and capacities, for which he owes nothing to society." I would add that it is equally significant that this individual owes nothing to the natural order, except to "improve" it. Macpherson, *Possessive Individualism,* p. 263.

68. Polanyi finds no application for the idea before the Industrial Revolution. Polanyi, *Great Transformation.*

century England developed over many centuries. Indeed, the social relationships of production of nineteenth-century English capitalism "had their roots in the soil of Locke's England."[69]

As an initial example of the difference, consider how Thomas and Locke justify the claim that other species are intended for the use of humans. Both refer to God's granting of dominion. But Thomas, following Aristotle, reads that dominion in terms of a preeminence within a common membership. Therefore, he sees a need to provide an argument for human preeminence on the assumption of continuity between humans and other creatures.[70] In human development we see that humans grow from imperfect to more perfect. The earlier stages, shared with all living things, are for the sake of the later, more perfect ones. Just as the imperfect is for the sake of the more perfect, the lower species are for the sake of the higher. Thomas needs such an argument precisely because he begins from the common membership in the natural order that humans share with all other species.

Locke, on the other hand, seems to assume that human origins are quite of another kind from those of all other creatures. He adds to the appeal to God's grant of dominion simply that "men, being once born, have a right to their preservation."[71] It never occurs to him that other living things, once generated, might have a similar right, so that the superiority of the right of "men" must be justified. Rather, he seems to see no common membership shared by humans and other living things. On the one hand are "the fruits [the world] naturally produces and beasts it feeds"; on the other hand are human beings.[72] For them, in place of the organic overtones of being "produced" and "fed," Locke uses the language of artifice: they are "the workmanship of one omnipotent and infinitely wise Maker."[73] Rather than God bringing forth one natural order of which humans are preeminent members, God brings forth human beings, on the one hand, and the fruitful processes of nature for their sustenance, on the other. The Lockean self is a kind of foreigner to the membership of the natural order to which other animals belong. The "right" of humans to their sustenance is intro-

---

69. Neal Wood, *John Locke and Agrarian Capitalism* (Berkeley: University of California Press, 1984), p. 92.

70. *ST* II-II 64.1.

71. Locke, *Second Treatise*, chap. 5, § 25.

72. Locke, *Second Treatise*, chap. 5, § 26.

73. Locke, *Second Treatise*, chap. 2, § 6.

duced as if from another dimension, heedless of the deference that befits membership.

To characterize the Lockean self as a "foreigner" is perhaps too stark. Locke clearly understands that the human being is "at home" in the world, a world that God has graciously fitted for his habitation.[74] But if both Aquinas and Locke imagine that the human being belongs in the world, in Locke this belonging is construed in a different way. While the Aristotelian and Thomistic account characterizes belonging as membership, the Lockean account imagines belonging as ownership. It is in this sense that the Lockean self is a foreigner. He relates to the other things in the world not first of all via a common fabric of membership they share but via the proprietary claims he introduces that have their own independent and prior legitimacy.

Legitimate Appropriation and the Origin of Property

This difference continues as one digs deeper into their apparently similar accounts of property. A close reading reveals that Thomas differs from Locke by distinguishing the rationale for legitimate appropriation from the account of *proprietas*. Thomas discusses the institution of property in several places, but the most compact summary of his own position is found in the first two articles of the question on theft in the *ST*.[75] What is striking is that the first article, on legitimate appropriation, prescinds from any notion of property. Human dominion in Thomas is originally a non-proprietary notion; and this original dominion is limited by the sovereignty exercised over all things by God, the pattern and guarantor of the natural order.[76]

This distinction between divine and human dominion is easy to overlook, but it plays a crucial function. We tend to think of limits on property in terms of social constraints and responsibilities. Thomas intro-

---

74. Locke, *Second Treatise*, chap. 5, §§ 25-27.

75. For interpretations of Thomas on property, see William J. McDonald, *The Social Value of Property according to St. Thomas Aquinas* (Washington, DC: The Catholic University of America Press, 1939), and Anthony Parel, "Aquinas's Theory of Property," in *Theories of Property: Aristotle to the Present*, ed. Anthony Parel and Thomas Flanagan (Waterloo, ON: Wilfrid Laurier University Press, 1979), pp. 88-111.

76. *ST* II-II 66.1.

duces those kinds of limits in the next article, on property. Here Thomas insists that even the original social *dominium,* on which the institution of *proprietas* is based, is limited. It is an adjunct to the *dominium* of God, who "directed certain things to the sustenance of man's body."[77] Therefore, a rationale derives from the divine ordering, with which human *dominium* must conform. Just as Aristotle's account of wealth is characterized by a yielding to the provision offered by nature for human sustenance, so Thomas subordinates human *dominium* to the divine purpose of nourishing human beings.

The nonproprietary character of original *dominium* can be clarified by seeing how Thomas's notion of *dominium naturale* responded to certain prominent views at the time.[78] There was a tradition, rooted in Augustine and recently recast by Joachim, that saw the institution of property as a kind of concession, a consequence of the sinful state of humanity, that appeared less than perfectly just in light of the perfect sharing of the paradisal state.[79] Even more recently, the Franciscan order, more or less influenced by this tradition, had come to insist that there was no human *dominium* in Eden or in the early church, and that its friars imitated this complete poverty by living without any *dominium,* including over the food they ate.[80] Maintaining this rejection of *dominium* required all kinds of juridical gymnastics, but the crux was a legal distinction, approved by the papacy, between *dominium* and *simplex usus facti.* The friars could have

---

77. *ST* II-II 66.1 ad 1.

78. Joan Lockwood O'Donovan is correct in recognizing a difference between a Franciscan-Wycliffite ideal of natural nonproprietary community and Thomas's account, which shifts more weight onto distribution as opposed to common use, and which sees a kind of *dominium* as natural even apart from sin. But it is easy to misread Thomas's *dominium naturale* in overly proprietary terms, especially in light of how Thomas was used by subsequent papal opponents of the Franciscans. In my reading, Thomas is trying to reckon with the fact that for many human needs, an account of common use analogous to our use of the sun is inadequate. In the case of some goods, appropriation is a condition of their use. Joan Lockwood O'Donovan, "Christian Platonism and Non-Proprietary Community," in O'Donovan and O'Donovan, *Bonds of Imperfection,* pp. 73-96, esp. p. 94, n. 77.

79. Paul J. Weithman, "Justice, Charity, and Property: The Centrality of Sin to the Political Thought of Thomas Aquinas," Ph.D. diss., Harvard University, 1988, pp. 117-26. Cf. Joan Lockwood O'Donovan's appreciation of this Augustinian tradition in "Christian Platonism and Non-Proprietary Community."

80. M. D. Lambert, *Franciscan Poverty: The Doctrine of the Absolute Poverty of Christ and the Apostles in the Franciscan Order, 1210-1323* (London: S.P.C.K., 1961).

this most basic kind of use without acquiring *dominium* over the goods they used.

It is against this background that we see Thomas Aquinas affirming a natural *dominium* of use proper to humans even in Eden. First, Thomas is attempting to account for the text of Genesis 1:26-28. Second, he is surely resisting what he sees as some of the excesses of the most extreme representatives of the Franciscan position.[81] The extreme rejection of *dominium* was increasingly associated with an idealization of poverty that, in Thomas's view, was losing sight of poverty's instrumentality. Third, part of the difference has to do with diverse perceptions of what *dominium* properly denotes. Franciscans tended to reject *dominium* because they took it to convey an absolute power of control, according to the meaning it often had carried in Roman law.

Duns Scotus would reject Thomas's affirmation of the compatibility of *dominium* with the state of innocence, for he "took *dominium* to be necessarily private, something which . . . could . . . be defended against the claims of the needy."[82] But some in the field of canon law had attempted to match the concept to the complexity of feudal practice by extending it to cover any power of use, inventing the notion of a *dominium utile*.[83] Whereas Franciscans tended to identify *dominium* with a possessive lordship, others viewed it as any allowance conferring legitimacy on use. Thomas incorporates *dominium* into the state of innocence by understanding *dominium* in a more minimal sense as any power — however limited and subordinate — to use goods.

It is now frequently recognized that these debates over *dominium* played a role in the evolution of modern natural rights-theories such as Locke's.[84] But we should not think of Thomas as pressing in that direction.

81. As Kelly Johnson points out, though the heart of the Franciscan position was a salutary "economic pacifism" that bore witness to the eschatological destiny of all things, when renouncing rights becomes a primary criterion of faithfulness, humility conflicts with charity and rights are severed from duties. Kelly S. Johnson, *The Fear of Beggars: Stewardship and Poverty in Christian Ethics*, Eerdmans Ekklesia Series (Grand Rapids: Eerdmans, 2007), pp. 57-63.

82. Richard Tuck, *Natural Rights Theories: Their Origin and Development* (Cambridge, UK: Cambridge University Press, 1979), p. 21.

83. Tuck, *Natural Rights Theories*, pp. 15-17.

84. In addition to Tuck, see Brian Tierney, *The Idea of Natural Rights: Studies on Natural Rights, Natural Law, and Church Law 1150-1625* (Grand Rapids: Eerdmans, 1997), in the Emory Studies in Law and Religion series, ed. John Witte, Jr.; see also Virpi Mäkinen, *Prop-*

Tuck suggests that a crucial step was the later identification of *dominium* with *ius* that occurred because of the expansion of the notion of *dominium* by the lawyers. *Dominium* continued to connote "private control," affecting the notion of *ius*, until the pivotal figure, Jean Gerson, identified *ius* as a definite, personal faculty.[85] A further, perhaps complementary, factor is the outcome of the debates about Franciscan poverty. As the disruptive and ecclesiastically explosive potential of the rejection of *dominium* became clearer, the papacy under John XXII moved to declare the rejection of all *dominium* heretical. In the midst of the controversy, the opponents of the Franciscans argued that there had to be *dominium* even in the state of innocence.[86] What was momentous was that these opponents generally accepted the Franciscan understanding of *dominium*. Affirming *dominium* in the state of innocence thus pushed notions of "absolute power" into that state.

John XXII and his supporters are sometimes supposed to have adopted a "Thomistic" understanding to combat the Franciscans. But Thomas never understood *dominium* in the way many Franciscans did. If he had, he would have been just as wary as they were of attributing it to the state of innocence. The *dominium* Thomas affirms of the state of innocence is limited, social, and defined by the power of use that is necessary to human beings in order to accomplish the purpose of sustenance established for them by the divine order. It is a *dominium* whose contours are defined by a yielding to the prior fabric of natural and social membership that encompasses human beings. In short, this *dominium* is nonproprietary.

One may ask why, if market society was still a long time in coming, other notions of *dominium*, notions more reflective of the nonreceptive, self-justifying proprietary claims that I have said are linked with the ascendancy of exchange value, came rather rapidly into some prominence not long after Thomas's day. The question is beyond the scope of this work, as well as beyond my expertise. But I venture that the answer has at least something to do with the growth of what Lester K. Little calls a "profit economy" during the High Middle Ages, the economy to which the mendi-

---

erty *Rights in the Late Medieval Discussion on Franciscan Poverty,* Recherches de Théologie et Philosophie médiévales, Bibliotheca, 3 (Leuven: Peeters, 2001).

85. Tuck, *Natural Rights Theories,* pp. 25-28.

86. Mäkinen, *Property Rights.*

cant movements were a reaction.[87] This economy, characterized by fairly rapid monetization, had perhaps already begun to foster the patterns associated with the gravitational pull of a dominating exchange value, at least in some pockets. It is a question that requires more research.[88]

What is clear is that the notion of *dominium* that Thomas proposes resists any pressure toward displacing the sense of an antecedent natural and social membership with primordial claims of individual propriety. In contrast to Thomas's position, Locke's account of property makes no bones about beginning with proprietary claims that have independent and prior legitimacy. One grasps a faint echo of Aquinas in Locke's admission that human beings belong to God: they are "his property whose workmanship they are."[89] But whereas the reference to divine sovereignty in Thomas conditions human claims, Locke's remark seems aimed at securing the noninterference of others in one's pursuit of such claims. Further, Thomas uses a broad yet limited notion of *dominium* to account for the social fact of human appropriation of necessities, while Locke roots such appropriation in a prior and individual claim of ownership: "Every man has a property in his own person."[90]

The difference between Locke's "labor theory of property" and Thomas's approach could hardly be more striking. Thomas justifies human appropriation of necessities in limited and social terms before he ever

87. Lester Little, *Religious Poverty and the Profit Economy in Medieval Europe* (Ithaca, NY: Cornell University Press, 1978).

88. A very illuminating piece of research on these questions has recently come from Joel Kaye. Kaye argues that economic change provides an important piece of the background for understanding the form that the revival of natural philosophy took in the fourteenth century. Scholars' growing recognition of the mechanistic character of the movements of money, and their willingness to accept the corresponding displacement of arithmetic equivalence and exact equalization by geometric approximation and probability, produced much of the mathematical language that would then be applied to the study of natural (and supernatural!) phenomena with such zeal. This argument suggests that the circulation of exchange value had reached a sort of "critical mass" by the end of the thirteenth century. In light of such a suggestion, it seems plausible that the pivotal developments toward modern natural rights language and the pivotal developments toward modern scientific naturalism both reflected the emerging predominance of exchange values. I discuss Kaye's work further in the concluding chapter. Joel Kaye, *Economy and Nature in the Fourteenth Century: Money, Market Exchange, and the Emergence of Scientific Thought* (Cambridge, UK: Cambridge University Press, 1998).

89. Locke, *Second Treatise*, chap. 2, § 6.

90. Locke, *Second Treatise*, chap. 5, § 27.

introduces the notion of *proprietas*. Only after the question of appropriation has been resolved does Thomas ask how this common and naturally limited *dominium* coheres with the institution of property. Locke, on the other hand, invokes an assumption of property to answer the question of legitimate appropriation. Because one owns oneself and hence one's labor, to mix one's labor with external goods through appropriating them is to attach something to those goods "that excludes the common right of other men."[91] The importance of proprietary claims Locke sees in the economy of seventeenth-century England is "read back into the nature of the individual."[92] Reading Thomas well demands resisting any such "reading back."

Property and Community

The *dominium* Thomas Aquinas proposes is both common and strictly limited by God's ordering of things to human sustenance. As he relates the institution of *proprietas* to that of *dominium,* the sense of an antecedent community embraced by an antecedent order of nourishment remains prevalent.

Thomas's remarks about property in the second article on theft have frequently been understood by modern interpreters, particularly by economic historians, to anticipate some of the fundamental individualistic assumptions of modern economics. It will be illuminating to look briefly at those interpretations. Thomas offers three reasons that *proprietas* is an appropriate institution for the sake of "procuring and dispensing." They are largely traditional, derived from Aristotle as interpreted by Thomas's teacher, Albertus Magnus, and from patristic sources. First, the institution of property promotes greater care *(sollicitudo)* in the necessary work of procuring, since otherwise each would seek to leave such work to others. Second, the institution of property provides an order for human affairs in place of the confusion that would arise if responsibility for goods were not assigned determinately. Third, allowing property yields a more peaceful community, for common possession leads to quarreling.

The first thing to note about these reasons is that Thomas, along

91. Locke, *Second Treatise,* chap. 5, § 27.
92. Macpherson, *Possessive Individualism,* p. 3.

with most of the tradition he inherits, sees a need to make them. Locke, we notice, makes no arguments of this kind. For Thomas, property is a social institution: it is devised by human communities and is capable of explanation. It is not dictated by natural law, but is a kind of addition to it devised by reason, a part of the "law of nations" *(ius gentium)*.[93] For Locke, property is a given of human existence: it is rooted in the individual constitution of every person. What needs to be explained is not its rationale but the mechanism for extending it from its original habitation in the individual outward to encompass other things.

Of the reasons Thomas offers, the one that is most often taken as the anticipation of modern economic wisdom is the first, which is sometimes misleadingly called the "argument from efficiency." As the interpretation goes, Thomas acknowledges that a social institution might find legitimacy in harnessing economic self-interest for the sake of greater productivity. Of course, such intuitions are hardly present in the original version of the argument in Aristotle. However, "[i]n the hands of St Thomas Aquinas and his successors, this line of reasoning . . . provides a major rationale for their acceptance of a free market economy as a framework for economic analysis."[94] Odd Langholm is more careful: he notes that, as Thomas states it, the argument is not about efficiency at all, but about incentive. But Langholm simply shifts the anticipation of modern wisdom from the *ST* into Thomas's commentary on Aristotle's *Politics,* where he remarks, "It is a good thing that each one shall enlarge his possessions more, applying himself to them more carefully *[insistens ei sollicitius]* as being his own."[95] It is difficult to see how this statement goes beyond the argument in the *ST*. But the normally judicious Langholm becomes quite tendentious: "Granted that Thomas had set out merely to explain the text of the *Politics,* . . . he cannot have been quite unaware of the far-reaching implications of what he was saying. It is impossible to suppress the inference that just as material wealth is an instrument from a personal point of view, so self-interest regarding wealth is now being accepted as an instrument from a social point of view. This is a fundamental principle of analysis in econom-

93. *ST* II-II 66.2 ad 1; 57.3.

94. Barry Gordon, *Economic Analysis before Adam Smith: Hesiod to Lessius* (New York: Barnes and Noble, 1975), p. 53.

95. As quoted in Odd Langholm, *Economics in the Medieval Schools: Wealth, Exchange, Value, Money and Usury according to the Paris Theological Tradition, 1200-1350* (Leiden: Brill, 1992), p. 215.

ics. . . ."[96] Despite how far Langholm has to reach to grasp it, there is some plausibility to this interpretation. The argument implies that people will be lazy unless, realizing that they will reap their own fruit, they see how their sloth harms their own interests. The incentive of self-interest then leads to more diligent work and consequent increases in productivity (to "enlarge his possessions"). That society should be organized to derive this benefit from the pursuit of self-interest is then hailed as a good thing. It is not a complete mystery why this argument is mistaken for a precursor to Adam Smith.

But the economists' reading is a mistake. As I have suggested above, it is important to distinguish the economic self-interest that everyone actually does share, that is, the need to do what is required for the "ordinary business of life," from that peculiar economic self-interest that is produced by the predominance of exchange value, according to which every individual faces the exigency, antecedent to all social commerce, to secure exchange value. Thomas's argument merely acknowledges that, given that sinful people tend toward sloth, the institution of property can teach them to appreciate the importance of that "ordinary business of life" that is incumbent on us all if we are to receive the sustenance God directs toward us. As Paul Weithman points out, the development of virtue requires us to appreciate the usefulness of material things for the ends that are appropriate to us. Property is a reasonable political development because it is better than mere common possession at training sinful people to grasp that usefulness and apply themselves to it accordingly.[97] Therefore, far from turning avarice to good use, or using social institutions to harness individualistic desires, Thomas's argument is about a moral education that will produce a more virtuous community.

We also see Thomas's receptivity to natural and social order — in contrast to Locke's priority on individual proprietary claims — in Thomas's adoption of the traditional Christian notion of the *ius necessitatis*. Goods, as we have seen, have an end in the common sustenance of human beings. That is why property is truly lawful only as a matter of "procuring and dispensing." With regard to the use of things, each person "ought to possess external things, not as his own, but as common, so that, to wit, he is ready to communicate them to others in their

---

96. Langholm, *Economics in the Medieval Schools*, p. 215.
97. Weithman, "Justice, Charity, and Property," pp. 126-66.

need."[98] Thomas envisions this proper distribution of things as far as their use to be largely a matter of the exercise of the virtues of liberality and charity.[99] But the notion of *proprietas* is conditioned by the common *dominium* in a further way that depends less on the various dispositions of those with property. Specifically, in extreme need, where the institution of *proprietas* mortally threatens the end of the common *dominium*, the common *dominium* takes over, and the power of *proprietas* is that far suspended. In other words, to take from another out of extreme need is not stealing, even if done secretly, and no matter whether the need is one's own or a neighbor's.[100]

This power of the poor may appear to be another point of similarity between Thomas and Locke. For Locke insists on the right of the poor to others' surplus:

> God the Lord and Father of all, has given no one of his children such a Property, in his peculiar Portion of the things of this World, but that he has given his needy Brother a Right to the Surplusage of his Goods; so that it cannot justly be denied him, when his pressing Wants call for it. . . . As *Justice* gives every Man a Title to the product of his honest Industry, and the fair Acquisitions of his Ancestors descended to him; so *Charity* gives every Man a Title to so much out of another's Plenty, as will keep him from extreme Want . . . and a Man can no more justly make use of another's necessity, to force him to become his Vassal, by withholding that Relief God requires him to afford the wants of his Brother, than he that has more strength can seize upon a weaker, master him to his Obedience, and with a dagger at his Throat offer him Death or Slavery.[101]

---

98. *ST* II-II 66.2. Langholm suggests that this stipulation on property is inconsistent with Thomas's first argument for the institution of property, for common use upsets the incentive to solicitous work. But given that, for Thomas, one's responsibility to direct goods to common use begins with the needs of one's own household, and that Thomas reserves the *ius necessitatis* for cases of extreme need, the objection seems excessively fastidious. Langholm, *Economics in the Medieval Schools*, pp. 216-17.

99. For an interesting argument about the questionability of governmental redistribution from Thomas's perspective, see Paul J. Weithman, "Natural Law, Property, and Redistribution," *Journal of Religious Ethics* 21 (1993): 165-80.

100. *ST* II-II 66.7.

101. Locke, *First Treatise*, pp. 205-6.

The flavor here certainly smacks of patristic exhortations to charity. But what might not be noticed in the rhetoric is that Locke never actually countenances the *ius necessitatis*. The exhortations remain aimed at alleviating need through charity alone. We see no conditioning of property here that does not depend on the dispositions of those with property. And in the subsequent section Locke hits on an answer to poverty that bolsters proprietary claims rather than conditioning them: "The Authority of the Rich Proprietor, and the Subjection of the Needy Beggar began not from the Possession of the Lord, but the Consent of the poor Man, who preferr'd being his Subject to starving. And the Man he thus submits to, can pretend to no more Power over him, than he has consented to, upon Compact."[102] The needy beggar who sells his labor finds some sustenance, and the voluntary nature of the arrangement distinguishes it from the slavery against which Locke warned in the previous passage. Perhaps offering employment, then, is a suitable response to the demand for charity.

In Locke the ancient right of the poor to others' surplus retains its rhetorical weight, but it is transmuted from a communal discipline that both obliges the wealthy to deeds of charity and absolves the extremely poor of the charge of theft, into a duty of relief whose responsibility falls one-sidedly on the shoulders of the wealthy individual. If in Thomas the *ius necessitatis* marks the extent to which the notion of property is conditioned by the shape of divine order, in Locke the right of the poor to sustenance fails to crack the impregnable fortress of antecedent proprietary claims. Locke's words about government appropriation of property seem to apply equally to appropriation of property by the poor: "Nobody has a right to take their substance or any part of it from them without their own consent; without this, they have no property at all, for I have truly no property in that which another can by right take from me when he pleases, against my consent."[103] The unquestionable nature of the Lockean proprietary claim is here reflected in his all-or-nothing conception of property: there can be no property if my voluntary control of it is conditioned. In Thomas, on the other hand, all human *dominium* is circumscribed and limited. This does not mean there can be no property, but that he conceives of property otherwise than does Locke. Locke abstracts the ancient

102. Locke, *First Treatise*, § 43, cited in Wood, *Locke and Agrarian Capitalism*, pp. 89-90.

103. Locke, *Second Treatise*, chap. 11, § 138.

right of the poor from the fabric of social recognition and membership that once presided over all property claims, and he reconstitutes it as a responsibility attaching to property where property claims themselves now reign supreme.

What we begin to see through these comparisons of Thomas and Locke is the depth of the difference between their respective views of nature. Thomas's Aristotelian approach is based on a receptivity that acknowledges the priority of a natural and social order, a membership that encompasses and conditions the economic activity of the human being. In Locke, on the other hand, an individual whose proprietary claims have an independent and prior legitimacy confronts the world as a kind of foreigner, introducing self-justifying (and thus from Thomas's perspective, presumptive) desires. Nature is thus strangely bifurcated in Locke. On the one hand, it is the tillable wilderness, as yet not fully commensurate to human need. It is the raw materials, the "almost worthless materials" that "nature and the earth furnished."[104] On the other hand, it is the source of the rights inhering in individuals unconditioned by that network of "materials." Nature is both the wilderness awaiting human labor and the legitimater of the "improvement" that proprietary humans impose on that wilderness. In contrast to this dualism of "natural man" and "natural raw materials," Thomas, like Aristotle, assumes one harmonious natural order that antecedently penetrates and commensurates "external goods" and the human beings for whose sustenance they are intended. As with Aristotle, so in Thomas, this natural order evokes a very nonmodern deference and trusting receptivity. Grasping this difference between Thomas's view and a modern view like Locke's is crucial to understanding Thomas's economic teachings. Only in light of that difference can we imagine the human action that Thomas joins Aristotle in calling "natural" as action that is fulfilled rather than frustrated in the consummation embodied in the charity of the poor Christ.

104. Locke, *Second Treatise*, chap. 5, § 43.

CHAPTER 2

Usury, Just Price, and Natural Order

Thomas Aquinas sympathizes with much of Aristotle's economic thought in large part because he recognizes in it a deferent receptivity that strikes a chord with his own account of our ontological poverty and dependence. In contrast, market society tends to produce unconditioned individuals, related to the rest of the natural order across the distance defined by ownership rather than embedded in one and the same membership. In this respect, Locke's understanding of nature as the source of individual rights, on the one hand, and the range of raw materials over which those rights are exercised, on the other, is more familiar to us. Our nearness to Locke marks our distance from Thomas. If we do not recognize these differences, do not recognize the peculiar blind spots induced by modern market society, it will be easy for us to misread Thomas's economic answers as addressing our economic questions.

In this chapter I argue that Thomas's economic answers challenge the assumptions behind our economic questions on issues of justice in exchange. The same fault lines between typically modern assumptions and Aristotelian ones that I traced in the previous chapter are crucial for understanding Thomas's teachings on usury and just price. These teachings are best understood as reflections of Thomas's concern to safeguard the deference involved when humans acknowledge the priority of membership in an external order that precedes and encompasses them. We misunderstand these teachings when we read them as attempts to analyze the "economic laws" that arise from the exchanges of a collection of proprietary individuals.

In modern market society, the movements and fluctuations of exchange value produce certain regularities that we can describe as "economic laws." These regularities can have the appearance of being timeless truths that constrain human economic activity in all times and places. But that appearance is an illusion. From the nonmarket society perspective of Aristotle or Thomas, exchange value is an important but nonetheless secondary and subordinate phenomenon. The primary context for imagining where wealth has come from and where it is going is the antecedent fabric of natural and social co-membership, dominated by use values, that encompasses human beings and intends their flourishing. This context disciplines and conditions all economic activity. Therefore, exchange value remains inscribed within and defined by a more comprehensive circuit that runs from nature's provision of useful things toward an end in the sustenance nature intends. In modern market society, on the other hand, this predominance of use values is superseded as exchange value itself becomes the regulatory factor in economic activity. Because of the ascendancy of exchange value, there appears to be no more comprehensive circuit of economic activity than that which exchange value itself traverses and conditions. Consequently, the regularities and cycles of exchange value define the ultimate context that disciplines and constrains economic activity. The apparent comprehensiveness of this context gives these regularities and cycles a finality that suggests their universality. But in fact the finality of that context only displaces the Aristotelian deference that acknowledges a more comprehensive economic circuit exceeding and embracing the conventions of exchange value.

The apparent inevitability of these "laws" makes it tempting to search for an awareness of them in St. Thomas, or in any thinker who takes up economic issues. In his remarkably comprehensive and admirably sympathetic account of the economic ideas of the Paris theologians around Thomas's time, economic historian Odd Langholm helpfully describes this tendency: "It has proved to be very tempting for economists to postulate the existence of certain universal laws, a set of relations between variables which will manifest themselves in different shapes depending on the social framework but which are themselves the identifiable and immutable objects of economics as an abstract science. If this view is adopted, the history of economic reasoning becomes the study of the gradual and piecemeal *discovery* of these laws."[1] Such an "anticipatory" approach to economic history has

1. Odd Langholm, *Economics in the Medieval Schools: Wealth, Exchange, Value, Money*

come under fire, Langholm says, but he points out that finding awareness of these laws in earlier writers gains plausibility the more the economic context of a given writer shares important features of our own. It is more likely, for example, that Thomas recognized the determinants of the price mechanism if the market dynamics we associate with the price mechanism were prevalent in his society.

The possibility of some "marketization" of Thomas's society is not far-fetched. I have remarked about the growth of a profit economy in the High Middle Ages, which had perhaps already begun to foster the patterns associated with the gravitational pull of a dominating exchange value — at least in certain pockets. Because of that growth, finding some inklings of modern economic rationality in Thomas cannot be dismissed out of hand as wishful thinking. Nevertheless, interpretations of Thomas's thought on usury and just price have tended to overplay this possibility. Scholarship in these areas has been characterized not only by a tendency to read market-society wisdom into nonmarket thinkers and to keep pushing the historical beginnings of market-society wisdom further back; it has also been characterized by a general failure to appreciate the depth of the difference between market and nonmarket thought, even when a given writer resists the former tendencies, as Langholm does.

This failure has obscured the challenge Thomas's teachings on usury and just price offer to contemporary economic wisdom. The literature on just price has made clear how far Thomas recognized the variations and common estimations we associate with the supply-and-demand mechanism. But finding in Thomas an appreciation of the competitive equilibrium of conflicting subjectivities distorts his thought. Specifically, it ignores the degree to which Thomas assumed that the common estimations associated with pricing would be shaped by the receptivity to an antecedent natural and social order he shares with Aristotle. Rather than assuming competition and conflict among proprietary individuals, that receptivity defers to the wider purposes carried by nature's provision and thus bends human economic activity in the direction of use values.

On usury, it may seem that the literature has been more attentive to the distance between Thomas and ourselves, because it is generally recognized that Thomas's usury prohibition cannot be made to fit our eco-

and Usury according to the Paris Theological Tradition, 1200-1350 (Leiden: E. J. Brill, 1992), p. 3.

nomic assumptions. But something of the same procedure has taken place even on the subject of usury. For in the attempt to render as much as possible of Thomas's thought amenable to market rationality, scholars have isolated the source of Thomas's incongruence with us in a primitive view of money. They have thus missed the more systematic challenge that Thomas's usury teaching also presents to the modern eclipse of deference.[2] Specifically, Thomas's usury teaching conveys his resistance to the presumption he sees involved in taking the conventions of exchange value to provide some security against the uncertainties of the future. The vulnerability he thus defends is one more aspect of the deference and trusting dependence he shares with Aristotle. The standard interpretations of Thomas's economic thought leave undiscovered both its true character and the questions it raises about fundamental assumptions of contemporary economic life.

Usury

The prohibition of usury has a rich pedigree in the traditions Thomas inherits: it has interesting articulations especially among the Socratic philosophers and among patristic theologians. In the medieval universities, especially since the beginnings of the economic growth dating from the twelfth century, the process of dialectical argument had honed and refined a number of anti-usury arguments. However, it seems that, in addition to prompting the flowering of such arguments, the changing economic context was also beginning to elicit recognitions of more and more titles to interest, in a gradual process of qualifying the usury prohibition that would continue for centuries. The tension between support for the traditional prohibition and the discovery of new titles that were more in tune with developing practice is the proper context for situating Thomas's own reflections on usury.

Scholars have often recognized that Thomas leans in the direction of

2. The assumption that Thomas's teaching here has been outgrown by new views of money is shared by economists and theologians. A typically casual dismissal by a theologian sympathetic to Thomas is Martin Rhonheimer's comment that Thomas's discussion of this issue "is now of merely historical interest." Martin Rhonheimer, "Sins Against Justice (IIa IIae, qq. 59-78)," trans. Frederick G. Lawrence, in *The Ethics of Aquinas*, ed. Stephen J. Pope (Washington, DC: Georgetown University Press, 2002), pp. 287-303, esp. p. 291.

the traditional prohibition. But modern interpreters often see an acknowl-edgment on Thomas's part of the emerging titles as a mark of empirical sensitivity to the realities of the market. Thus, since few want to question Thomas's intellectual integrity or his scholarly penetration — and particu-larly since readers have had apparent success finding awareness of market mechanisms in his teaching on just price — it seems that Thomas's primi-tivism on usury is in need of explanation. These interpreters typically lo-cate the error in Thomas's archaic understanding of money. If he had un-derstood money as a credit that signifies a claim on assets (which, of course, no one can fault him for failing to do), he would have been back to the drawing board on his usury arguments.

These interpretations fail because Thomas's position on usury de-pends, not on a particular way of configuring money, but on the very no-tion of abstractable exchange value that any understanding of money pre-supposes. Thomas argues that abstracted exchange value as such cannot have a vendible use value in addition to the exchange value it abstracts. To believe that it does indicates that a spurious "usefulness" humans can at-tribute to something has been mistaken for true use value. Further, Thomas goes on to consider other possible justifications for interest on a loan, and he faults them not for misconstruing the nature of money but for presumptively seeking a security against the future that denies the def-erent receptivity necessary to humans as members of an antecedent natu-ral order that sustains us. Thus, we can see Thomas's adherence to the usury prohibition not as evidence of his obscurantism in the face of "eco-nomic realities," but as his resistance to the presumption inherent in emerging economic practices, practices that only become "realities" as hu-mans abandon Aristotelian deference.

Thomas's Usury Teaching in Modern Scholarship

Two of the most representative and influential interpretations of Thomas on the subject of usury in the last fifty years are those of John T. Noonan and Odd Langholm.[3] Noonan's is the seminal contemporary reading, while Langholm has more recently revised our understanding of the sig-

---

3. John T. Noonan, Jr., *The Scholastic Analysis of Usury* (Cambridge, MA: Harvard University Press, 1957); Langholm, *Economics in the Medieval Schools.*

nificance of medieval Aristotelianism for the history of economic thought. Reviewing their interpretations will acquaint us with the relevant texts in St. Thomas's work. While they have their differences, both find the crux of Thomas's usury arguments in a primitive view of money.

For Noonan, Thomas's view of money plays a large role because Thomas is trying to penetrate behind mere legal pronouncements to discover the natural-law basis for the case against usury. Thus, in his earliest stab at it in his commentary on Lombard, Thomas produces the legal reference — but then goes beyond it. The juridical background is the Roman law treatment of a *mutuum*. The *mutuum* was an exchange contract dealing with fungible items (commodities whose quantities are interchangeable, such as wine, oil, or grain).[4] In a *mutuum*, of which a loan of money is an example, ownership necessarily transfers to the borrower; therefore, Thomas reasons, to charge additionally for the use is to sell what already belongs to the buyer. But Thomas goes beyond this legal reference by showing why usury is contrary to the nature of money. Thomas cites Aristotle's *Nichomachean Ethics* to the effect that money measures the worth of other things. He concludes that taking more for less money is to "diversify the measure."[5] Noonan makes much of this statement, claiming that Thomas thus roots his usury doctrine in this formal conception of money "as having one constant, fixed value — its legal face value."[6]

The main argument Thomas uses in all his later work is a little different, but Noonan still finds in it a fixation on the formal and legal character of money. The argument is known as the "consumptibility argument," and the primary articulations of it are in *De Malo* and in the *ST*. Believing *De Malo* to be the later of the two documents, Noonan cites the argument from there:

> [I]n those things whose use is their consumption, the use is not other than the thing itself; whence to whomever is conceded the use of such things, is conceded the ownership of those things, and conversely. When therefore, someone lends money under this agreement that the money be integrally restored to him, and further for the use of the money wishes to have a definite price, it is manifest that he sells sepa-

---

4. Barry Gordon, *Economic Analysis before Adam Smith: Hesiod to Lessius* (New York: Barnes and Noble, 1975), p. 162.

5. *In Sent.*, III:37:1:6, cited in Noonan, *Scholastic Analysis of Usury,* p. 52.

6. Noonan, *Scholastic Analysis of Usury,* p. 52.

rately the use of the money and the very substance of money. The use of money, however, as it is said, is not other than its substance: whence either he sells that which is not, or he sells the same thing twice, to wit, the money itself, whose use is its consumption; and this is manifestly against the nature of natural justice.[7]

Here Thomas makes even more headway toward showing the natural-law basis for the usury prohibition. Some things, by their very nature, are consumed in use, so that to charge for the use in addition to the worth of the thing is to charge for the same thing twice. Here money is conceived as being "consumed" through being alienated in exchange, even if the borrower who consumes it obtains something of equal value. Therefore, Thomas makes no distinction between loans made for consumption goods and those made for production goods. Regardless of the borrower's ends, the money is changed for something else, and so is completely gone. Noonan brings out the importance of the formal and legal character of money in this argument by comparing a loan at usury with the medieval practice of lending money *ad pompam,* that is, for ostentatious display by the borrower. In accord with the standard opinion of the time, Thomas allows a charge beyond the worth of the money itself in such cases.[8] What we learn here is that the opposition to usury is not based on the sterility of money, for money is certainly even more unproductive in the *ad pompam* case, where use can be charged. Consequently, the scholastics' "opposition is only to profit on a transaction where money is formally and legally sterile, that is, where it is consumed in the sense of being alienated from its possessor by being spent."[9] Therefore, as different as the consumptibility argument is from Thomas's arguments in the *Sentences* commentary, we still see Thomas depending on a formal and legal conception of money to make the case against usury.

Just as Noonan restricts the fault in Thomas's usury arguments to an outdated conception of money, he manages to find in other areas a good deal of accommodation to market rationality in Thomas. The just price, for example, is "mutable, imprecise, [and] radically subjective."[10] (We will further explore the just price argument below.) At other places, Thomas

7. *De Malo,* 13.4, cited in Noonan, *Scholastic Analysis of Usury,* pp. 53-54.
8. *De Malo,* 13.4 ad 15.
9. Noonan, *Scholastic Analysis of Usury,* p. 56.
10. Noonan, *Scholastic Analysis of Usury,* p. 89.

begins to show signs of breaking out of traditional concepts, but he refuses to follow them through and ends up in inconsistency. With regard to other titles to interest, we see in the *ST* that Thomas is "the first major authority, either theological or canonical, to express himself in such a way as to seem to favor interest from the beginning of a loan."[11] Noonan refers to Thomas's acceptance of *damnum emergens,* the notion that lenders may charge extra to indemnify themselves against an actual loss. Thomas says that "a lender may without sin enter an agreement with the borrower for compensation for the loss he incurs of something he ought to have, for this is not to sell the use of money but to avoid a loss."[12] However — contra Noonan — it is not clear that this concession involves interest from the beginning of the loan. By saying the two people may agree on compensation for actual loss, Thomas could simply mean that the lender may contract to be compensated in the case where, for example, a delay in payment keeps the lender from using his money for a dowry he owes. But Noonan sees more of a concession to market principles here, and hence he finds Thomas's rejection of interest from the beginning of a loan in *De Malo* to contradict his more liberal position in the *ST.* But it is precisely damage for delay of payment that Thomas accepts in *De Malo,* and he may mean nothing more in the *ST.*[13] Noonan's resolve to find market rationality in Thomas produces a contradiction that is not otherwise apparent.

A further example of the inconsistency Noonan finds when Thomas is unable to follow through his concessions to the market comes in his discussion of the *societas.* Thomas allows the legitimacy of what was called a *societas,* a partnership in which a financier entrusts his money to a merchant or craftsman for the sake of a share in the profits of the trade or craft. He distinguishes this financier, who may receive a return on his money, from the lender at usury. The lender transfers ownership of the money, and thus bears none of the risk of it and is entitled to no benefit from its use. The financier, on the other hand, does not transfer ownership, but bears the risk and thus lawfully benefits from any profits made with it.[14] According to Noonan, Thomas here accepts capitalist investment, yet vainly tries to distinguish it from usury through ad hoc arguments that

---

11. Noonan, *Scholastic Analysis of Usury,* p. 117.
12. *ST* II-II 78.2 ad 1.
13. *De Malo,* 13.4 ad 14.
14. *ST* II-II 78.2 ad 5.

contradict Thomas's earlier arguments against usury.[15] In accepting the *societas,* Thomas reverses his earlier contention that use and ownership are inseparable; in fact, he reverses his conception of money as inherently unproductive. Since his arguments against usury, based on that other conception of money, are now falling apart, he grasps onto incidence of risk as the distinguishing factor, but we find no basis for that move in Thomas's understanding of property. Noonan reads Thomas's position on usury as a sort of primitivism inconsistent with Thomas's important concessions to market rationality, and he explains the discrepancy in terms of an inadequate view of money.

Odd Langholm shows less haste about attributing an acceptance of capitalist practice to Thomas, and yet he still sees the crux of Thomas's usury argument in an archaic conception of money. Langholm begins his discussion of Thomas on usury by offering a more sympathetic reading than Noonan does of Thomas's *Sentences* commentary. The comment about "diversifying the measure," he says, need not mean that Thomas is thinking of money only formally and as having a constant, fixed value; it may simply indicate that a medium of exchange needs to be intrinsically consistent. In this way, the statement may anticipate the notion of the self-valuation of fungibles.[16]

Langholm further improves on Noonan's reading by attending to *damnum emergens* more carefully and by emphasizing Thomas's non-modern concern for protecting those suffering economic duress. Langholm notes that the passage on *damnum emergens* in the *ST* is ambiguous regarding interest from the beginning of a loan, and instead of seeing tension or contradiction, he looks to the similar principle of indemnity articulated in Thomas's discussion of pricing for help in interpreting.[17] Langholm makes much of Thomas's concern with economic duress; indeed, he sees this concern as one of the primary legacies of scholastic economics.[18] Langholm highlights how Thomas, especially in *De Malo,* argues that the apparent voluntary nature of the loan contract does not render it just, for the borrower only chooses to pay usury under the compulsion of economic duress.[19]

Langholm shows greater interest than does Noonan in appreciating

---

15. Noonan, *Scholastic Analysis of Usury,* pp. 143-45.
16. Langholm, *Economics in the Medieval Schools,* p. 240.
17. Langholm, *Economics in the Medieval Schools,* p. 246.
18. Langholm, *Economics in the Medieval Schools,* pp. 577-79.
19. Langholm, *Economics in the Medieval Schools,* p. 247.

medieval thought in its difference from modern thought, and he rejects Noonan's suggestion that Thomas fixes on the formal and legal character of money. Still, other than the concern with economic duress, Langholm does not find a broader intelligibility to Thomas's usury arguments, but associates those arguments specifically with the limitations of an ancient conception of money. Unlike Noonan, he finds a metallist conception of money expressed in the consumptibility argument. Langholm sees in Aristotle an association of money with specie, with particular pieces of precious metal, and supposes that such a conception drives Thomas's argument. Money is "consumed" in exchange because the actual pieces of coin are lost, given over to the process of circulation. Thus, money can have no separate use in addition to its substance, because to use it is to lose its substance, and the borrower is "unable to repay (the loan) in the actual coins borrowed."[20] This archaic view of money explains why Thomas did not see the legitimacy of charging interest: "In terms of a modern credit transaction, which does not involve specie at all, the consumptibility argument is meaningless."[21] Like Noonan, Langholm explains Thomas's apparent naïveté on usury by pinning the blame on his outdated view of money.

The Usury Prohibition and the Defense of Deference

These modern interpretations fail to capture the sense of Thomas's arguments. In order to penetrate them, we need to perceive the relationship between Aristotelian deference and Thomas's account of justice. Thomas's economic teachings reflect an assumption that justice in exchange depends on commensurating the terms of exchange with the shape of the provision God unfolds for human beings. When Thomas says, "one man cannot overabound in external riches, without another man lacking them," we are tempted to read it as a mere pious assertion to shame the rich.[22] But it is firmly rooted in Thomas's assumptions about how God provides for human beings through the fruitfulness of nature.[23] The common *telos* of cer-

---

20. Langholm, *Economics in the Medieval Schools*, p. 243.

21. Langholm, *Economics in the Medieval Schools*, p. 242.

22. *ST* II-II 118.1 ad 2.

23. On the biblical background to the image of God as provider, see L. Juliana M. Claassens, *The God Who Provides: Biblical Images of Divine Nourishment* (Nashville: Abingdon, 2004).

tain of nature's goods is to meet the needs of human sustenance, and so they ought to find their way to those who lack. To make a claim to wealth that outstrips that provision, as usury does, is to produce injustice.

Thomas's centerpiece argument attacks the very notion of usury, but he supports it with other arguments about a variety of possible titles to interest. In both cases his arguments are meant to preserve justice by rejecting inordinate claims to wealth. First, I will show that Thomas's centerpiece argument does not hinge on an antiquated understanding of money. Thomas sees in the very notion of an abstracted exchange value the possibility of economic activity that obscures the primacy of use values. Such economic activity would be unconditioned by the deference that inscribes human action within the comprehensive circuit extending from nature's provision of goods to the flourishing nature intends. Second, I will show (*pace* Noonan) that Thomas's teachings on other possible titles to interest do not pull in the opposite direction. What all of Thomas's positions on titles to income from money show is an insistence that profit can only come from nature's goods, which always requires the patience and vulnerability that waits to see what nature offers. Thomas refuses the presumption against God's providence that would seek to secure a claim to wealth that outpaces that provision.

It would seem from our modern interpreters that the logic of the consumptibility argument depends on a particular construal of the nature of money. As Noonan has it, there is no price for the use of money because money, as a formal and legal implement, is considered used up, consumed, as soon as it is changed from its form as legal tender into some object of exchange. A more up-to-date account of money would see in money the potential presence of whatever it can be exchanged for.[24] In Langholm's interpretation, the use of money cannot be reckoned separately from its substance because money just is the particular piece of metal that is exchanged. When it has been exchanged, it is considered consumed.

However, the key to the consumptibility argument is not seeing what kind of conception of money Thomas had, but grasping the role of the Aristotelian distinction between use value and exchange value. The goal of the argument is to distinguish a loan of money from a rental situation. The most obvious defense of interest on a loan is to compare it to rent. If I hand my house over to you for a while, I can then demand it back along

---

24. Noonan, *Scholastic Analysis of Usury*, p. 56.

with the rents for the time you used it. The analogy suggests that, in the same way, if I hand my money over to you for a while, I can then demand it back along with interest for the time you used it. The consumptibility argument is meant to show that, since money does not share the crucial feature houses have that makes them rentable, it has no vendible use.

The Aristotelian distinction between use value and exchange value helps us understand the force of the identification of some things as "consumptibles." A house, for example, has both a use value (it can be lived in) and an exchange value (it can be exchanged for something else). A glass of wine, similarly, has both a use value (it can be drunk) and an exchange value (it, too, can be exchanged). But there is a crucial difference in the relationship between use value and exchange value in each. In the case of the house, not only can the whole house be exchanged, but, alternatively, a temporal duration of the use can be exchanged without prejudice to the exchange value of the house itself. Because the house persists through the use, the passage of time produces an accumulation of potential uses, and the use itself can be temporally divided and exchanged. It is exactly because the potential uses accumulate with time that the owner can charge rent that is completely additional to the exchange value of the whole house. With respect to the glass of wine, on the other hand, there are no accumulating potential uses: there is no way to exchange the use of the glass of wine without exchanging the glass of wine itself. Therefore, use and ownership are inseparable, and the glass of wine is unrentable. That is why, "if a man wanted to sell wine separately from the use of the wine, he would be selling the same thing twice, or he would be selling what does not exist, wherefore he would evidently commit a sin of injustice."[25]

The crucial issue, of course, is whether Thomas is right that money is like the glass of wine and not like the house. Noonan and Langholm suggest that it is not necessarily unlike the house, and that Thomas's primitive view of money kept him from imagining how that could be so. If he had envisioned the possibility of money as credit, he might have seen that a single sum can be used again and again.

Money appears to Thomas like the glass of wine, not because of a particular conception of money, but because of the condition of possibility of all money, the very notion of abstracted exchange value. All money derives from the fact that people exchange and from the need for a conven-

25. *ST* II-II 78.1.

tion that abstracts exchange value from useful things. Thomas's point is that insofar as money is nothing more than that convention — nothing but pure exchange value — there is no way to exchange the use of it without exchanging it. It has no separable use such that the potential uses of a sum of money could accumulate with time. Some might object that its use should be imagined not as a single exchange but as a circuit of exchanges that sends the money into an investment and then returns it (or perhaps an increased amount) to me, so that I could think of using the same sum again. But this suggestion hides what actually happens in the midst of the circuit, mystifyingly chalking up the possible increase to the "use" of the money. In fact, in this scenario I have used the money to obtain a share in an investment, and then I have used that share to exchange for money. Neither of these transactions involves a use of money that is separable from its exchange.

This clarification of the consumptibility argument helps us understand why Thomas thought it lawful to collect rent for a loan of money *ad pompam*. Such a loan treats money in an alternative way, as something that can be used (displayed) in such a way that its exchange value persists through that use. Hence, in this way money can be rented.

It is thus surprising that the consumptibility argument does not reduce to a sterility argument. Both Noonan and Langholm assert that it does. Roger E. Backhouse summarizes contemporary economic historiography in the same way: "The fundamental idea underlying all [medieval] discussions of usury was that money is sterile."[26] But what could be more sterile than a house? The distinction is not between things that bear fruit and things that do not, but between diverse ways in which things are used. Some uses of things are such that the use cannot be sold without selling the thing. Other kinds of use can be sold without selling the thing. Money can be the object of either kind of use.[27] But if the borrower is going to do anything with the money that does not keep it out of circulation, then money, by the very nature of abstracted exchange value, has no separate use. It cannot be rented.

---

26. Roger E. Backhouse, *The Ordinary Business of Life: A History of Economics from the Ancient World to the Twenty-First Century* (Princeton, NJ: Princeton University Press, 2002), p. 46.

27. Money as credit is different only in that it is not subject to the latter sort of use, the *ad pompam* use. Money as credit is even more reduced to pure exchange value, and thus Thomas's argument against usury applies to it all the more fittingly.

If Thomas's analysis of money-lending is correct, then to contract a price for the use of money in addition to the principal is to sell a use that does not and cannot exist.[28] It creates a spurious "use" based on human agreement that is incommensurate with true use value. Therefore, it contravenes the receptivity that would recognize the origin of all wealth in the use values that nature produces and the ordering of all wealth toward the procuring of the use values required for human flourishing. Thomas's concern to protect this deference is even more evident in his comments regarding other titles to income from money.

The consumptibility argument is not meant to destroy all possible arguments for a return on one's money. It only dispatches the muddled notion that the reason interest is legitimate is the same reason that collecting rent for a house is legitimate. Aside from that notion, there are other considerations for why a lender might charge extra beyond the principal. Thomas addresses some of them, and he consistently rejects the presumption that would seek to secure claims to sustenance in advance of suffering the contours of nature's temporally unfolding provision.

Witness this concern of Thomas in his discussions of other titles to income from money. If money has no separable use, the most obvious alternative justification for interest is the separable use of that for which the money is exchanged. Such separable use may attach to the exchanged object either actually or potentially. Take the actual separable use first: in that case, perhaps the lender has a right to a portion of the profits from that use. Say the borrower buys a house, which he rents out for a time and then sells, enabling him to pay back the lender and retain a nice profit. Should the lender not have a share in that profit? This is the place to invoke Thomas's approval of the *societas*. Thomas approves of a share in that profit if the principal transfer was construed as an investment and not as a

---

28. Joan Lockwood O'Donovan laments that Thomas's arguments omit much of the patristic concern for charity to the needy, focusing instead on the equality of value in things exchanged. What her reading fails to notice is that Thomas's arguments, by uncovering the most basic reason against usury (that it sells a metaphysical impossibility), confirm the rationale of the usury prohibition even in productive loans where the borrower is not needy. Thomas is concerned not only for charity, but for keeping all exchanges answerable to the contours of real wealth. Joan Lockwood O'Donovan, "The Theological Economics of Medieval Usury Theory," in Oliver O'Donovan and Joan Lockwood O'Donovan, *Bonds of Imperfection: Christian Politics, Past and Present* (Grand Rapids: Eerdmans, 2004), pp. 97-120, esp. pp. 109-12.

loan. Noonan is concerned that Thomas's introduction of incidence of risk here as the distinguishing factor is merely a convenient device that has little coherence with Thomas's broader views.[29]

In fact, however, the reference to risk shows Thomas's concern to resist presumption. The lender at interest presumes by staking a claim to wealth — possible future wealth — that is not disciplined by any receptivity to what God's providence may actually end up providing. The investor does not presume, but takes the risk of waiting to see what comes of it.[30] He does not hold title to the return of all his money, but rather makes himself vulnerable to the contingencies of how God's provision may or may not smile on the efforts of the merchant or craftsman to whom the money is entrusted. While the investor entrusts his money at his own risk, the usurer transfers risk to the borrower, so that the borrower "holds the money at his own risk and is bound to pay it all back."[31] The usurer thus claims a title to a return that neglects any attempt to conform to God's actual provision. Furthermore, in a *societas* one is not compensated for one's risk as for a loss.[32] Rather, to the extent that the dangers inherent in such a venture actually thwart it, causing real loss, the investor simply suffers the loss; that is what it means to have borne the risk. If the venture yields a profit, the investor

29. As mentioned above, Noonan also thinks that here Thomas reneges on his trademark insistence that use and ownership of money are inseparable. But Thomas does not attribute the use of money in a *societas* to the craftsman, while the ownership remains with the financier. The point of the *societas* is to create a partnership in which each aspect of the enterprise is shared.

30. Thus, lending at interest appears as a manifestation of our changing attitude toward time: "The whole attitude toward time that we take is moving away from living in time as exclusively a matter of *waiting*, and toward living in time as a matter of industrious exploitation of time, of *making* time." Charles Mathewes, "On Using the World," in *Having: Property and Possessions in Religious and Social Life*, ed. William Schweiker and Charles Mathewes (Grand Rapids: Eerdmans, 2004), pp. 189-221, here p. 196.

31. *ST* II-II 78.2 ad 5. Herman Daly and John Cobb suggest that the abstraction of our financial markets from real wealth has led to reckless and destructive investing in a modern version of "moral hazard" similar to the problem Aquinas identifies: "[T]he costs of imprudent risk taking are borne by someone other than the risk taker." Herman E. Daly and John B. Cobb, Jr., *For the Common Good: Redirecting the Economy toward Community, the Environment, and a Sustainable Future*, 2nd ed. (Boston: Beacon, 1994), p. 411.

32. Cf. D. Stephen Long's claim that Thomas permits "receiving of interest for losses incurred in a joint-enterprise." D. Stephen Long, *Divine Economy: Theology and the Market*, Radical Orthodoxy series, ed. John Milbank, Catherine Pickstock, and Graham Ward (New York: Routledge, 2000), p. 77.

gains, not as compensation for his risk, but as the fruit of a venture in which he had a stake, a stake certified by his acceptance of risk.[33]

In the second case, perhaps it should not matter so much what the borrower actually does with the money or what actually becomes of it. Perhaps the lender should be compensated for the potential separable use that could be gotten with the money regardless of what the borrower actually does. What if the borrower is an incompetent businessman, while the lender could quite reliably have turned a profit with his money somewhere else? This argument Thomas rejects, again because of its presumption. This is the notion of *lucrum cessans*, the notion that a lender has a title to compensation beyond the principal for forgoing the gain he might have otherwise made with his money. The mounting pressure to accept such titles is evident in that the first canonist to endorse it, Thomas's contemporary Hostiensis, was only the first trickle of what would become a flood of both canonists and theologians.[34] The reason Thomas finds it presumptive is that, unlike a risky investment, a loan involves a contract obliging the borrower in advance to compensate the lender for a potential gain the actual realization of which could only be determined by waiting to see. Thomas insists that a lender cannot enter an agreement for *lucrum cessans*, "because he must not sell that which he has not yet and may be prevented in many ways from having."[35] However reliable the alternative investment, it would involve vulnerability to the contingencies of the unfolding of God's provision, a vulnerability that *lucrum cessans* circumvents.[36] To es-

---

33. The danger of transport that may yield compensation, discussed in II-II 77.4 ad 2, is of the same variety. It is not that the seller is rewarded for bearing risk regardless of how it turned out. The only reason he has the thing for sale now is that it turned out well. His compensation for risk figures into price the same way labor and expenses do, which we will look at in relationship to the just price. That is, estimates of usefulness to the buyer, by which prices are determined, will partially consist of an estimate of how much it is worth to avoid the risk the buyer would undertake to procure the good herself, a risk she avoids by buying it from this seller.

34. Hostiensis, *Commentaria,* V, *De Usuris,* 16; see Noonan, *Scholastic Analysis of Usury,* p. 118.

35. *ST* II-II 78.2 ad 1.

36. One contemporary manifestation of this drive toward invulnerability is the imperative "to convert wealth into debt in order to derive a permanent future income from it — to convert wealth that perishes into debt that endures, debt that does not rot, costs nothing to maintain, and brings in perennial interest." Daly and Cobb, *For the Common Good,* p. 423.

tablish a title to such wealth irrespective of the actual possibilities and provisions the future may turn out to hold is to set up an artificial invulnerability that only guarantees that any unforeseen shortfall in God's provision will fall exclusively and hence disproportionately on the borrower. Thomas's rejection of other titles to interest bears witness to his concern to protect the deference of economic activity that acknowledges its circumscription by an antecedent natural order.[37]

Thomas's consumptibility argument and his other arguments about titles to a return on money all support his claim that usury is a matter of injustice. Since money has no separable use, contracting to rent out its use is "to sell what does not exist, and this evidently leads to inequality which is contrary to justice."[38] But further, the injustice of usury is evident in, for example, its distinction from the arrangement of the *societas,* which respects justice by returning to the investor only what actually comes, through God's provision, of the money entrusted. Lending at usury, on the other hand, involves injustice because it prepares a claim of what is "due" to the lender that fails to fit itself to God's provision. If God provides what is required for human flourishing, but not necessarily more than that, then to claim a "due" that outpaces that provision is to rob from what is due to another. It is money, especially, that provides the occasion to suppose that such an illusory "due" is legitimate. Money especially finalizes the detachment of the sustenance that is "due" from its otherwise necessary inscription within the circuit of natural wealth by crystallizing it within the abstractive capacity of money. Furthermore, money's abstractive capacity, the fact that it can abstract exchange value from useful goods, occasions the presumption that the price of future uses can be abstracted from them and contracted for in the present. This presumption contributes to the creation of an unconditioned claim on nature's goods, a claim that produces injustice by undermining acknowledgment of an antecedent order circumscribing and sustaining us.

---

37. Daly and Cobb stop short of Aquinas's prohibition, but they articulate a similar concern to inscribe economic activity within the contours of natural order, and they affirm as an aspect of such inscription that "money should not bear interest as a condition of its existence, but only when genuinely lent by an owner who gives up its use while it is in the possession of the borrower." Daly and Cobb, *For the Common Good,* p. 426.

38. *ST* II-II 78.1.

Just Price

Thomas's concern for receptivity to our place in the natural order, for seeking justice through refusing to make claims on sustenance incommensurate with the shape of that order, is equally relevant in interpreting the just price. For Thomas, prices must be shaped by a proper deference and acknowledged dependence in order to be just.

This point has been largely missed in the various battles over the last hundred years concerning the meaning of just price. The history of interpretation of Thomas on exchange during most of the last century can be characterized, with only slight exaggeration, as a series of investigations into whether Thomas is a precursor to Karl Marx or to Adam Smith. Early in the twentieth century, interpreters more suspicious of capitalism looked for an account in Thomas of the value of exchangeable goods minimally related to fluctuations in the market and more largely based in the cost, especially the labor cost, of production (the "cost" interpretation).[39] In the latter half of the twentieth century, those more suspicious of Marxist modes of thought tried to insist instead that, for Thomas, just price is determined primarily by the fluctuations in the market (the "competitive market" interpretation).[40] At least one scholar has found the arguments of both sides plausible enough to suggest that Thomas actually has no consistent view of the determination of price, but applies various criteria depending on the problem he is addressing.[41]

Each of these interpretations reminds us of important aspects of Thomas's approach to pricing and trading. Adherents of the cost interpre-

---

39. Prominent examples include W. J. Ashley, "Just Price," in *Dictionary of Political Economy,* ed. R. H. I. Palgrave (London: Macmillan, 1896), vol. 2, p. 500; R. H. Tawney, *Religion and the Rise of Capitalism: A Historical Study* (London: John Murray, 1926), pp. 40-41.; and Selma Hagenauer, *Das "Justum Pretium" bei Thomas von Aquino: ein Beitrag zur Geschichte der objectiven Werttheorie* (Stuttgart: W. Kohlhammer, 1931).

40. Most influentially and forcefully, Raymond de Roover, "The Concept of the Just Price: Theory and Economic Policy," *Journal of Economic History* 18 (1958): 418-34, esp. pp. 421-3. But see also Noonan, *Scholastic Analysis of Usury,* pp. 84-89; John W. Baldwin, *The Medieval Theories of the Just Price: Romanists, Canonists, and Theologians in the Twelfth and Thirteenth Centuries* (Philadelphia: American Philosophical Society, 1959), pp. 71-80; S. T. Worland, *Scholasticism and Welfare Economics* (Notre Dame, IN: University of Notre Dame Press, 1967); and Langholm, *Economics in the Medieval Schools,* pp. 229-31.

41. Samuel Hollander, "On the Interpretation of the Just Price," *Kyklos* 18 (1965): 615-34.

tation have particularly emphasized how circumspect we should be about finding a principle of competition in Thomas that would only project the social atomism of modern society back onto scholastic thought. On the other hand, competitive-market interpreters have rightly insisted that Thomas makes important concessions to the practice of traders and clearly acknowledges the legitimacy of fluctuations in price due to nothing other than changes in market configuration.

What is uniformly missing in these discussions, however, is a recognition of the importance Thomas attaches to economic activity yielding to the contours of the antecedent natural order. In fact, it is in this light that we can discern the unity of Thomas's thought on justice in exchange. When economic activity conforms to the natural circuit of nourishment aimed at human sustenance, prices reflect cost via the common estimate of the community, even as that estimate fluctuates in various ways. This interpretation of Thomas shares some affinities with that of Bernard Dempsey, who suggests that the common estimate itself, while variable, will reflect social solidarity rather than competition if it is disciplined by the proper sense of membership in a social organism.[42] Yet Dempsey's view still fails to see the inseparability of that sense of social membership from a sense of natural membership that inscribes human economic activity within the comprehensive circuit of use values extending from nature's provision to nature's goal of human flourishing.

The Just Price in Modern Scholarship

British socialist R. H. Tawney enlisted Thomas as one of his own predecessors when he affirmed that the last of the schoolmen was Karl Marx.[43] Tawney's view was not novel, but followed the dominant scholarly consensus, based on the cost interpretation of the just price. Nor was that consensus without some textual basis.

The case begins with attention to Thomas's commentary on Aristotle's *Nichomachean Ethics*. The key text is in *NE* V.5, on justice in exchange. As I noted in the preceding chapter, this section of the *NE* is pri-

---

42. Bernard W. Dempsey, *The Functional Economy: The Bases of Economic Organization* (Englewood Cliffs, NJ: Prentice-Hall, 1958), esp. pp. 412-31.

43. Tawney, *Religion and the Rise of Capitalism*, p. 36.

85

marily focused on the question of commensurability, of how qualitatively distinct commodities can be compared quantitatively for the purpose of exchange. Aristotle comes up with no completely satisfactory conclusion, but he explains that money, as a conventional representation of human need, allows goods to be commensurated "sufficiently." Along the way, Aristotle proposes several examples of simple exchange situations, trying to suggest how exchangers could achieve justice. Of course, given the difficulty of commensuration, we should not be surprised to find that determining whether justice has been done in exchange is a bit of a mystery. We know that strict equality of quantity does not do it, for in an exchange between a builder and a shoemaker, one shoe is obviously too little to give for one house. Aristotle proposes this enigmatic relationship: a proportion must be found between the builder and the shoemaker such that by the same proportion so many shoes equal one house.[44] What is it that marks the difference between builder and shoemaker? Aristotle does not say; however, Thomas, following his teacher, Albert, ventures a suggestion. He interprets the proportion between builder and shoemaker in terms of the extent to which the builder "exceeds the shoemaker in labor and expenses *[in labore et expensis]*."[45] It would seem that cost is the primary determinant of price. Allowing the going market rate to determine the just price would seem to invite injustice, especially under the possibility that the market rate may fall below cost.

The cost interpretation has also often incorporated an element of attention to social status. If cost includes whatever is required for the producer to make a living, what constitutes "a living" will vary with one's station. In his discussion of almsdeeds, Thomas uses two different senses in which things can be called "necessaries." On the one hand, some things are so necessary that to reject them is to throw away life. Such things should be given as alms only in the rarest of circumstances. On the other hand, some things are necessary for living at a certain social rank. Alms can be given from such necessities, although in the absence of an extremely needy recipient, one should not give too much, for "it would be inordinate to deprive oneself of one's own, in order to give to others to such an extent that the residue would be insufficient for one to live in keeping with one's station and the ordinary occurrences of life: for no man ought to live unbe-

---

44. Aristotle, *NE*, V.5; 1133a22-23.
45. *Sent. Eth.*, V.9, to Aristotle, 1133a22-23.

comingly."[46] Such social stratification may suggest that just pricing depends more on what is required to maintain one's social station than on the fluctuations of market determination. Indeed, W. J. Ashley affirms that according to common scholastic teaching, it should be possible in principle for each individual producer to determine for himself the just price of his product "by reckoning what he needed to support his rank."[47]

According to this view, the just price is a standard of justice from which to criticize going market rates. It favors the protection of the worker and assumes an understanding of society as a highly stratified but nevertheless somewhat harmonious whole in which the claim to a reward for labor can be understood independently of market estimations of labor's value. Here Thomas is apparently bearing witness to a society quite different from ours, in which the shape of exchange could be "determined by the hierarchies of producers."[48]

It is interesting and probably not incidental that scholarship on the just price began to reject this earlier line of interpretation and affirm Thomas's concessions to market determinations in the 1950s and 1960s, when the Cold War made Marxism the great enemy of North Atlantic societies. But for all the ideological warfare hidden in the scholarly shifts, the new wave of interpretation came to some compelling conclusions about how price is determined, according to Thomas.

In an article published in 1958, Raymond de Roover points out that interpretations of the just price had mistakenly taken a passage in Henry of Langenstein (1325-1397) to be representative of scholastic consensus. Henry affirmed that no producer should charge more for his labor and expenses than he needed to maintain his status. De Roover argues that Henry was a marginal figure, and that mainstream scholasticism followed the legal tradition, which equated just price with market price. Indeed, the legal tradition, reflecting Roman and then Carolingian legislation, identifies the just price with whatever something can be sold for and insists that a price is unjust not when it fails to reflect cost but when it diverges too much from the common estimate due to idiosyncratic affections.[49] De Roover interprets Thomas accordingly, and he contends that even though neither

46. *ST* II-II 32.6.

47. Ashley, "Just Price," cited in Hollander, "On the Interpretation of the Just Price," p. 624.

48. Hollander, "On the Interpretation of the Just Price," p. 628.

49. Noonan, *Scholastic Analysis of Usury*, pp. 82-83.

Thomas nor any other scholastic before the sixteenth century mentioned "competition," "the whole discussion on the just price assumed the existence of competitive conditions."[50]

Similarly, and almost contemporaneously with de Roover, Noonan's landmark monograph on usury asserts that the scholastic notion of the just price was "mutable, imprecise, [and] radically subjective."[51] Noonan notes with respect to Thomas's commentary on the *Nichomachean Ethics* that the comment about "labor and expenses" is not determinative, for the conclusion of V.5 is in fact that value is determined by human need. And human need, he says, is a matter of subjective human evaluations. No change is introduced by Thomas's interpretation of Aristotle's "need" in terms of human usefulness, for "'usefulness' is basically dependent on man's purposes: to value a good because it fills a need or to value it because it is useful are identical acts."[52] Not only does Thomas recognize the importance of variable human appraisals of utility in pricing, but he also understands the correlative importance of supply. In an article insisting that sellers disclose defects in their products, Thomas considers whether a seller must disclose information that would lower the price though not on account of a defect.[53] Suppose the seller, in a place where his product fetches a high price, knows of other sellers coming behind him, the knowledge of whose approach would drive down the price. Thomas responds that this case differs from disclosing a defect because the latter involves a deception about the value of the product now. The tight-lipped seller trades at the value of the product now, and so is not unjust, although he would show exceeding virtue if he would tell. Obviously, the just price in this instance is understood to fluctuate simply with a change in the relative abundance of a commodity. The just price appears to be simply the market price. Therefore, de Roover insists that "this passage destroys with a single blow the thesis of those who try to make Aquinas into a Marxist, and proves beyond doubt that he considered the market price as just."[54]

Noonan further undermines the picture painted by the cost interpretation by highlighting the imprecision and variability of the just price. In the first article on cheating by buyers and sellers in the *ST*, Thomas admits

50. De Roover, "The Concept of the Just Price," p. 425.
51. Noonan, *Scholastic Analysis of Usury*, p. 89.
52. Noonan, *Scholastic Analysis of Usury*, p. 83.
53. *ST* II-II 77.3 obj. 4.
54. De Roover, "The Concept of the Just Price," p. 422.

that the just price is not an exact and identifiable point. The article contends that selling high, except to indemnify against actual losses resulting from the sale, is always a sin. The first objection points out that civil law allows selling high. Thomas replies that civil law, which allows discrepancies from the just price up to half the value of the thing, cannot punish everything contrary to virtue; but divine law does, and so to avoid sin one must strive for no discrepancy. Indeed, if there is a discrepancy, the one who gained must make restitution. But here Thomas makes a qualification. Restitution is required only if the loss is "considerable," for "the just price of things is not fixed with mathematical precision, but depends on a kind of estimate, so that a slight addition or subtraction would not seem to destroy the equality of justice."[55] And not only is the just price imprecise, but it is also variable. We have already seen how it may vary with supply. Later in the question on cheating, Thomas allows that a change in the just price can be due merely to "the change of place or time."[56] Arguments such as these by de Roover and Noonan permanently changed the way Thomas's just price teaching has been understood.

Samuel Hollander, in an article published in 1965, recognizes the force of these arguments, but he faults scholars such as de Roover for failing to take the full measure of the weight of the cost interpretation. De Roover interprets Thomas's remarks about "labor and expenses" as an anticipation of the modern realization that "market price could not fall permanently below cost." Thus, those remarks do not undermine de Roover's interpretation, because "market price would then tend to coincide with cost or to oscillate around this point like the swing of a pendulum."[57] This reading presents Thomas as a neoclassical economist, recognizing that if price falls below cost, it must eventually either recover or it will drive production away from that commodity, in which case it will recover anyway. On the contrary, Thomas seems to insist that price *ought always* to reflect cost. Therefore, "while it is certainly true that price cannot fall permanently below cost it is not by means of a classical or neo-classical mechanism that this fact is assured."[58]

Hollander proposes that the tension can be resolved by positing two

55. *ST* II-II 77.1 ad 1.
56. *ST* II-II 77.4 ad 2.
57. De Roover, "The Concept of the Just Price," p. 422.
58. Hollander, "On the Interpretation of the Just Price," p. 629.

versions of just price in Thomas. On the one hand is the cost version, which fits the social structure with which Thomas was most familiar. On the other hand is the market version, which Thomas invokes when discussing the particular problems faced by traders in situations where the traditional "stratified social relationships had presumably far less meaning."[59] Hollander's dichotomous reading admirably tries to grapple with all the texts, but the identification of two distinct versions of the just price seems uncalled for. On the one hand, it grants too much to the cost interpretation, though Thomas never indicates that status has any role in just pricing. On the other hand, it grants too much to the competitive market interpretation, implying that Thomas's "ethical" concern to protect workers could find no application in those special cases when he was faced with the realities of the market.

Warnings like those of Hollander have dampened the enthusiasm, evident in de Roover and Noonan, to find "Thomas the theorist of capital." Nevertheless, their basic point, that Thomas identifies the just price as the current competitive market price, has carried the day. Langholm provides a carefully nuanced example. He acknowledges the texts used to support a status- or labor-based interpretation, but reads them not as rules for determining every just price but as examples of a broader principle of indemnity that Thomas applies consistently.[60] He sees this principle not only in Thomas's comments about "labor and expenses," but also in his most prominent set of rules about what counts as justice in exchange. In the first article of the question on cheating in buying and selling, on the subject of whether selling high is a sin, Thomas articulates what Langholm calls a "double rule of just pricing."[61] The article assumes that there is one price (or a small range of approximations) that is the just price. Langholm first notes that the most straightforward reading is that this price is the current competitive market price. Thomas's language of what it is worth "in itself" *(valeat secundum se)* need mean nothing more than its "normal" or prevailing price. Thomas suggests that sometimes the special need affecting the buyer and special disadvantage affecting the seller by the proposed sale make a higher price possible. The double rule of just pricing states that such an elevated price may be just only in view of the seller's indemnity:

59. Hollander, "On the Interpretation of the Just Price," p. 626.
60. Langholm, *Economics in the Medieval Schools,* pp. 225-29.
61. Langholm, *Economics in the Medieval Schools,* pp. 232-34.

the seller can raise the price to compensate for actual losses. The other side of the rule is that if there is no such loss to the seller, the special need of the buyer alone cannot justify charging a higher price.

Neither Thomas nor Langholm offers an example of such "special needs" and "actual losses," but imagining what Thomas might mean concretely can help us understand his teaching here. Say that a man begs to buy my horse because he has just learned that his true love left this morning by carriage for Milan, where she will wed another man. If he catches her before she gets there, he can marry her himself and settle with her on his estate in Verona. Here where I live, near Paris, such a fine horse would go for 100 pounds, but because of his special need, the man is willing to pay much more. As it happens, I only have two horses fit for draft work, and I need both to start plowing next week. Selling will be a significant loss to me, in terms of both my losing time to get the plowing done and the special need I will suffer by having to buy another horse quickly. That loss makes the horse worth 140 pounds to me, and to in-demnify myself, I may justly charge 140. On the other hand, if I have five fit horses and would be in no hurry to replace one if I sold it, I suffer no actual loss by selling one at 100 pounds. In that case, I may not justly charge more, no matter what the lovestruck man is willing to pay, for "the advantage accruing to the buyer, is not due to the seller, but to a cir-cumstance affecting the buyer. Now no man should sell what is not his, though he may charge for the loss he suffers."[62]

If the first half of the rule expresses Thomas's principle of indemnity, the second half shows his concern to protect the buyer from economic compulsion. As in his discussion of usury, Langholm makes much of Thomas's insistence that no one should be pressured into exchange through deception, through coercion, or through one party taking advan-tage of the special need of the other. He thus sees much of Thomas's dis-cussion as aiming to establish the conditions of free bargaining, which, if it is observed, will end up producing an agreement that in fact matches the just price.[63] Langholm presents a much more careful depiction of Thomas than does Noonan, but he affirms Noonan's main point: that the just price is the competitive market price. Thus, Roger E. Backhouse not only echoes Langholm but summarizes contemporary economic scholarship when he

---

62. *ST* II-II 77.1.
63. Langholm, *Economics in the Medieval Schools*, pp. 234-36.

says, "The main idea underlying the scholastic discussion of the just price was that the market offered protection against economic compulsion."[64]

Just Price, Usefulness, and Deference

There can be little doubt that Thomas identifies prevailing prices with the just price. Nothing else can explain a statement in a letter addressing the practice of Florentine merchants who customarily delivered goods on three months' credit. The letter, probably composed in 1262, is known as "On Buying and Selling on Credit."[65] Thomas lays out the guideline that, if the just price is charged, there is no usury involved in such credit. In discussing one of the four cases proposed to him, he specifies that if the merchants "sell the cloth for more than it is worth in the general market [secundum communem forum], there is no doubt that this is usury. But if they sell it, not at more than its worth but at its worth, yet at more than they would take for it if payment were made immediately to them, there is no usury."[66] Thomas seems to acknowledge the justice of the prevailing price with little fanfare. Perhaps this text seals the case in favor of the competitive market interpretation.

This view might seem to have the best chance of incorporating all the textual evidence. Just price is determined by a common estimation arrived at through the normal workings of the market. That common estimation is an expression of human appraisals of the usefulness of things. Such appraisals will vary with supply. We might expect them also to vary with "changes of time or place." Dependence on such appraisals can even cohere with Thomas's counsel that prices should indemnify producers against their cost, because it is likely that Thomas expected such appraisals to be partially constituted by an estimate of how difficult and costly it would be for the buyer to produce the commodity for herself. Since I have some idea what it would take to build my own house or make my own shoe, my estimate of usefulness will assign greater value to the house in proportion as the builder exceeds the shoemaker in costs. This reading, which sees a cor-

---

64. Backhouse, *Ordinary Business of Life*, p. 45.

65. See the text and English translation by Alfred O'Rahilly in *The Irish Ecclesiastical Record* 31 (1928): 159-68.

66. Aquinas, "On Buying and Selling on Credit," p. 165.

respondence between the measure of usefulness and the measure of cost, gains support from the apparent congruity between relative cost and relative usefulness in Aristotle.[67] Relative usefulness reflects relative cost; thus cost gets built into Thomas's understanding of how common estimates work.

All of this is, I think, unassailable. But something crucial is missing if we leave it at that, or if we mistake this common estimate based on usefulness for a *competitive* market price. The implication of all the "competitive market price" interpreters is that what safeguards the just price is the existence of competition. Interpreters suppose that buyers and sellers are out to bargain for the best price they can get, that justice is determined by the compromise arrived at by the interplay of these competing interests, and that justice is threatened primarily by any irregularities in the playing field of free bargaining.

Thomas certainly relies on a common estimate that is variable and based on appraisals of human usefulness. But the usefulness Thomas envisions is not whatever usefulness buyers and sellers can agree to, but the true usefulness of things as such things are intended by God for the sake of human flourishing. What we think of as "utilities" will only reflect Thomas's sense of "usefulness" when agents possess the virtue to seek only what flourishing truly requires. Furthermore, that usefulness will determine prices if the appraisals that jointly form the common estimates refuse presumption and suffer to be inscribed within the circuit of nourishment that runs from nature's provision to nature's goal of human sustenance. As we saw in the discussion of usury, exchange must be deferent if it is to be just.

Adherents of the competitive market price interpretation assume that Thomas's understanding of usefulness is identical with modern notions of "utility." Utility refers to the subjective and highly elastic human preferences, the conflict among which produces the aggregate estimation of a thing's value. The private and variable character of these preferences is what Noonan seems to invoke with his assertion of the "radically subjective" nature of the just price.

Thomas had no such notion. Indeed, this view of "utility" seems tied to

---

67. Barry Gordon argues for the coincidence of relative cost and relative utility in Aristotle, in "Aristotle and the Development of Value Theory," *Quarterly Journal of Economics* 78 (1964): 115-28.

the predominance of exchange value in a market society. In Aristotle's analysis, use values are natural, incommensurable, and rooted in the diversity of natural kinds. Exchange values, on the other hand, are metaphysical oddities that somewhat mysteriously commensurate these things while raising the specter of acquisitive activity no longer aimed at use values at all, but rather at the accumulation of exchange values. Even where such acquisitive activity rears its head, however, so long as use values remain the predominant organizers of economic activity, use values will exert pressure on all human appraisals of usefulness to reflect that dominance. On the other hand, where exchange value has become regulative and determinative, such appraisals become answerable not to the origin and *telos* of use values, but only to the conventions of exchange value itself. The movement of exchange value takes on a logic of its own, and human appraisals of "utility" become legitimated not by their conformity to natural order but by their ability to make themselves effective in exchange. In this sense, human assertions of value are no longer seen as evaluatable in terms of their conformity to a prior order; rather, they seem to be self-legitimating and unquestionable. This notion of "utilities" is an adjunct of the proprietary self.[68]

68. This argument points toward the role of economic change in the development of an ethics of obligation. It has for some time been noticed in moral philosophy that much modern reflection on morals assumes that human purposes can only be evaluated by a notion of obligation that is external to them and imposed on them. Philosophers since Anscombe have argued that all attempts to root morality in obligation have failed and that what is needed is a notion of human purposes as internally appraisable by reference to a notion of human flourishing. Such philosophers have made extensive use of Aristotle, and have thereby contributed to the recovery of the importance of human flourishing and hence of internally appraisable human purposes in the interpretation of Thomas. To the extent that the ascendancy of exchange value contributes to construing human purposes as not internally appraisable, economic change may play a role in the rise of modern ethical problematics. My argument further suggests that only when human flourishing is understood as inscribed within an antecedent natural order is the alienation of ethical evaluation from human purposes fully overcome. Alasdair MacIntyre has recently suggested something similar. In *After Virtue,* he tried to recover internally appraisable human purposes without reference to nature by locating human flourishing in shared practices. He has since recanted the attempt to avoid claims about nature. In *Dependent Rational Animals* he points out that his former approach neglects what it is about human animality that makes flourishing possible and therefore leaves important elements out of its account of the virtues. I take MacIntyre's account of the "just generosity" and vulnerability that his new recognition involves to be quite amenable to my own emphasis on deference and trusting dependence. See G. E. M. Anscombe, "Modern Moral Philosophy," *Philosophy* 33 (1958): 1-19. For a brief introduction

In Thomas, on the other hand, human claims of usefulness are fully evaluatable. There is real and apparent usefulness, and the difference between them is determined by whether the usefulness is directable to the pursuit of virtue. Things are useful if they are means to some end that is apprehended as good.[69] Just as ends apprehended as good can be either really or only apparently good, so things apprehended as useful can be either really or only apparently useful, depending on the end to which they are means.

It is important not to mistake what Thomas means by "apparent goods." He does not mean that we are deceived to think the thing is good in any respect. Indeed, everything is good in some respect. Further, humans incline to goods that are the objects of their various faculties. Every inclination directs "to something like and suitable to the thing inclined."[70] More specifically, insofar as we consist of various faculties — of sensing, of reasoning, and so on — we incline toward the objects of those faculties. Thus certain sensible and intellectual pleasures are desirable to us.[71] That is why Thomas's account of human action requires that the achievement of human purposes always issues in pleasure, or delight.[72] Nothing could be desirable to us if it did not fit our natures in such a way.[73]

What determines whether a good that is really desirable in this sense becomes a merely "apparent good" is whether in this particular circumstance this desire for a generically good thing fits with the achievement of the flourishing of the whole human being.[74] For that flourishing, some goods must be subordinated to others according to the hierarchy of ends that reflects the hierarchy of human capacities. Since all human action

---

to the directions this argument has taken since Anscombe, see *Virtue Ethics,* ed. Roger Crisp and Michael Slote (Oxford: Oxford University Press, 1997). Cf. Alasdair MacIntyre, *After Virtue: A Study in Moral Theory,* 2nd ed. (Notre Dame, IN: University of Notre Dame Press, 1984), and *Dependent Rational Animals: Why Human Beings Need the Virtues* (Chicago: Open Court, 1999).

69. *ST* I 5.6; cf. II-II 145.3.

70. *ST* I-II 8.1; cf. *Sent. Eth.,* II.3, to Aristotle 1104b3-9.

71. *ST* I-II 10.1.

72. *ST* I-II 31.

73. It is possible, in Thomas's view, to delight in something that is strictly unnatural, but that can only result from some injury to the faculties that makes the unpleasant seem pleasant. It is interesting to note that Thomas considers here not only physiological injuries such as disease, but also the damage done to the soul by perverse customs that could make even cannibalism or bestiality seem pleasant (*ST* I-II 31.7).

74. *ST* I-II 10.2.

seeks to actualize these capacities, and succeeds in doing so more or less depending on how far the agent is perfected by virtuous habits, all human action bears within itself the structure of its own evaluation. By the same token, all human acquisitive activity, as it seeks things useful for the ends of human flourishing, is good or bad acquisitive activity as it seeks things of either real, or only apparent, usefulness.

Since the same God who constituted human beings with these desires and capacities also brings forth from the earth the goods required for human sustenance, we should not be surprised to find a coincidence between the external goods needed for human flourishing and the goods nature's provision brings forth. These things are the necessities of human living: they are human use values. It is to these that Thomas refers when he says that the common estimate of value reflects human usefulness.[75]

Just as the competitive market interpretation of the just price assumes a notion of "utility" foreign to Thomas, so its concept of justice cannot be squared with Thomas's. Since the utilities determined by the market are unquestionable, the concept of justice has no work to do except to ensure that the compromise among them is fair and uncoerced. For Thomas, on the other hand, justice has to do with rendering dues that are determined by the mutual benevolence God intends to characterize a flourishing human community, not by compromises among conflicting human desires.

Thomas says the object of justice is the due *(ius)*, what is right and due in one's relations with others.[76] It can only be understood in terms of the order God intends for human community, an order constituted not only by cooperation but by benevolence.[77] Justice seeks not only not to harm the neighbor, but to do good to her. It is thus evident that avarice, which seeks more than its due, is contrary to justice.[78] Therefore, justice in exchange must be a matter of seeking the level of exchange that will both

---

75. Daly and Cobb excoriate contemporary price theory for taking the "utility function" of *homo economicus* to be an adequate basis for establishing prices. This approach, they say, abstracts from the concerns real people have that are not expressed in market activity. Daly and Cobb, *For the Common Good,* pp. 85-87.

76. *ST* II-II 57. For an insightful explication of the role of the "due" in considerations of justice, see Josef Pieper, *The Four Cardinal Virtues: Prudence, Justice, Fortitude, Temperance* (New York: Harcourt, Brace, & World, 1965), pp. 43-63.

77. Rhonheimer, "Sins Against Justice," p. 288.

78. *ST* II-II 117.1.

render the due to the neighbor and avoid the avarice involved in seeking more than one's own due.

According to the competitive market interpretation, justice in exchange comes about quite differently. It results from accepting the market price, which is presumed to be set as a byproduct of many processes of bargaining between buyers and sellers, each of whom has little or no interest in protecting the due of the other. What protects the justice of the just price is not the virtue of the exchangers, nor their attention to directing use values to human sustenance, but the level nature of the playing field on which all try to attain their best bargaining position. On the contrary, in Thomas's discussions of the just price he clearly thinks that exchangers should seek justice rather than whatever they can bargain for.

In this respect, Thomas's neglect of the problems of monopoly is especially instructive. That neglect corresponds to a broader lack of concern for the "competitiveness" of prices that characterizes all the scholastics of his day. The competitive market interpretation supposes that the reason Thomas identifies the just price with the prevailing price is because the competition of the open market is what protects justice. As Langholm says, "medieval buyers were thought to be protected by the competitive market." He further extrapolates a reason for the persistence of the usury prohibition: markets in money were not extensive enough to provide the competition that would protect borrowers.[79]

It is strange, then, as de Roover uncomfortably notes, that no scholastic mentions competition before the sixteenth century.[80] Indeed, when Aristotle mentions monopoly in his discussion of wealth-getting in the *Politics,* he invokes it not to disparage it, as he does trade, but to commend it as a technique useful to politicians and others.[81] In his commentary on the *Politics,* Thomas lays forth Aristotle's remarks with no hint of chafing at Aristotle's failure to attack monopoly. When Thomas lays out his own position in the *ST,* it is striking that in four articles dealing with how prices can diverge in one way or another from the common estimate, he never thinks of monopoly.

Not that monopolistic abuses were unknown. An earlier thirteenth-century Summa, attributed to Alexander of Hales, condemns those

---

79. Langholm, *Economics in the Medieval Schools,* p. 592.
80. De Roover, "The Concept of the Just Price," p. 425.
81. Aristotle, *Politics,* I, 1259a6-37.

"greedy rich people who frequently take over the whole marketplace for commodities, in order later at will to sell them to others at a higher price than they would have been sold at in the market if these people had not bought them, and this they do with grain and other things necessary for human life; such people should be expelled from the Church as detestable to God according to the example of the Lord."[82] While our modern assumptions might incline us to read here an attack on monopolies as such, it is important to read more closely. We have here an attack on those who orchestrate a monopoly out of greed and in such a way as to threaten the human sustenance for which nature's provision is intended. Monopolies are not bad in themselves for any of Thomas's contemporaries, as if the absence of competition itself means the demise of justice. Rather, monopolies are bad when they are used to thwart a justice that is not defined as the absence of monopoly.

This much has been recognized by some, particularly by representatives of the cost interpretation of the just price. Bernard Dempsey, in particular, has done a great service for scholarship on the just price by showing sensitivity to the broader contours of Thomas's understanding of justice, while acknowledging the importance of the variations and social determinations involved in Thomas's acceptance of the common estimate as the just price.[83] Yet we will not fully grasp Thomas's teaching on the just price and its implications for how nature is understood unless we recognize the role Thomas assigns to our situatedness within the natural circuit of nourishment. Dempsey is right to emphasize the location of exchangers within a coherent social body organized by the wisdom of God's providence, a context that itself requires a degree of deference and receptivity.[84] But we do not fully understand what Thomas means by the "common good" if we miss how this social belonging is rooted in and inseparable from our membership in an antecedent natural order. The criteria Thomas most clearly invokes to protect justice in exchange refer not so much to social context as to the context of nature's provision of useful things. As clearly as Thomas invokes these criteria, they are almost never noted by modern interpreters. This blindness, I think, bespeaks the difficulty of recovering Thomas's view

---

82. Alexander of Hales, *Summa Theologica*, 724, cited in Langholm, *Economics in the Medieval Schools*, p. 131.

83. Dempsey, *Functional Economy*, pp. 412-31.

84. Dempsey, *Functional Economy*, p. 422.

in light of the strong hold of modern economic assumptions. In Dempsey, this blind spot is evident not only in his failure to attend to the natural circuit of nourishment, but equally in his assumption that Thomas shares the modern concern with "progress," a concern inveterately hostile to suffering the contours of an antecedent natural order.[85]

What protects justice in Thomas's account of exchange is not competition, nor attention to a common good that can be abstracted from its membership in natural order, but rather the deference that inscribes economic activity within the natural circuit from nature's provision to nature's goal of human sustenance. I will illustrate these claims by looking more closely at the fourth article of the question on buying and selling in the *ST*. This reading will provide an example of how Thomas invokes conformity to natural order as a criterion of justice. Further, it will show how recognizing that criterion sheds light on an otherwise difficult article.

In II-II 77.4, Thomas asks whether the vocation of the trader, which involves selling things for more than he paid for them, is lawful. This question poses special difficulties for Thomas. On the one hand, he wants to affirm the legitimacy of the trading profession. He is presumably attending to the social importance of trade in his own day, but he also draws support from Augustine, who attests that the greed and deceit often associated with trade are not in fact necessary to it. On the other hand, three considerations constrain his enthusiasm for trade. First, much patristic tradition seems to condemn trade *tout court*, and the prevailing rule that clerics must not participate in trade seems to tarnish that activity. Second, Thomas accepts much of Aristotle's thought on economic matters, and Aristotle associates trade with the unnatural form of wealth-getting that is rightly condemned. Third, Thomas's own teaching on just price, which he articulates in the first article of this question, rules out both selling high and buying low, and it seems difficult to account for the trader's profit without assuming one or the other. Thomas navigates these constraints by

---

85. Dempsey, *Functional Economy*, p. 423. Concern for sustainability has led a wave of recent writers to question whether unlimited growth is a legitimate economic goal. Margrit Kennedy, for example, contrasts natural and exponential growth. Natural growth starts quickly but then levels off when maturity is reached. Exponential growth, as represented in today's financial markets, begins slowly but then continually accelerates. Such growth, she points out, is not a sign of health but of cancerous sickness. Margrit Kennedy, *Interest and Inflation Free Money: Creating an Exchange Medium That Works for Everybody and Protects the Earth*, rev. and exp. ed. (Philadelphia: New Society Publishers, 1995), pp. 18-24.

distinguishing acceptable trade from illegitimate trade. Thus he interprets the church fathers and Aristotle as attacking only the illegitimate kind, and he appeals to the acceptable kind to show why selling at a higher price than one paid need not mean an abrogation of the just price.

If the competitive market interpreters were correct, we might expect Thomas to base his distinction between two kinds of trade on the attention the trader pays to the exigencies of the free market. He does not. If Dempsey told the full story, we might expect Thomas to base the distinction solely on the trader's concern for the common good. He does not. He bases the distinction entirely on whether the trading activity is patient of its location in a prior natural order. Thomas invokes two criteria: does the trader recognize the origin of all wealth in nature's provision, and does the trader direct his or her acquisition to the ends nature intends?

In the body of the article, Thomas invokes Aristotle's distinction between natural and unnatural exchange. Natural exchange, whether involving money or not, originates in useful commodities and aims "to satisfy the needs of life." Unnatural exchange necessarily involves money, sometimes seems to make money from money, and always aims not at necessities but at profit. The latter type has to do with traders, and justly deserves blame. At this point Thomas tweaks Aristotle: the latter leaves it there, with trade as unnatural and blameworthy; but Thomas envisions another kind of trade, a kind that, even though it seeks profit, orders its activity within the constraints of natural order. This trader would seek only a "moderate gain," intended for the ends of nature's sustenance — "for the upkeep of his household, or for the assistance of the needy, or . . . lest his country lack the necessaries of life." Further, this trade would not squeeze a suspicious profit from the very conventions of exchange value, but would seek only the gain that can be justified "as payment for his labor." The criteria of being rooted in nature's provision and ordered to nature's ends determine what is just in trading.

This distinction between two kinds of trade enables Thomas to address the objections. Chrysostom says that Christ's cleansing of the Temple was a judgment on all traders who sell the same commodity at an increased price to make a profit. Thomas invokes the "source" and "end" criteria to interpret. It is trade that seeks gain as a last end, rather than as ordered to nature's goals, that Chrysostom describes. And contravening that criterion goes hand in hand with contravening the other, for seeking gain as a last end seems especially to be the case where no additional contribution from nature's provision changes the thing and justifies the higher price. But "if he sells at a higher price something that has changed for the better, he would seem to receive the reward of his labor."[86]

The other particularly telling objection is the second, which claims that selling at a profit must mean that one has bought too low or has sold too high and thus destroys the just price. Thomas's reply is worth quoting in full:

> Not everyone that sells at a higher price than he bought is a tradesman, but only he who buys that he may sell at a profit. If, on the contrary, he buys not for sale but for possession, and afterwards, for some reason wishes to sell, it is not a trade transaction even if he sell at a profit. For he may lawfully do this, either because he has bettered the thing, or because the value of the thing has changed with the change of place or time, or on account of the danger he incurs in transferring the thing from one place to another, or again in having it carried by another. In this sense neither buying nor selling is unjust.[87]

The objection focuses attention on the source of wealth. Regardless of the ends toward which profit is directed, what can be the source of the increase in price, so that the just price when one sells is higher than when one bought? As in the *respondeo,* the increase must be reckoned as a sort of payment, and not merely justified by the seller's desire to multiply his exchange value. In this way, trade can be acceptable if the profit on a sale is legitimated with reference to some addition from nature's provision, paradigmatically in the form of the labor of the seller.

However, this logic of claiming profits only when the source of the increase in nature's provision is somehow identifiable runs into trouble when a thing's worth changes simply with a change of place or time. We have seen that abundance can depress prices at one time, while dearth inflates them at another. In this case, a seller can, by timing his buying and selling well, buy at a low just price and sell at a high one, with hardly any of his own labor to justify the increase. The possibility of such exchange is built into the very character of exchange value. Nothing unjust can be identified in it so long as the profit obtained remains aimed at nature's ends.

---

86. *ST* II-II 77.4 ad 1.
87. *ST* II-II 77.4 ad 2.

As just as such exchange may be, considered in itself, it bears within it a dangerous potential. Traders grow skilled at judging the timing that maximizes the increase. The more widespread the practices of traders, the more prominent buying low and selling high become. Even if done justly, the spread of such practices creates a momentum, so that buying low and selling high begin to become imperatives to which all economic activity must submit. Samuel Hollander suggests that this is why Thomas allows these concessions to selling at a higher price only for nontraders. The concessions, he says, are limited to situations "where the individual is not strictly a trader at all."[88] But on this interpretation, the reply undermines the thrust of the article, which contends that trade can be a legitimate occupation, even though it involves selling at a profit. Thomas does not mean for these concessions not to apply to traders. His remarks about those who buy not for trade but for possession must be understood as invoking a noncontroversial example of selling at a profit in order then to extend the legitimacy of certain forms of selling at a profit also to traders. Thomas's answer to the dangers of trading is not to allow selling at a profit to nontraders while prohibiting it for traders. Rather, his answer, which he spells out not here but in *De Regno*, is to insist that trading, though a legitimate profession, must be kept to the margins of economic activity. To modern ears, Thomas sounds downright prophetic in his assessment of the danger involved if a king allows more than a "moderate use of merchants": "Since the foremost tendency of tradesmen is to make money, greed is awakened in the hearts of the citizens through the pursuit of trade. The result is that everything in the city will become venal; good faith will be destroyed and the way opened to all kinds of trickery; each one will work only for his own profit, despising the public good; the cultivation of virtue will fail since honour, virtue's reward, will be bestowed upon the rich. Thus, in such a city, civic life will necessarily be corrupted."[89]

For Thomas, justice is protected not by competition, nor only by attention to the common good. Justice in exchange is protected by the deference that keeps economic activity inscribed within the natural order that directs all wealth from nature's provision to nature's goal of human suste-

---

88. Hollander, "On the Interpretation of the Just Price," p. 627.

89. *De Regno*, II.7. This translation is from *On Kingship to the King of Cyprus*, trans. Gerald B. Phelan, rev. I. Th. Eschmann, O.P. (Toronto: Pontifical Institute of Mediaeval Studies, 1949).

nance. Microeconomic signs of that deference include seeking a source in nature's provision to legitimate any claim to an increase in wealth and determining to direct all acquisitive activity to ends conducive to human flourishing. But such discreet practices are not enough in the end. Because of the possibility that exchange value creates for gains whose origin in nature's provision is obscure at best, and because of the power social arrangements have to direct economic activity into certain patterns, ultimately the deference that protects justice is only maintained at the macroeconomic level by regulating the scope of trading activity.[90]

This explains why Thomas could have such confidence in the justice of prevailing prices in his own day. He understood trade to be sufficiently marginal and use values to be sufficiently supreme that the requisite deference was basically determinative of the common estimates that set prices. Correlatively, he was sufficiently confident of the sway that a true (or true enough) estimate of human flourishing held in his society. Whatever the vices of the individual buyers and sellers, their trades are ultimately directed toward the usefulnesses that are determinative for the broader community, since it is the members of such a community from whom they must buy or to whom they hope to sell. Nor must such community members be predominantly virtuous in order to keep prices honest. Thomas knew that folks generally seek to buy low and sell high, a trait he attributed to the fact that they "walk along the broad road of sin."[91] All that is required is that their lives be sufficiently governed by a true reckoning of human flourishing to render their valuations of exchangeable things, by and large, directable toward that flourishing. In other words, exchange values simply need to be governed by the predominance of use values. Indeed, it seems fair to suppose that one would have no reason to doubt the broad justice of prevailing prices except where community members generally have abandoned a sufficiently true estimate of human flourishing.

90. The kind of regulation Thomas envisions may seem utopian today, but Daly and Cobb make a serious suggestion in a similar vein: "[Oikonomia] finds the market an excellent instrument for certain function, especially the allocation of resources. It also finds it dangerous. The management of the community so as to increase use value to all members over the long run requires that the market be of the right size to make its positive contributions while minimizing its harmful effects." Daly and Cobb, *For the Common Good*, p. 158.

91. *ST* II-II 77.1 ad 2.

Conclusion

In many interpretations of Thomas's economic thought, the teachings on just price and usury seem to stand in some tension with one another. On just price, Thomas seems to anticipate much modern wisdom about how pricing works, while on usury he holds on to an ancient prohibition in conflict with those anticipations. My reading of Thomas in this chapter suggests, on the contrary, that Thomas's understandings of just price and usury are of a piece. In both areas, Thomas seeks to stave off economic practices that threaten to undermine the deference and trusting vulnerability to an antecedent natural order that he sees as crucial to human flourishing and to maintaining justice in human relations of exchange. Recognizing the importance of this deference is the key to avoiding anachronistic readings of Thomas and to understanding the character of Thomas's appreciation of Aristotle's writings on economics. It is also crucial for understanding how Thomas's teachings on justice in exchange reflect his account of our ontological poverty. In the next chapter I will begin to explore this ontological poverty and how it orients action involving external goods toward its *telos*.

CHAPTER 3

Ontological Poverty
and the Priority of the Counsels

The teachings on property, usury, and just price that we have been investigating are found within Thomas's treatment of the virtue of justice. Many aspects of Thomas's discussion of justice depend on what he has learned from Aristotle. But here, as elsewhere, Thomas transforms Aristotle in light of his theological commitments. Some of these transformations are evident in the account of justice. For example, Thomas situates original human *dominium* within a biblical account of God's providence, giving human appropriation of necessary goods a less proprietary flavor than it has even in Aristotle. To see the full extent of those transformations, though, we must attend to other virtues that work along with justice to order human economic activity.

What we find is that in Thomas the deferent wonder commended by Aristotle is deepened into an acknowledgment of our fundamental ontological poverty before God. This has everything to do with Thomas's account of creation. The receptivity to an encompassing order evident in Thomas's teachings on justice in exchange is revealed to be an aspect of the humble vulnerability appropriate to creatures. But we cannot separate Thomas's understanding of this ontological poverty from his grasp of the self-offering charity taught by Christ, the *telos* of all human action. This humble vulnerability reflects both the status of the creature before God and the movement of love beyond itself. We could see ontological poverty as a sort of hinge that accounts for how Thomas can simultaneously appreciate Aristotle's deferent dependence and see all human action involving wealth as culminating in the poverty of the crucified Christ.

When Aristotle's deferent dependence is transformed into Thomas's ontological poverty, the human agent is placed within the movement of Christian life toward greater participation in the divine charity. Believers grasp their ontological poverty in the course of being summoned to the beatitude opened up by Christ. And activity that accords with ontological poverty is activity on the way to that beatitude. So when we recognize that Aquinas's account of justice assumes not just Aristotelian deference but Christian ontological poverty, we not only leave behind Aristotelian metaphysics, but also set the human agent on the road to a perfection Aristotle never contemplated.

In this chapter I will explore this ontological poverty and the corresponding calling to evangelical perfection from two directions. First, I will discuss the implications for Thomas's economic teachings of some of his comments about specific theological virtues, namely hope and charity. Hope, and particularly its correlative gift of fear, show how one's grasp of ontological poverty derives from the summons to beatitude. It also reveals how the humble vulnerability that results is the root of all virtuous action with external goods. Charity is the fulfillment of all virtuous action, and yet Thomas's comments about the order of charity may seem to suggest that he ultimately legitimates the drive to secure oneself. I argue that even charity's concern to care for oneself is part of the self-abandonment that directs Christological, humble vulnerability toward its completion.

Second, I will say more about how the life of theological virtue is oriented toward a perfection whose contours are better specified by the counsels of religious life. Thomas makes a number of general comments about the relationship between the commands, which prescribe the acts of the virtues, and the counsels. He frequently insists that keeping the counsels is not required for perfection. Interpreters could come away with the impression that counsels such as poverty are helpful adjuncts to the commands, but that they do not do significant work in specifying good action. I will probe these comments to show that, although the counsels are merely instrumental to perfection, they specify more concretely the direction pointed by the commands.[1] Thomas's general comments on this issue sup-

---

1. In other words, the counsels help spell out the virtues made possible by the New Law in Christ. And this New Law is "the summit of the Christian moral life toward which all paths and precepts lead." Servais Pinckaers, *The Pinckaers Reader: Renewing Thomistic Moral Theology,* ed. John Berkman and Craig Steven Titus (Washington, DC: The Catholic University of America Press, 2005), p. 381.

port my interpretation of the poverty of Christ as the *telos* of human action involving external goods.

The Gift of Fear, Charity, and Thomas's Economic Teachings

Thomas's teachings on justice are sometimes taken to cut in the opposite direction from an evangelical focus on selfless love and nonproprietary sharing. Justice seems to imply asserting one's claims rather than giving unconditionally. Even when he discusses charity, it is thought, Thomas reaffirms natural self-possession. Contrary to such readings, I will suggest that what Aquinas says about justice does not domesticate his evangelical focus. Rather, the teachings on justice investigated in earlier chapters fit into an account of Christian life that begins in an evangelical fear of the Lord and aims at a charity that imitates Christ's self-giving. Deferent wonder in Thomas's hands reflects Christian humble vulnerability. From first to last, a humble vulnerability echoing Christ on the cross conditions Christian economic action.[2]

Humble Vulnerability and the Gift of Fear

Thomas's discussion of the gift of fear may not seem the most obvious place to begin a discussion of what Christians do with their wealth, but in Thomas's estimation, any proper disposition toward wealth must be rooted in the fear of the Lord. Fear of the Lord is the beginning of the requisite degree of humble trust.

The very notion of a "gift of fear" might be difficult for modern readers to accept. We like to praise boldness and confidence, entrepreneurial daring, and undaunted scientific advance. The technological conquest of the natural world has been motivated in great part by a desire to banish

2. These connections are not lost on Joan Lockwood O'Donovan, who comments that the economic and philosophical transformations that doomed scholastic usury teaching were part of one movement that both eroded older assumptions about justice and undermined the force of the counsels at the same time. Joan Lockwood O'Donovan, "The Theological Economics of Medieval Usury Theory," in Oliver O'Donovan and Joan Lockwood O'Donovan, *Bonds of Imperfection: Christian Politics, Past and Present* (Grand Rapids: Eerdmans, 2004), pp. 97-120, esp. p. 99.

fears — that the triumph of human reason may lead to there being nothing left to fear. The notion that fear might be a gift is foreign indeed. Josef Pieper identifies two sources of this discomfort with fear: "One is an enlightened liberalism that relegates fearfulness to the realm of the unreal and in whose worldview, accordingly, there is no room for fear except in the figurative sense. The other is an unchristian stoicism that is secretly allied with both presumption and despair and confronts in defiant invulnerability — without fear, but also without hope — the evils of existence, which it sees with admirable clarity."[3] For such reasons, modern readers are often deaf to the significance of the claim that the "fear of the Lord is the beginning of wisdom" (Ps. 110:10).

I suspect that modern attitudes toward fear have much to do with the rise of the proprietary self. Acknowledging our ontological poverty is particularly uncomfortable for us: as I have noted in the introduction, it can seem to be a kind of violence. But for Thomas the fear of the Lord is given graciously by the Holy Spirit, and it is the beginning of economic wisdom. Thomas's account of the gift of fear shows how ontological poverty goes beyond Aristotelian deference and how it starts the Christian life on the path of self-abandonment to which mendicancy bears concrete witness.

To understand ontological poverty and its evangelical character, we must explore the gift of fear to show how it is a kind of attachment to God. Thomas links fear with hope. It may seem odd to link hope and fear, since hope draws up toward a good, while fear recoils from some evil. But this fear is, perhaps surprisingly, a kind of attachment to God, the kind that strengthens and perfects the attachment to God we have through hope. But how can fear be a kind of attachment to a good while still remaining fear?

Thomas distinguishes worldly, servile, initial, and filial fear.[4] *Worldly* fear is the fear of losing some created good such that one flees from God for the sake of that good. Such fear is always sinful and completely differs from the fear of the Lord.[5] The other three fears together form a movement that turns us more and more toward the love of God. The most important distinction is between *servile* and *filial* fear, *initial* fear being a

---

3. Josef Pieper, *Faith, Hope, Love,* trans. Richard and Clara Winston and Sister Mary Frances McCarthy, S.N.D. (San Francisco: Ignatius Press, 1997), p. 130.
4. *ST* II-II 19.2.
5. *ST* II-II 19.3.

transitional state that includes both.[6] Servile and filial fear both recoil from some evil and turn us toward God; but servile fear turns toward God out of fear of punishment. This fear perhaps accords better with our common sense understanding of what a "fear of the Lord" would be. One fears God through aversion, not strictly to God, but to the evil of punishment one might expect for sinning against God.[7] If servile fear fits fairly well our expectations of the fear of the Lord, for Thomas the most proper fear for the Christian is filial fear. This fear turns to God not through fear of punishment but through fear of offending a beloved Father. If servile fear fears God as the cause of punishment, filial fear fears God as "the term wherefrom it shrinks to be separated by guilt."[8]

It is perhaps clear how filial fear can be a kind of attachment to God, but unclear how it is still fear *of God*. It is not God from whom we recoil in filial fear. On the contrary, connection with God is precisely the good we love, because of which we fear the opposite. Therefore, is not filial fear just another name for charity, which helps Thomas interpret some otherwise troublesome biblical texts?

What filial fear brings out that is not evident from charity by itself is the disproportion between our wretchedness and God's grandeur. Filial fear may have more in common with charity than with servile fear, since it emphasizes our attachment to God as our good who is loved so much that the importance of our own well-being, which may be threatened in some way by punishment, pales in comparison. But filial fear remains fear, and retains an important kinship with servile fear, insofar as the sense of subordination to one who is able to punish is brought to perfection in a rever-

---

6. *ST* II-II 19.4, 5, and 8.

7. Such fear can be sinful if one's attachment to the goods that punishment threatens is so great that punishment itself is feared as the greatest evil. Such disproportionate fear of punishment shows that God is not appreciated as one's ultimate end. But one can turn from sin through a fear of punishment that is ordered toward God as final end (art. 4). Romanus Cessario tries to detach servile fear from the notion of an "avenging God" by noting that, since sin is its own punishment, recoiling from the punishment could simply mean fearing to return to the state of enslavement the sin generated. But this interpretation seems to lose exactly what is distinctive about servile fear. Thomas's taxonomy of fear shows that simplistic fears of an "avenging God" may be useful in turning us toward God, but they give way to a filial fear that recoils above all else from losing the great good of friendship with God. Romanus Cessario, *The Virtues, or the Examined Life* (New York: Continuum, 2002), pp. 52-59.

8. *ST* II-II 19.5 ad 2.

ent submission that more fully reflects and acknowledges how great is the disproportion between our lowliness and the exceeding majesty of God. It is this disproportion that underlies our fear of falling away from God. William Hill comments that while filial fear's act is something like reverence before God's eminence, which seems more like an attachment to — rather than a fear of — God, it remains fear insofar as an evil is dimly sensed. There are hints that "this eminence may be too far beyond one; its absolute purity may be such that it cannot endure contact with anything impure — and so the fear arises that one may lose contact with the very source of one's being."[9] If filial fear still sounds more like fear of *losing* God than fear of God, note that filial fear remains even among the blessed. Fear's act changes somewhat, but what remains is its subordination in view of the disproportion between us and God. Thomas likens this fear to "wonder at God's supereminence and incomprehensibility."[10]

Filial fear is the habit of embracing our ontological poverty. It is a kind of attachment to God that heightens our grasp of the distance between us and God. Filial fear does not denote less subordination than servile fear does, for our sense of the disproportion *increases* as we grow closer to God. The closer we come to God, the greater our awareness of God's majesty. Knowledge of our disproportion to God, who is above us, results in humility.[11] And the greater our nearness to God, the greater we know the truth uttered by Abraham, "I will speak to my Lord, whereas I am dust and ashes," and by Isaiah, "All nations are before him as if they had no being at all."[12]

If filial fear, this profound sense of our lowliness before God's greatness, is a wellspring of humility, it also prompts dependent trust. For the more one's own insignificance before the Almighty impresses him, the more vehemently he "casts himself into God's omnipotent arms."[13] As we will see in more detail when discussing mendicant poverty, humility and dependence are two sides of one coin. Thus, Thomas takes our perfect subjection to God to be expressed in the words of trust in Psalm 19:8: "Some trust in chariots and some in horses; but we will call upon the name of . . .

9. William J. Hill, O.P., *Hope. Summa Theologiae IIa IIae. 17-22*, Blackfriars edition, ed. Thomas Gilby et al., vol. 33 (New York: McGraw-Hill, 1966), p. 170.

10. *ST* II-II 19.11.

11. *ST* II-II 161.2.

12. *ST* II-II 161.1 ad 1 and ad 4. Cf. Gen. 18:27 and Isa. 40:17.

13. Hill, *Hope*, p. 170.

our God."[14] As we sense our lowliness and God's greatness, we also recognize the extent of our dependence. So the gift of fear shores us up for the arduous task of trusting God for all our needs. Thomas sees the fortitude fear engenders expressed in the petition of the Our Father that requests our daily bread: "This fortitude which is given by the Holy Ghost so strengthens the heart of man that he does not fear for the things that are necessary for him, but he trusts that God will provide for all his needs."[15] Filial fear, therefore, both strengthens and completes the movement of theological hope, which clings to God for help to reach a difficult end.

The humble trust of filial fear belongs to all Christians. Although servile fear is a sort of *terminus a quo* to filial fear's *terminus ad quem*, filial fear is not a later stage of the Christian life; rather, it belongs to its very beginnings.[16] Thomas thus affirms the teaching of Psalm 110:10, "The fear of the Lord is the beginning of wisdom," by noting that wisdom involves following divine law, for which "man must first of all fear God and submit himself to Him: for the result will be that in all things he will be ruled by God."[17]

This subordination, lowliness, and wonder is the "fear of the Lord" that we moderns are so disposed to qualify, reinterpret, or forget. The centrality of charity for Thomas is more amenable to us. If we attend to filial fear, it is probably to point out its similarity to charity. But our discussions of charity would do well to reflect more on filial fear and to remember that it remains a kind of fear. It is this notion of the fear of the Lord, of the unfathomable disproportion between us and God, that keeps Thomas's talk of our friendship with God in charity from becoming a modern-style domestication of God instead of an ineffable mystery.[18]

The fear of the Lord is not only a stumbling block for modern thought; it also evokes a sense of our ontological poverty that goes beyond Aristotelian deference. A philosopher such as Aristotle could recognize a

---

14. *ST* II-II 19.12.

15. *The Catechetical Instructions of St. Thomas Aquinas*, trans. Joseph B. Collins (New York: Joseph F. Wagner, 1939), p. 155.

16. *ST* II-II 19.8; cf. I-II 68.2.

17. *ST* II-II 19.7.

18. For an intriguing account of how thinking about God was subtly domesticated, especially in the seventeenth century, see William C. Placher, *The Domestication of Transcendence: How Modern Thinking about God Went Wrong* (Louisville: Westminster John Knox Press, 1996).

kind of disproportion between human beings and the First Cause. Ancient philosophers certainly acknowledged that God is infinitely above us.[19] Furthermore, philosophy can grasp that God is our cause, that God is not part of what is caused, and that our distance from God is not due to a defect in God, but to the fact that God super-exceeds everything that is caused.[20]

But the lowly dependence of an Aristotle is nowhere near as deep as the sense of disproportion we have by faith, and this for two reasons. First, a Christian sense of this disproportion reflects the teaching of *creatio ex nihilo*. Our lowliness and dependence before God corresponds to our originating from nothing. For Aristotle, nature is the necessary, the entirety of what is; it encompasses us and merits our admiration. Within nature we find our place and suitably seek to live with the dignity of those endowed with that precious divine attribute of reason. If nature is necessary, our place within nature is not to be questioned. Despite the need for deferent dependence, no reason could be imagined for us to pursue a movement of self-abasement. For Thomas, on the other hand, nature in itself is nothing. It has a certain dignity, called into being by God. But its existence, and ours as members of it, is due to a gratuitous gift. For Aristotle, nature is simply there, calling forth admiration; for Thomas, nature directs our attention to God its author, and it calls forth our gratitude.[21] Here humility makes sense, for the giver of that gift owes us nothing; rather, we owe all. Our proper estimation of ourselves is to grasp the "poverty" of our place in relation to that giver.

The depth of this disproportion is not naturally available, but is a matter of revelation. Indeed, it is fitting that the fear of the Lord is reckoned among the gifts of the Holy Spirit, because it is only by being brought near to God that we see the true scope of the disproportion emerge. Only in friendship with God do we attain such an awareness of God's majestic glory and of our utter insufficiency.[22] The sense of disproportion we re-

19. *ST* I 7.1.

20. *ST* I 12.12.

21. For more on the distinction between ancient pagan and Christian conceptions of the way things are, see Robert Sokolowski, *The God of Faith and Reason: Foundations of Christian Theology* (Notre Dame, IN: University of Notre Dame Press, 1982), pp. 12-19 and *passim*. See also David B. Burrell, *Aquinas: God and Action* (Notre Dame, IN: University of Notre Dame Press, 1979).

22. On our insufficiency, see *ST* II-II 161.6 ad 1.

ceive is itself disproportionate to our nature! Filial fear "is a gift that entirely surpasses the potentialities of natural man."[23]

The second reason Thomas's account of humble vulnerability surpasses any Aristotelian analogue is that Thomas sees the fear of the Lord as a summons that is part of Christ's invitation to beatitude. Through our response to this invitation we are drawn near to God, and the excessive degree of this nearness deepens our sense of disproportion between us and God. And Christ proposes this beatitude by calling us to renunciation and self-abandonment, casting the shadow of the cross on the Christian practice of humble vulnerability.[24]

Thomas aligns each gift of the Holy Spirit with a beatitude. While Thomas understands the gifts as habits that dispose us to receive the action of the Holy Spirit,[25] the beatitudes are acts that correspond to those gifts.[26] The beatitudes are taken from the Sermon on the Mount, and Thomas understands them as Christ's progressive path toward our final beatitude.[27] Just as the fear of the Lord is the beginning of wisdom, Thomas follows Augustine by connecting it with the first beatitude, poverty of spirit. Making such connections may seem an overwrought medieval obsession, and certainly there is some arbitrariness in the connections made. But Thomas invests great thought into the assignments, and "this penchant for symmetry should not conceal the intellectual penetration which occurs beneath such convenient scaffolding."[28]

It is not difficult to see why Thomas associates this beatitude with this gift. The profound sense of lowliness before God causes us to cast off all our aspirations to greatness, whether in ourselves or in honors and riches. Thus the gift of fear finds its proper act in poverty of spirit, whether that be understood as an inward humility and lowliness, as in Augustine, or as the voluntary renunciation of worldly goods, as in Ambrose or

---

23. Pieper, *Faith, Hope, Love*, p. 136.

24. A humble vulnerability deeper than anything in Aristotle is to some extent shared among the three scriptural religions that confess a similar account of creation — Judaism, Christianity, and Islam. But within Christianity, the cross of Christ draws that humble vulnerability toward a level of renunciation rarely found in Judaism or Islam. I am grateful to Fritz Bauerschmidt for helping me clarify this point.

25. *ST* I-II 68.1.

26. *ST* II-II 69.1.

27. Pinckaers, *The Pinckaers Reader*, p. 104.

28. Hill, *Hope*, p. 168.

Jerome.[29] Poverty of spirit may be understood in either way not because we may neglect the other interpretation, but because this beatitude refers to our "despising altogether" either honor or riches, whichever stands for us as an obstacle to blessedness.[30] Thus, as William Hill suggests, poverty of spirit empties the soul "of all superficial exaltation of spirit feeding upon honours or wealth. Fear focuses the spirit upon the ineffable grandeur of God thereby unveiling this creaturely self-sufficiency as the nothingness it is."[31]

Poverty of spirit is the root of any properly Christian disposition toward wealth. All are thereby called to a pattern of renunciation that can have many forms but is specified especially well by the poverty of religious life. Although everyone need not take vows of poverty, notice how the abandonment of possessions actualizes the habitual renunciation required of all Christians in the following passage from *Contra Impugnantes:* "The Gloss on Luke 14:33, 'If anyone does not renounce all he possesses . . . ,' says, 'There is a difference between renouncing everything and abandoning everything. For they renounce everything who lawfully use the worldly things they possess, while yet their minds tend toward eternal things. But to abandon belongs only to the perfect, who disregard all temporal things and long for eternal things alone.' Therefore to abandon, which involves actual poverty, belongs to evangelical perfection, but to renounce by this habitual poverty is necessary for salvation."[32] Voluntary poverty displays a material pattern of life that actualizes the direction in which poverty of spirit points. The sense of ontological poverty that is part of Christian life from its beginnings sets us on a path toward the poverty of Christ.[33]

29. *ST* II-II 19.12.

30. *ST* I-II 69.3.

31. Hill, *Hope*, p. 173.

32. "Luc. XIV 33 'Nisi quis renuntiaverit omnibus quae possidet,' Glosa Hoc distat inter renuntiare omnibus et relinquere omnia, quia renuntiare convenit omnibus qui ita licite utuntur mundanis quae possident ut tamen mente tendant ad aeterna, relinquere est tantum modo perfectorum qui omnia temporalia postponunt et solis aeternis inhiant; ergo relinquere, quod pertinet ad actualem paupertatem, est evangelicae perfectionis, sed renuntiare, quod pertinet ad habitualem secundum glosam praedictam, est de necessitate salutis." *CI*, chap. 6, § 3, 318-29. (Translations from the polemical works, *CI, CR,* and *DP,* are my own unless otherwise noted.)

33. Whereas virtue apart from Christ's call in the beatitudes teaches moderate use of external goods, life in the Spirit "goes further and would have us scorn material goods en-

Humble Vulnerability and the Acts of Charity

We have seen some connection between filial fear and charity, and so we may expect to find that charity points in the same direction, toward a self-abandonment that refuses to secure itself. But, on the other hand, a look into Thomas's discussion of charity might give pause to such a claim. For charity does not imply a straightforward and unambiguous self-denial. Rather, charity observes a certain order. Within that order, love of oneself holds a special place.[34] Further, among our neighbors, one should especially love those proximate either to us or to God.[35] For these reasons, when yielding up one's material goods for the sake of others through almsdeeds, one should give out of one's surplus, for "each one must first of all look after himself and then after those over whom he has charge, and afterwards with what remains relieve the needs of others."[36] It seems that the order of charity qualifies rather than confirms the movement of self-abandonment that I have been outlining.

But I argue that charity, even in its order, is driven by a movement of self-abandonment for the sake of others. It has something about it of what Augustine called "love of God extending to contempt of self."[37] Therefore, Thomas appeals to Augustine's formulation in his account of the care of common things among religious orders.[38] He is trying to show that having such common things is no detriment to perfection. Perfection consists in the operation of charity, and poverty is meant to remove obstacles to charity. Entering religion deals a definitive blow to the love of riches, which grows with possession, and to the vainglory that accompanies them. But it may seem that keeping even the most minimal common things marks a failure to remove the obstacle of the care riches bring, for even a few things require some solicitude. First, Thomas notes that if the things are few enough, the minimal solicitude they require is no hindrance to perfection. Second, Thomas contends that if such things are held in common, the very

---

tirely, so as to detach our heart from them without reserve. Such was the evangelical poverty actually practiced by St. Dominic and St. Francis." Pinckaers, *The Pinckaers Reader*, p. 128.

34. *ST* II-II 25.4; 26.4.

35. *ST* II-II 26.6.

36. *ST* II-II 32.5.

37. Augustine, *The City of God against the Pagans*, XIV.28. See the translation by R. W. Dyson (Cambridge, UK: Cambridge University Press, 1998), p. 632.

38. *ST* II-II 188.7.

care exercised over them, rather than being a hindrance to charity, can be an expression of it. For whereas care of one's private goods pertains to self-love, care of things held in common pertains to the love that does not seek its own. And this is proper to the perfection of religious orders, for charity is perfected in the love of God extending to contempt of self.[39]

If that love, oriented beyond the self, is the perfection of charity, such self-abandonment must belong in some measure to all charity. Note that if charity involves self-abandonment, it is never our own striving for God that is abandoned. For Thomas, the existential form of all our action is to desire the good and to seek the fulfillment of that desire.[40] We cannot annul our fundamental identification with our own deepest desires. As Thomas says, we must love our own spiritual good above that of others, for the very character of the movement of love requires it. If a certain union with others is the basis and reason for loving them, our love for ourselves must excel that love just as unity surpasses union.[41] In this basic and benign sense, we are all inescapably "self-centered." And yet, in the charity that is friendship with God, our striving attains its fulfillment precisely in being drawn out of itself. Only in this way are we so transformed through divine action that we are capable of being friends with God.[42]

This "being drawn out of itself" places our obligation to care for ourselves in a new light. Hence, Thomas gives two reasons why charity demands that we love ourselves.[43] The first takes self-love in the inescapable existential sense described above. Charity is a kind of friendship. If it involves loving friends, we must recognize that we are more than friends to ourselves. A person could not relate well to friends more removed from her if she did not relate well to that nearest of friends, herself. This reason merely indicates that we must have that fundamental identification with our own deepest desires if we are to be the subjects of any love at all. It does not tell us much about whether charity will be served or not by our efforts to secure ourselves. The

---

39. Thomas acknowledges that such care, while an expression of charity, can hinder some higher act of charity, such as contemplation or instruction. For this reason, orders with few things, devoted to such higher acts, are higher orders, although other orders remain perfect for all that.

40. *ST* I-II 10.1.

41. *ST* II-II 26.4; 25.4.

42. Paul J. Wadell, C.P., *The Primacy of Love: An Introduction to the Ethics of Thomas Aquinas* (Mahwah, NJ: Paulist Press, 1992), p. 75.

43. *ST* II-II 25.4.

second reason Thomas gives tells us more about charity's effect on the way we care for ourselves. Thomas's comments are worth quoting at length: "Secondly, we may speak of charity in respect of its specific nature, namely as denoting man's friendship with God in the first place, and, consequently, with the things of God, among which things is man himself who has charity. Hence, among these other things which he loves out of charity because they pertain to God, he loves also himself out of charity."

There is a breach between ourselves and our self-love. In charity the primary object of love is God. We love other things for God's sake and in light of their directedness toward the God whom we love.[44] Our love for ourselves is therefore indirect. It is not a spontaneous embrace of ourselves because of our own nearness, but it is a consequence of our love for God, as is our love for all our neighbors. Thomas does not say that in charity our immediate and untutored self-love is supplemented by concern for others and a more intense connection with God. Rather, our self-love is transformed by being refracted through our participation in the divine charity. Thus our necessary (and in a sense necessarily self-affirming) striving for God finds that the true way to love the self is by losing oneself in participating in divine charity.[45]

This transformation conditions our self-love, since we now arrive at it the same way we arrive at our love for our neighbors — via love for God. But the result is not a flattening of our loves into "equal regard." Two considerations block such a result. First, we love everything for the sake of God, but God does not love everything the same, and so neither will we. This assertion shocks modern sensibilities, but Thomas has good reason for it. Since God's love is the cause of goodness in things, no thing would be better than another if God loved everything equally.[46] This is why, for

---

44. *ST* II-II 25.1.

45. In the words of a certain contemporary conversation, eros is fulfilled rather than negated by agape. It is beyond the scope of this work to expound the contemporary controversies over the relationship between eros and agape. Two of the seminal works that play up the distinction between them are Anders Nygren, *Agape and Eros,* trans. Philip S. Watson (New York: Harper and Row, 1969), and Gene Outka, *Agape: An Ethical Analysis* (New Haven: Yale University Press, 1972). Stephen Post, *A Theory of Agape* (Lewisburg, PA: Bucknell University Press, 1990), offers a revisionist view. For a recent summary of the issues involved, see David Matzko McCarthy, *Sex and Love in the Home: A Theology of the Household* (London: SCM Press, 2001), esp. chap. 7.

46. *ST* I 20.3.

example, God loves Christ, even in his human nature, above all created things.[47] Second, the preferences for what is nearer to us that God built into our nature are good and thus not overturned by charity.[48] This point does not suggest that our self-love does not have to traverse the breach that charity marks, for charity repeats in a new key the good ordering of nature rather than simply sanctioning or supplementing it.

One sign of the new situation of our self-love is that the reason we must care for our own first is that, as Augustine says, such care falls to us "as if by lot."[49] It is as though, in God's loving assignment of responsibility for the care of each thing, God fittingly assigns the care of you to you. After all, you are right there! In this way the order of charity reflects the natural ordering of love, even if such love has been transformed and perfected. Josef Pieper explains the continuity within transformation in this way. We are created to love the good we encounter (and he might add that we encounter ourselves as goods early on), and therefore to reenact the primordial affirmation of creation attributed to God in Genesis 1. Our love says, "It is good that this thing is!" But our little reenactments do not reach the profundity of God's love. Yet, through faith we can attain communion with the depths of God's love. Then, by virtue of our love for the "First Lover," we come to identify with God's affirmation of all nature. Hence "our own love . . . would receive a wholly new and literally absolute confirmation. And the beloved, though still altogether incomparable, still someone personally and specially intended for us, would at the same time suddenly appear as one point of light in an infinite mesh of light."[50] This interpretation begins to evoke what Thomas is trying to get at when he says that, "according to right reason and natural instinct, each one orders himself towards God, as a part is ordered toward the good of the whole. This order is perfected through charity, by which a man loves himself for God's sake."[51]

Our care for our own material needs is merely the servant of our participation in the divine charity. And our subordination to that self-

47. *ST* I 20.4 ad 1.
48. *ST* II-II 26.6.
49. *ST* II-II 32.9.
50. Pieper, *Faith, Hope, Love*, p. 276.
51. "Secundum rectam rationem et naturae instinctum, unusquisque se ipsum in Deum ordinat sicut pars ordinatur ad bonum totius: quod quidem per caritatem perficitur qua homo se ipsum propter Deum amat." *DP*, chap. 14, 173-77.

abandoning love is in fact the highest affirmation of our fundamental love of self. Ultimately, therefore, our truest self-care is to foster whatever draws us more deeply into the love of God. These reflections shed interesting light on Thomas's discussion of the virtue of liberality. Liberality regulates the affections associated with the possession of money, such that we are always ready to make a proper use of money, that is, to part with it.[52] So liberality is related to our ability to act justly. Since liberality is directed toward providing for others, it may seem that it cannot be a virtue, because virtues do not contradict natural inclinations, and we are naturally inclined to provide for ourselves more than for others. Thomas's reply reflects the lessons learned from his account of charity.[53] He says that since one person needs few things, it is good to spend more on others. But let no one misunderstand: looking out for the welfare of others *is* a matter of providing for ourselves, with regard to our spiritual good. Our natural inclination here is transformed in light of our participation in the divine charity.

Thomas affirms that in charity's movement away from ourselves and toward others (for the sake of our own good!) we must remember to care for ourselves. We should not look out for others so much that we neglect ourselves and those in our care. And yet, because our good of participating in the divine charity is the very rationale for our care of ourselves, the good of that participation allows and even at times demands that our material well-being be quite strikingly jeopardized. Thus, for the sake of a more perfect participation in the divine charity, one may indeed give away not only one's surplus but also one's necessaries, as is the case with those who enter religious orders.[54] Such abandonment, in fact, does not go beyond the measure of liberality into prodigality, but exhibits the most perfect liberality.[55] Moreover, while we normally exercise care for our own bodies, we may at times be obliged to set the good of our bodies aside for a neighbor's welfare, since we must love the neighbor more than our own body. And the absence of obligation makes such an offering not unlawful, but an act of charity's perfection.[56]

In the normal course of affairs we should care for our own, and even

---

52. *ST* II-II 117.2.
53. *ST* II-II 117.1 ad 1.
54. *ST* II-II 32.6 sed contra.
55. *ST* II-II 119.2 ad 3.
56. *ST* II-II 26.5 ad 3.

maintain not only our subsistence but whatever is required by our social station.[57] But as we have seen, even that care is but a service to God's care of all things, and hence bears within it the pattern of self-abandonment that Christ has revealed at the heart of the divine charity. We care even for ourselves out of that charity that by its nature diffuses itself.[58]

The lowly exposure of the mendicants only more concretely specifies the self-abandonment, the humble vulnerability that characterizes all Christian action involving wealth. Such a refusal of security is what divine law has always tried to teach. We see even in the Old Law, which takes for granted the importance of caring for one's property for the sake of community welfare, that this welfare is ordered toward the mutually self-effacing interdependence of the divine charity. That is why the Old Law went beyond the demands of antique justice by including precepts aimed at charity, such as, "Going into thy neighbor's vineyard, thou mayest eat as many grapes as thou pleasest" (Deut. 23:24), and "He to whom any thing is owing from his friend or neighbor or brother, cannot demand it again, because it is the year of remission of the Lord" (Deut. 15:2). Such precepts were meant to foster not merely temporal tranquility, but the readiness to give to others, and the refusal to secure ourselves against them, that would embody the divine charity.[59] Christ deepens this lesson, drawing us nearer to God through a humble vulnerability that draws us out of ourselves with abandon.

The Priority of the Counsels

When we set Thomas's account of justice within its context among the theological virtues, we see how Thomas's agreements with Aristotle are part of a more abased practice of humble vulnerability than Aristotle

---

57. *ST* II-II 32.6.

58. We learn that divine charity is self-diffusive primarily from the Incarnation. See *ST* III 1.1. Further, in his commentary on the hymn to charity in 1 Corinthians, Thomas notes that this love "causes one not to hoard his goods just for oneself but to diffuse them among others." See the translation in *Thomas Aquinas: The Gifts of the Spirit,* trans. Matthew Rzeczkowski, O.P., ed. Benedict M. Ashley, O.P. (New York: New City Press, 1995), p. 62.

59. *ST* I-II 105.2 ad 1, ad 4. See Matthew Levering's appeal to these aspects of the Old Law to show its direction toward charity. Matthew Levering, *Christ's Fulfillment of Torah and Temple: Salvation According to Thomas Aquinas* (Notre Dame, IN: University of Notre Dame Press, 2002), pp. 115-16.

would countenance. In Thomas, that practice participates in a movement aimed at the perfect charity of the poor Christ.

Yet it may seem that Thomas minimizes the role Christlike voluntary poverty plays in grasping the shape of this movement. Thomas apparently downplays the importance of the counsels. As we will see in more detail in the following chapter, Peter Olivi objected to Thomas's account of the counsel of poverty because poverty seems so marginal to Thomas's account of perfection. Indeed, in Thomas's view all the counsels are merely instrumental to perfection. But I will argue that the counsels are more than mere handmaids to the commands. It is not enough to understand Thomas's view of the Christian life without looking at the counsels. Though Thomas speaks of the counsels as helps to keeping the commands, the counsels help us see what the commands mean.

Interpreters of Aquinas do not often recognize the role of the counsels in illuminating human action.[60] In the introduction I have noted some possible reasons for this neglect. Now I offer some of the negative consequences of it. First, neglecting the religious life suggests that this optional discipline is somehow an "extra" set of activities added on to the content of morality. This implication underwrites modern assumptions that only a certain delimited set of activities counts as the "moral realm."[61] The "moral" is thus divided from the "spiritual" and from other "realms" in a way that belies Thomas's concern with the ordering of all human actions to their true end.

Second, when the religious life is neglected, those pieces of advice gleaned from the gospel that have come to be called "counsels" are implic-

60. This is most surprising with regard to scholars who wish to emphasize the specifically theological character of Thomas's ethics. In his introduction to Aquinas, Joseph Pieper utters what is no revelation to those familiar with Thomas, that the character of his thought derives from his choice not to choose between the Bible and Aristotle, but to choose both as providing legitimate vocabularies for articulating the truth. Both Thomas's evangelicalism and his appreciation for Aristotle were cutting-edge movements to which he became exposed when he went to Naples as a boy. And Thomas embraced evangelicalism in the form of the voluntary poverty movement. Therefore, Thomas's defense of voluntary poverty seems a promising, and even an obvious, place to look to bring out the specifically theological rationale at work in his thought. Josef Pieper, *Introduction to Thomas Aquinas*, trans. Richard and Clara Winston (London: Faber and Faber, 1962), pp. 22-32.

61. For a critique of such a notion of morality from a position sympathetic with Aquinas, see Charles R. Pinches, *Theology and Action: After Theory in Christian Ethics* (Grand Rapids: Eerdmans, 2002).

itly dismissed as superfluous and excluded from the content of ethics. But those counsels are most closely associated in Thomas with the *sequela Christi*. Excluding them makes Thomas's moral theology seem a more moderate and less passionately evangelical enterprise than it is.

Third, neglecting the religious life fails fully to address our normal assumptions of a chasm between nature and grace. Thomas affirms that the commands are determinations of the law of nature.[62] Excluding the role of the counsels underscores an apparent autonomy to nature. Recognizing how the counsels illuminate the trajectory of the commanded acts of virtue helps us see all human action as summoned toward the beatitude that is in Christ.

Commands, Counsels, and Perfection

In his discussion of the state of perfection in the *ST*, Thomas asks whether the perfection of this life consists in keeping the commandments or the counsels. He replies that everything that is needful for perfection is contained in the commands.[63] The perfection of Christian life consists chiefly in charity, because perfection involves attainment of the end, and charity attains our end, which is God.[64] This charity, love for God and neighbor, is a commandment. The counsels, he says, relate to perfection instrumentally, for they "remove things that hinder the act of charity."[65] In other words, perfection requires charity, which is commanded, but the counsels foster a freedom that conduces to charity's actualization. The commands are sufficient for perfection, and the counsels are instrumental to perfection. We could easily read this article as affirming a disjunction between the commands, which really deliver Thomas's ethical thought to us, and the counsels, which are helpful adjuncts that are completely dispensable for understanding what Thomas's ethics calls for.

But such a reading would be too hasty. True, the commands are sufficient and the counsels are mere instruments. But the counsels' role in specifying the content of ethics is not negligible. Rather, the commands are suf-

---

62. *ST* I-II 99.3 ad 2; cf. 107.3 ad 2.
63. *ST* II-II 184.3.
64. *ST* II-II 184.1.
65. *ST* II-II 184.3.

ficient and the counsels are instrumental because the counsels help to specify what the commands already imply.

The chief impediment in the way of grasping the true relationship between the counsels and the commands is a failure to keep the progressive dynamism of the life of charity in view. As Torrell points out, charity is "a virtue of a being in motion."[66] We are teleological beings, and our movement toward our ultimate end can never stop in this life without mortally disrupting our orientation to that end. We cannot be charitably directed to that end in a static manner; we must always be making progress toward it. Charity "can never turn back or pause without denying itself, because the desire for its completion belongs to charity's very nature."[67] And since charity itself is commanded, we are commanded to a pursuit that by its nature is always seeking to keep the command more perfectly.[68]

In the article on commands and counsels, Thomas adverts to this progress in the third objection. It seems that perfection is in the counsels rather than the commands, for there are stages of charity leading up to its perfection, while the commandments are required at every stage. Thomas's reply suggests that seeing the counsels as mere aids to an end that is fully grasped apart from them is inadequate. He likens the growth of charity to the growth of a human being. The one who observes charity in accord with the counsels has that perfection that comes with growth. The commands remain constitutive of perfection "just as a man has a certain perfection of his nature as soon as he is born."[69] If a person is commanded to be a human being, in one sense she has fulfilled the command at birth, for she has in fact the essence of humanity. But as she matures she fulfills the command with another perfection — an even more perfect perfection — since humanity is understood primarily according to its maturity. In her maturity she is in one sense fulfilling the command better than in her youth, but

---

66. Jean-Pierre Torrell, *Saint Thomas Aquinas,* vol. 2, *Spiritual Master,* trans. Robert Royal (Washington, DC: The Catholic University of America Press, 2003), p. 354.

67. Torrell, *Saint Thomas Aquinas,* vol. 2, p. 366.

68. As Pinckaers points out, an ethics of obligation has difficulty accounting for this movement. Obligatory systems inquire about minimum requirements and static limits. But the Christian calling to charity involves a dynamism well captured in the Sermon on the Mount, which "is animated by a continuous tendency toward exceeding and surpassing, a tendency toward the progress and perfection of love in imitation of the Father's goodness." Pinckaers, *The Pinckaers Reader,* p. 52.

69. *ST* II-II 184.3 ad 3.

at the same time she is doing no more than fulfilling the command. Similarly, a Christian fulfills the command of charity as soon as the Christian life begins, for she has the essence of charity. But as she grows in charity, she attains another perfection that is still no more than a fulfilling of the command. Just as in the case of the command to be human, however, the latter perfection does have a heuristic function in relationship to the former, for charity is primarily understood according to its maturity.

It is important to recognize that both the beginner and the mature Christian are perfect for the same reason: because they fulfill the commandment of charity. Perfection consists in the observance of the commands. But the mature Christian is not perfect in virtue of loving just as the beginner does, such that his maturity is supplemental to his perfection. His perfection consists rather in his greater love, but that greater love is no less the love that is commanded. For "the love of God and of our neighbor is not commanded according to a measure, so that what is in excess of the measure be a matter of counsel. This is evident from the very form of the commandment . . . *Thou shalt love the Lord thy God with thy whole heart.*"[70] As long as one loves God with the whole heart, the commandment is fulfilled, but the degree of that love may differ depending on the maturity of one's heart. Thomas spells out this implication in *Contra Retrahentes*. There he repeats the point that the counsels do not propose more than the commands, for the command to love God cannot be exceeded. Rather, he says: "Everyone observes this command according to his ability, one more perfectly, but another less perfectly. He totally departs from observing this precept who does not prefer God above all things in his love. But he who prefers Him above all things as his final end fulfills the precept either more or less perfectly according as he is more or less held back by his love for other things."[71] Perfection consists in charity, but one can have that charity more or less perfectly. Those who prefer God above all things have the perfection of charity. But those who abandon other things for the love of God exhibit a more perfect perfection.

Thomas's discussion of these issues near the end of the *ST* II-II ech-

---

70. *ST* II-II 184.1, resp.

71. "Unusquisque autem hoc observat secundum suam mensuram, unus quidem perfectius, alius autem minus perfecte. Ille autem totaliter ab observantia huius praecepti deficit, qui Deum in suo amore non omnibus praefert. Qui vero ipsum praefert omnibus ut ultimum finem, implet quidem praeceptum vel perfectius vel minus perfecte, secundum quod magis vel minus detinetur aliarum rerum amore." *CR*, chap. 6, 65-73.

oes his treatment of charity nearer the beginning. In the treatise on charity, he affirms two distinct kinds of perfection possible in this life.[72] First he shows the imperfection of all charity *in via* by setting it within the context of higher charities. Only God has perfect charity in an unqualified sense. Charity is most perfect if the most lovable object is loved as much as it is lovable. God is infinitely lovable, and only God can love God infinitely, so only God's charity is truly perfect. But others can be said to love perfectly if they love God as much as they can. Even in this respect our charity *in via* is limited, for only the blessed in heaven, who are not subject to the weakness of this life, can have hearts that are always actually moved by love toward God. In this life someone loves God as much as she can if she "makes an earnest endeavor to give [her] time to God and Divine things, while scorning other things except in so far as the needs of the present life demand." Or, in another way, one loves as much as she can when she is habitually, if not always actually, directed to the love of God, so that she thinks or desires nothing contrary to the love of God.

This account of the two perfections of charity possible *in via* supports my point that mature perfection helps us understand what is meant by the life of charity in general. For habit is ordered to act.[73] Indeed, it is by means of the distinction of acts that we are able to distinguish habits.[74] Therefore, it is in light of the actualization of charity that we can grasp what having charity habitually means. And the higher the perfection of charity, the greater its actualization.[75]

Further, Thomas tells us that just as charity must always move toward its end, so the stages of the lower perfection are directed toward the higher. The beginner in charity begins, after all, for the sake of growing in maturity.[76] We can easily be misled to think that the two *in via* perfections Thomas has introduced are two distinct and unconnected paths. That the one is in fact ordered to the other is made clear by Thomas's following of the patristic tradition in dividing the lower perfection into the stage of the

---

72. *ST* II-II 24.8; cf. II-II 184.2; see also *DP*, chaps. 3-7.

73. *ST* I-II 49.3.

74. *ST* I-II 54.1.

75. Charity's actualization is not merely a matter of adding up distinct acts of charity, but of marking the increase of charity's intensity and degree — i.e., we begin to love things more as we participate more completely in the Holy Spirit and thus in God's love for them. *ST* II-II 24.4 ad 1; 24.5 ad 3; 24.7.

76. *ST* II-II 184.5 ad 1.

beginners and the stage of the proficient who are advancing toward maturity.[77] Thomas notes that the three stages are perhaps more tidy than our actual lives, but that all movements do, after all, involve a beginning, a middle, and an end.[78] The connected movement of the three stages is evident in Thomas's characterization of them: the beginner stage is focused on avoiding sin, on resisting any movement opposed to charity; next, the proficient make progress in goodness and in the development of virtue; finally, the perfect "aim chiefly at union with and enjoyment of God."

The mature perfection that the counsels help to specify provides a direction for all who live the life of charity. Thomas is thus quite explicit that the counsels embody more fully the end aimed at by the commands. In the *ST*, Thomas considers whether those who desire to enter religion should become practiced in keeping the commandments first.[79] One objection claims that the commandments must precede the counsels since they are more universal, and the universal precedes the particular. Thomas points out the fallacy here: the precedence of the universal is not necessarily chronological, since "a thing is not in the genus before being in one of the species." Besides, he says, from another point of view, the counsels are prior insofar as a perfection aimed at takes priority over the imperfections that fall short of it. For "the observance of the precepts apart from the counsels is directed to the observance of the precepts together with the counsels; as an imperfect to a perfect species, even as the irrational to the rational animal."

Thomas talks about the perfection of Christian life not only in terms of charity, but also in terms of the imitation of Christ. Indeed, the question "In what does perfection consist?" appears to have two interchangeable answers: *caritas* and *sequela Christi*.[80] A passage in *CR* makes clear how the counsels perfect the imitation of Christ begun in baptism. *CR* largely addresses the positions of Gerard of Abbeville, who argued, among other things, that new converts to the faith should be held off from religious life until they have become practiced in Christian living. Thomas's response suggests that religious life more perfectly embodies the following of Christ at which Christian life aims. "Who will be so shameless a disputant as to

77. *ST* II-II 24.9. These stages are derived from Thomas's patristic inheritance. See P. Pourrat, "Commençants," in *Dictionnaire de spiritualité*, vol. 2 (Paris, 1953), col. 1143-56.

78. *ST* II-II 24.9 ad 1.

79. *ST* II-II 189.1.

80. *ST* II-II 184.3 ad 3; 185.6 ad 1; 188.7.

dare to counsel these men to remain in the world, rather than to strive by observing religion to preserve the grace of baptism? What man of sound mind would hinder them from this intention, lest they be worthy to put on Christ by perfect imitation, when by the sacrament of baptism they have already been clothed with him?"[81] There could be no more fitting sequel to baptism than embracing the evangelical counsels. Not that the commands are insufficient, or that the counsels go further, for the commands to love God or to follow Christ are beyond measure and cannot be exceeded. But while the incipient *caritas* or *sequela Christi* of the beginner is already in one sense the attainment of the goal, at the same time it is undertaken in order to be deepened. The counsels invite us to a more perfect fulfillment of the direction in which the rudiments of Christian life already aim, and thus they helpfully specify that direction.

The Counsels as Instruments

If the counsels play such a role in specifying the direction of charity's perfection, how are they mere instruments? We see their instrumentality in that they are neither sufficient nor necessary for perfection. First, they are insufficient: keeping them does not entail perfection. Second, they are unnecessary: it is possible to attain perfection without them. Yet these qualifications do not undermine the counsels' role in clarifying the shape of Christian maturity. Specifically, they remind us that mature charity summons us to self-offering that bears itself out in action.

The insufficiency of the counsels makes clear that they are mere external aids to a perfection that is not defined by them. Keeping the counsels is no guarantee of perfection, or even of a beginner's charity. This fact may seem to sit ill with Thomas's idea that religious life is a state of perfection; but Thomas distinguishes one's ecclesiastical state from one's true character. A state, Thomas says, denotes a certain immobility of one's condition with respect to freedom or servitude.[82] In the church it is proper that such states be adopted, so that the church may be perfect in its variety,

---

81. "Quis autem erit tam improbus disputator, qui audeat eis consulere ut potius in saeculo remaneant, quam in religione perceptam baptismi gratiam studeant conservare? Quis sanae mentis ab hoc proposito eum impediat ne Christum, quem per sacramentum baptismi iam induit, perfecta imitatione induere mereatur?" *CR*, chap. 4, 30-36.

82. *ST* II-II 183.1.

that the diversity of persons may be adequate to the diversity of actions required in the church, and that the beauty of the church might be manifest in the order of higher and lower states.[83] But despite the fittingness of such states, the attainment of a high ecclesiastical state need not reflect one's state in the eyes of God. For ecclesiastical states are necessarily external and imposed with public solemnity, while God judges the heart.[84] The cases of wicked bishops and wicked religious make this distinction clear enough.[85] If one does not have charity, the counsels will not make him perfect.

Keeping the counsels may not indicate Christian maturity even for those who keep them with charity. Some in religious orders are not perfect, Thomas says, because the religious life includes Christians at every stage of progress. Even if one is not a wicked religious, to take the vows and adopt the immobility of the state of perfection does not necessarily indicate that one has attained the highest degree of charity possible in this life. Rather, the religious life includes many beginners and proficient. Therefore, it is called the state of perfection not because its members profess to be perfect, but because they profess to tend toward perfection.[86] The religious state does not enshrine those who have already attained perfection; rather, it is a "school or exercise for the attainment of perfection, which men strive to reach by various practices, just as a physician may use various remedies in order to heal."[87]

What of the role of the counsels for specifying Christian maturity if the same stages of charity that divide beginning Christians from more mature Christians are found among those who keep them? The answer is that charity's perfection is a matter of complete self-offering, but the counsels, properly understood, simply are an exercise in complete self-offering. Even a beginner who adopts them in that spirit shows a mature charity simply by doing so.

All beginners in Christian life undertake the life of charity for the sake of advancing toward the perfect charity of those whose chief aim is to be united with God, "to be dissolved and to be with Christ."[88] This starting point is common to beginners who immediately embrace religious life and

83. *ST* II-II 183.2.
84. *ST* II-II 184.4.
85. *ST* II-II 184.4, sed contra.
86. *ST* II-II 184.5 ad 2.
87. *ST* II-II 186.2.
88. *ST* II-II 24.9.

to those who remain in the world. But beginners who embrace the counsels in a sense already share the complete self-offering of the perfect. For their very act of committing to the religious life is a perfect offering of the self to God.[89] The counsels offer everything to God: first, the externals that one possesses; second, the near relations of spouse and family; and third, one's own will. By offering oneself completely to God through entrance into religious life, one already exhibits a greater degree of the charity that is commanded.

We have seen that the way of charity is undertaken in order to be deepened. But it seems that the abandon with which one gives oneself to the project of having it deepened reveals how perfect one's charity already is. The more intensely one has been affected by the brightness of God's charity, the more one's response anticipates the shape of that ultimate self-offering toward which all charity is directed.[90]

Keeping the counsels does not always indicate such a degree of charity. But keeping the counsels, as a road of renunciation and self-offering, particularly suggests what a material display of such utmost self-offering would look like. What better way to advance in giving oneself completely to God than to vow to keep the counsels, thereby giving oneself to God by giving oneself to the practice of giving oneself to God? That is why Thomas insists that adopting the counsels is the more certain and secure way to beatitude.[91] Though they do not guarantee perfection, they play a large role not only in conducing to it, but pointing out in which direction it lies.

Still, the counsels remain instrumental. Their instrumentality is evident in that they are not only insufficient, but also unnecessary. Not only do

89. *ST* II-II 186.1. Thomas frequently compares the religious life to Christian life in the world by analogy with the way a holocaust exceeds a regular sacrifice. See the catalogue in Jan van den Eijnden, O.F.M., *Poverty on the Way to God: Thomas Aquinas on Evangelical Poverty* (Leuven: Peeters, 1994), p. 157, n. 84.

90. The notion of charity as a brightness that dawns on us is derived from the commentary on the Lombard. *In Sent.* 17.2.2. Thomas says that, though the reception of charity is different in one person from another, the difference is not due to a diversity in God's action. Rather, the same charity affects some more and some less, just as the same radiance of the sun dispels a hindering haze to produce air that is in some places clear and in others still more clear. Van den Eijnden, *Poverty on the Way to God*, p. 147. Similarly, in *Summa contra Gentiles,* Thomas suggests that adoption of the counsels shows a special degree of participation in the charity toward which the counsels speed us. So the counsels are not only instruments of perfection, but also "effects and signs" of it. *ScG* III, 130.

91. *ST* I-II 108.4.

they not guarantee perfection; perfection is possible without them. Thomas does not think that all Christians should be moving toward the religious life. Further, there are those who are perfect apart from the counsels. Bishops more principally represent the state of perfection, yet they do not observe all the counsels (they have their own possessions). While those in religious orders merely tend to perfection, the bishops are professors of perfection.[92] Maintaining that the bishops are in a state of perfection is one important reason why the counsel of poverty can be no more than an instrument of perfection.[93] Furthermore, Abraham was a wealthy man who was said to be perfect.[94] Despite all I have said about the counsels' role in pointing the way to perfection, surely the example of Abraham shows that they can hardly be crucial for grasping what the life of charity looks like.

But Thomas suggests that we can only account for the fact that Scripture calls Abraham perfect by finding in his life a renunciation like that commended in the counsels. Since perfection requires that our affections be wholly withdrawn from worldly things, and since love of things grows with the possession of them, Thomas claims that voluntary poverty is the starting point for bearing oneself up for perfection.[95] Further, our love for God can be hindered from growing to its utmost simply by the distraction from divine things that is involved in caring for one's possessions.[96] If Abraham was both rich and perfect, it can only be because, despite his wealth, his affections remained unentangled in his possessions and because his love for God was so great that it was not diminished by the care his possessions required. Nor does the coincidence of wealth and perfection mean that detachment from worldly things is merely an inner disposition that needs no external display. For Abraham showed his detachment to the point of contempt for himself and all that belonged to him by his readiness to kill his own son.[97]

---

92. *ST* II-II 185.8.

93. Ulrich Horst argues that it is Thomas's interest in keeping mendicancy subordinated to the traditional self-understanding of the church that led to increasing tensions between his formulations and the interests of certain Joachimite Franciscans. Ulrich Horst, O.P., *Evangelische Armut und Kirche: Thomas von Aquin und die Armutskontroversen des 13. und beginnenden 14. Jahrhunderts* (Berlin: Akademie, 1992), pp. 93-119.

94. *ST* II-II 185.6 ad 1.

95. *ST* II-II 186.3.

96. *ST* II-II 188.7.

97. *DP,* chap. 8.

Thomas goes on to commend the counsel of poverty by comparing the might of Abraham's charity with the strength of Samson. Living the charity that the counsels foster apart from observance of the counsels is possible for those of heroic virtue. But we should not presume on Abraham's example to justify bypassing the counsel of poverty. For either way we are called to that charitable self-offering that we grasp best through attending to the evangelical counsels. While the counsels remain mere instruments, they help to specify what the commands intend by clarifying the self-offering in which the commands are fulfilled.[98]

98. I understand that my reading of the relationship between the counsels and the commands concurs with that of Pinckaers. Pinckaers faults readings of Thomas that see the commands as obligatory moral teachings and the counsels as superadded spiritual disciplines. Instead, he suggests that all of Thomas's teaching on the Christian life is for everyone, and within that teaching the counsels have a special role, even if not everyone can keep them. The religious state "became a special sign of adherence to the Gospel, because its way of life was more directly oriented to it through the chief counsels it implemented. The evangelical counsels were indeed addressed to everyone, but not all could practice them in the same way, for vocations differ and lead to distinct patterns of living." Servais Pinckaers, O.P., *The Sources of Christian Ethics*, trans. Mary Thomas Noble, O.P. (Washington, DC: The Catholic University of America Press, 1995), p. 187.

CHAPTER 4

Mendicant Poverty and Following Christ

Thomas's economic teachings aim human action at a *telos* that is best represented by the poverty of Christ. In earlier chapters, we have seen how Thomas appreciates Aristotelian deference and how he adopts some positions very similar to Aristotle's in view of our ontological poverty. We have also seen how this ontological poverty reflects Thomas's placement of the Christian life on the road toward a beatitude specified in terms of the self-abandonment of Christ's charity. Deferent dependence is perfected in Christological humble vulnerability. And my inquiry in this book has given reasons to expect that the mendicant life offers crucial insight into the material shape of this humble vulnerability.

In this chapter I wish to make good on that expectation. I explore Thomas's account of mendicancy to show its evangelical character and to suggest how it gets embodied. Along the way, we will see some of the illumination the mendicant life casts on the life to which all are called. In short, this humble vulnerability is lived out when one divests oneself in imitation of Christ and continually renews one's state of having-very-little by refusing to let past gifts become the guarantee of future security. Its characteristic virtues are a humility constantly drawn toward greater abasement and a receptive and patient trust always pulled toward a more threatening exposure. What summons us in this direction is the calling to conform to the cross of the poor Christ.

A Moderate Poverty?

The chief hurdle that my reading must overcome is the common impression that Thomas's account of mendicancy is neither particularly evangelical nor radical. To some readers, it may seem that Thomas's comments on voluntary poverty present a position hardly different from what Aristotle could approve. Aristotle admitted that possessions can be an obstacle to the contemplative life,[1] and Thomas's discussions of poverty in the *ST* may seem to argue nothing more. In his discussion of voluntary poverty in the treatise on states of life (II-II 183-89), Thomas insists that poverty, like the other counsels, is only an instrument of perfection, and not the thing itself. Not only does this help him account for the perfection of bishops and patriarchs such as Abraham, but he also employs this distinction to contend that the degree of an order's poverty does not determine the extent of its perfection.[2]

Further, in the face of the traditional mendicant claim to have abandoned even common possessions, Thomas argues not only that common possessions are compatible with perfection, but that all religious orders have some things in common. And whereas mendicants typically appealed to the example of Christ and the apostles as the authority for their poverty, finding ingenious ways to explain why Judas's purse was not evidence of common possessions among the disciples, Thomas seems to argue the opponents' case. He invokes Judas's purse to support his claim that keeping at least some minimal amount of common things *(res communes)* accords with the example of Christ.[3]

Thomas's discussions in the *ST* provoked a hostile reaction from some among the Franciscans who felt that Thomas was attacking voluntary poverty itself. Most notable among Thomas's Franciscan detractors was Peter Olivi in his commentary on Matthew's Gospel, written a few years after Thomas's death.[4] Olivi took particular offense at Thomas's interpretation of the content of the New Law. Thomas claims that the New Law is a law of liberty, none other than the power of the Holy Spirit, writ-

---

1. *ST* II-II 186.3 ad 4.

2. *ST* II-II 188.7.

3. *ST* II-II 188.7.

4. For Olivi's posthumous debate with Thomas, see Kevin Madigan, "Aquinas and Olivi on Evangelical Poverty: A Medieval Debate and Its Modern Significance," *The Thomist* 61 (1997): 567-86.

ing, as it were, the law on the hearts of believers.[5] For this reason the New Law proposes few concrete ordinances: just the sacraments and whatever pertains to virtue formed by charity.[6] One objection Thomas considers is that the New Law should have proposed more concrete observances for the laity, just as it proposes that ministers should not possess gold, nor silver, nor money (Matt. 10:9). Thomas replies that the ordinance in Matthew 10:9 is not a fixed and permanent command at all.[7] Rather, it could be a concession that allowed the disciples to accept their livelihood from their hearers, in place of the act of supererogation of providing for their own welfare, as Paul did. Or it could be a temporary command, revoked just before the passion (Luke 22:35f.), intended to train the disciples in freedom from care for temporal things, so that when the time of liberty came, they would be prepared to exercise mature judgment.

As Olivi was quick to point out, Matthew 10:9 had always been taken by the mendicants as a direct command they were obeying by renouncing property for the sake of preaching the gospel. In fact, the "concessions" interpretation of Matthew 10:9 had been used by the secular masters in their attempts to discredit the mendicant orders.[8] Thomas seemed to be taking up the arguments of the enemies of poverty.

While attacking Thomas's interpretation of Matthew 10:9, Olivi went on to condemn Thomas's careful distinction between the degree of an order's poverty and the degree of its perfection. Thomas offers two reasons why degree of poverty and degree of perfection might not directly correspond.[9] First, poverty is good insofar as it conduces to an order's end. It is important to consider both the common end of religious orders ("to devote oneself to the service of God") and the special end of each order (active works of charity, contemplation, or a mixed life). A religious order's poverty is more perfect the more it is "adapted to the end both common and special," so that a hospital order, for example, will need significant wealth to carry out its mission. Second, even if poverty be considered conducive to the common end of all orders, other means of perfection (chastity, obedience) are still more conducive. Thus, a more chaste order might be absolutely more perfect, although less poor.

5. *ST* I-II 106.1.
6. *ST* I-II 108.2.
7. *ST* I-II 108.2 ad 3.
8. Madigan, "Aquinas and Olivi," p. 576.
9. *ST* II-II 188.7 ad 1.

Olivi sees here more evidence that Thomas has become an enemy of poverty. Thomas gives the special end of an order altogether too much weight in determining its perfection, so that an order's degree of poverty becomes of no account. On the contrary, the common end alone should determine the perfection of each order. By implying that certain orders are imperfect if they have too little wealth, Thomas becomes an advocate of riches. And Olivi contrasts Thomas's ranking of poverty as least among the means of perfection with the estimate of Christ, who "extols it above all else."[10]

Olivi's criticism provides an apparently compelling account of Thomas as a reluctant devotee of poverty. Furthermore, Olivi's exaltation of poverty is mixed with a mistrust of the use of Aristotle, who Olivi thought gave entirely too much value to the senses and to sense knowledge.[11] Thus Olivi becomes the first outspoken interpreter of Thomas who sees him as granting a great deal to "nature," at the expense of, among other things, evangelical poverty. On this reading, poverty is always at the service of a prior appreciation of nature in Thomas. We can know naturally, after all, that contemplation of things above us is the highest good of our nature. And even pagans knew that renunciation of wealth could be useful for freeing us from certain dangers that would inhibit such contemplation. Therefore, "even certain philosophers are said to have done this."[12] Perhaps Thomas's comments on mendicant poverty are not so evangelical nor radical after all.

Origins of Dominican Poverty

Before I counter Olivi's interpretation and display Thomas's devotion to the poor Christ, it will be helpful to recall the historical context of the growth of mendicancy and offer some remarks about the character of its Dominican wing. That context will help situate Dominican poverty as part of a recovery of evangelical rigor in reaction to wide-ranging economic changes.

10. *Lectura super Matthaeum*, 81ra, cited in Madigan, "Aquinas and Olivi," p. 583.
11. David Burr, *The Persecution of Peter Olivi* (Philadelphia: American Philosophical Society, 1976), pp. 27-31.
12. *ST* II-II 186.3 ad 3.

It has long been recognized that a massive transformation of European society, sometimes called the "commercial revolution," can be traced at least back to the late eleventh century.[13] The causes of this change are understandably hard to pin down, and exploring that literature would take us beyond the scope of the present work. But for us to understand the rise of the mendicants, it is important to grasp something of what religious poverty meant prior to the shift, and what kinds of changes precipitated the new forms of religious life.

Poverty had been an ideal of religious life since Antony responded to the text of Matthew 19 by selling all and turning to the desert. In a sense, that act was already a protest against the increasing acceptance within the church of extra-ecclesial economic norms.[14] After the Germanic migrations and the collapse of the Empire in the West, a gift economy based on prestige and largess became the prevailing pattern. The monks who Christianized the Germanic peoples did not mount a comprehensive criticism of this economy. Indeed, in many places the pattern of prestige and largess continued, now with the monastery at the top of the hierarchy of prestigious institutions.[15] One change the monks effected was the cessation of burying treasure with the dead, presumably because of its association with pagan understandings of death and its sequel. But it is interesting to note that very frequently such hoards ceased in an area at about the same time that such metals were recognized as useful in the minting of coins. Monastic communities, which lived from their landed endowments, became managers of great wealth, and at times they stimulated the use of money to facilitate exchange.

After the invasions of Europe by Vikings, Magyars, and Muslims tapered off for a variety of reasons, and with the development of new agri-

13. Marc Bloch divides his epic medieval history by this shift. Marc Bloch, *Feudal Society*, 2nd ed., trans. L. A. Manyon (New York: Routledge, 1962). For a more recent discussion of the economic changes, see Lester Little, *Religious Poverty and the Profit Economy in Medieval Europe* (Ithaca, NY: Cornell University Press, 1978), and N. J. G. Pounds, *An Economic History of Medieval Europe*, 2nd ed. (New York: Longman, 1994).

14. See Justo L. González, *Faith and Wealth: A History of Early Christian Ideas on the Origin, Significance, and Use of Money* (San Francisco: Harper and Row, 1990), for an account of how dissatisfaction with the economics of the present age and a preference for the theme of material communion in the early church fathers gradually gave way to a concern with one's inner disposition toward wealth.

15. Little, *Religious Poverty*, p. 7.

cultural techniques, population began to expand — and towns with it. Industry developed, and the spread of coin-minting provided the conditions for the growth of trade and specialization. Monetization was not limited to trade centers; it included agricultural rents as well. Merchants and bankers became very important in the new economy. Lester Little draws an interesting parallel, noting that at the same time that Europe was expanding aggressively outward, sending troops to the Holy Land, to Spain, to eastern Germany, and to North Africa, another kind of plundering was taking off within Europe itself. Elsewhere, banking and commerce developed under the restraining watch of a strong state. "By contrast, European commerce came to maturity well in advance of the state, and as a result nurtured a peculiarly unrestrained aggressiveness, above all when it came to lending money."[16] Monasteries played a prominent role in these changes: they recognized how their surpluses could be translated into money, and how such money could be used in money-lending. By 1146, Peter the Venerable lamented, "Cluny has many debtors, but few benefactors."[17]

Despite their place in the changing economy, the monasteries remained the bearers of voluntary poverty. But poverty did not necessarily mean lack of riches. During the age of Christianization and persistent foreign invasions, "poverty" betokened not utter lack of wealth but social vulnerability, the abandonment of political and military power to pursue "poverty of spirit" in the form of complete dedication to religious matters. This older understanding of poverty persisted in the monasteries, even through these economic upheavals. Therefore, Little suggests, the monasteries generally failed to address the economic changes, accepting the new realities almost unthinkingly. Little helpfully characterizes the older notion of harmony between spiritual poverty and material wealth that persisted: "The essential meaning of 'poor' before the triumph of the commercial economy was 'weak' in relation to the powerful. The particular forms taken by monastic spirituality had developed in connection with the problems of power and violence in late Carolingian society. The monks, who were recruited from the warrior class, were men who had surrendered their weapons, who had made themselves voluntarily weak — or 'poor,' who thus felt no disturbing contradiction between 'wealth' and 'poverty'

---

16. Little, *Religious Poverty,* p. 8.
17. Peter the Venerable, Letter 131, cited in Little, *Religious Poverty,* p. 69.

while living by a rule in the setting of a materially comfortable, in some cases even magnificent and luxurious, monastery."[18]

There is no reason to think claims to poverty among such monks were hypocritical. According to the older taxonomy of religious poverty, these monks were indeed poor. But the tectonic shifts in wealth's social meaning were undermining the legitimacy of those claims in the eyes of many. Still, a religious poverty that could embody the traditional ideal of renunciation in a compelling way for a new social context was not easy to find. Dissatisfaction with the comfort of the monasteries led to a renewed eremitic movement and several attempts at monastic reform. Typically, reform movements like the Cistercians sought a more adequate path through a stricter life and a more zealous refusal of any attachment to city life. But the very discipline and organization of the Cistercians brought economic success that soon rivaled that of the older institutions. And because the new economic practices had already spread into the countryside, avoiding towns did not guarantee noncomplicity in the new and aggressive money economy. Within a hundred years of their founding, many of the new orders fell under some of the same opprobrium that they had heaped on their monastic forerunners.

The increasing scandal associated with ecclesiastical wealth derived in part from the changing situation of the involuntary poor.[19] In an earlier age, ties to the land and customs of social recognition provided the vast numbers who lived at or near subsistence levels with some protection from complete destitution. Misfortune or social isolation could occasion extreme poverty, but for the most part the fortunes of the poor depended on the quality of harvests as much as anything. The economic changes I have been detailing drove increasing numbers of the poor into the cities, where they were cut off from prior means of support. Further, even those who remained in the country found that the impersonal and unforgiving institution of money was gradually becoming the universal medium for obtaining necessities. The poverty in which so many had long lived began to involve a more acute vulnerability. Moreover, the new power that the spreading money economy gave to the emerging middle class made it possible to attribute such vulnerability not merely to the unpredictability of agricultural yields, but to subtle new forms of compulsion.

18. Little, *Religious Poverty,* p. 68.

19. The standard discussion is in Michel Mollat, *The Poor in the Middle Ages,* trans. Arthur Goldhammer (New Haven: Yale University Press, 1986).

If in an earlier age religious poverty had summoned warriors to lay down their military power, the convulsions of the twelfth and thirteenth centuries nursed a notion of religious poverty as the renunciation of monetary power.[20] The way was paved by lay groups such as the Humiliati and the Waldensians, who sought in a renunciation of possessions to embrace the *vita apostolica*.[21] Not much later, Francis rejected a career as a cloth merchant that had been prepared for him and embraced a poverty based on the refusal of any property, especially the "concrete, portable form of the right to command wealth" that he saw in money.[22]

This scenario of evangelical renewal and economic protest is the context for the origin of the Dominican order. The heart of the Dominican apostolate has always centered on preaching rather than on poverty. However, from the time of Dominic, poverty was closely associated with the evangelical purposes of the order. Dominic himself was a companion of bishop Diego of Osma, and was sent with the latter on a preaching mission among the Cathars. The Cathars were another lay group that sought the *vita apostolica*, characterized by contempt for wealth and property; but among them such contempt was often associated with complete contempt for the flesh and for all things material. Therefore, their teachings were treated as Manichaean, and Diego's mission was to recall these heretics to the true faith. Unsurprisingly, many of the Cathars, with their devotion to the poor Christ, were little moved by a preaching coterie that arrived on horseback — with retainers and plenty of evidence of expenditure. This was the same wealthy church the Cathars were hoping to recall to the poverty of the apostles. To eliminate the greatest liability of the preaching mission, Diego sent his belongings back to Spain and began preaching poverty, thereby "stopping the mouths of the wicked."[23]

Diego died in 1207, a year after that mission, but Dominic continued to preach in the south of France until 1215, and under his influence a small

---

20. Little, *Religious Poverty*, pp. 197-202.

21. The classic work on these lay movements is Herbert Grundmann, *Religious Movements in the Middle Ages*, trans. Steven Rowan (Notre Dame, IN: University of Notre Dame Press, 1995).

22. Kelly S. Johnson, *The Fear of Beggars: Stewardship and Poverty in Christian Ethics*, Eerdmans Ekklesia Series, ed. Michael L. Budde and Stephen E. Fowl (Grand Rapids: Eerdmans, 2007), p. 59.

23. Cited in Guy Bedouelle, O.P., *Saint Dominic: The Grace of the Word*, trans. Mary Thomas Noble, O.P. (San Francisco: Ignatius Press, 1987), p. 149.

band of followers gathered to preach in voluntary poverty. In contrast to the idealism of Francis, there was a more practical concern at the fount of Dominican poverty: poverty was at the service of the preaching mission. Sleeping in huts and caves, as many of the early Franciscans did, could be unconducive to the Bible study required for good preaching. Therefore, Dominic established a convent at Prouille, which became a center of material aid for Dominic's brothers. When Dominic and his fellows took up a preaching mission for the bishop of Toulouse in 1215, they were promised one-sixth of the parish tithes for their support.

But if Dominic's poverty was more prudent than was Francis's, it was no less rooted in devotion to the poor Christ.[24] Dominican poverty was not just a tactic to avoid being shamed by the heretics. It was an attempt to follow the poverty taught in the Gospels. Dominic's own commitment to that poverty is evident in his reluctant parsing of twelve pence to John of Navarre, who bereaved Dominic by refusing to leave for Paris with no money at all, despite the injunction in Matthew 10:9-10.[25] Indeed, Dominic began to move his order toward a more strict poverty. In 1219 he obtained from the pope a bull confirming the order's mendicancy and giving it a penitential significance. Poverty, travel, and begging would constitute austere hardships for which the pope granted indulgence. Then the General Constitutions of 1220 insisted that poverty be observed not only on preaching missions but also by the convents of the friars, and that subsistence needs be met through the acceptance of alms, and not through revenues from land or other goods. Dominicans were to observe not only individual but conventual poverty.

Still, Dominicans always considered it legitimate to own the convents in which the brothers lived and the land on which the convents stood. The Franciscans sought to forsake all such ownership, and hence ended up in the tortured distinctions between use and ownership we have observed above. But for the Dominicans, poverty did not mean that the order could own absolutely nothing. When the Chapter of 1228, seven years after Dominic's death, affirmed the "absolute prohibition of acquiring property and revenues,"[26] it was primarily moneymaking goods that it

---

24. For the following, see Bedouelle, *Saint Dominic*, pp. 151-53, and Jan van den Eijnden, O.F.M., *Poverty on the Way to God: Thomas Aquinas on Evangelical Poverty* (Leuven: Peeters, 1994), pp. 10-13.

25. "Take no gold, or silver, or copper in your belts, no bag for your journey, or two tunics, or sandals, or a staff; for laborers deserve their food."

26. Cited in Bedouelle, *Saint Dominic*, p. 152.

meant. Yet, even goods that were to be directly used by the order were to be limited to what was necessary for the day. From 1220 on, Dominic wanted them "to live solely on alms and sparingly, for when they had enough in the house to enable them to last the day, he did not want them to accept anything or to send anyone out looking for alms."[27]

Clearly, Dominican poverty was different from the older religious poverty of the monks. At least four meanings stand out. First, it was a following of Christ, who humbled himself and who bade his followers to entrust themselves to God's providence. In contrast to the monks, who entrusted themselves by yielding military power, Dominicans committed themselves to trust providence by renouncing monetary power. Since they did have to accept their nourishment for the day, this commitment required that the abandonment of goods be renewed daily, for in a money economy they could compromise such trust by accepting a little extra and laying it up for the future. Second, Dominican poverty was an imitation of the life of the apostles, freed for devotion to the evangelical task. Whereas monastic poverty demanded a stable connection to the monastery and its lands, Dominican poverty abandoned such connections to be free to go where preaching was needed. Dominicans' poverty did not mean having no possessions at all, for their very preaching required some. They could have the books and the priories required for their specific tasks, but they were to renounce all other possessions that might distract them from those tasks with worldly concerns. Third, Dominican poverty was penitential: it sought through an austere life to show the humility appropriate to sinners before God. In contrast to monastic poverty, this poverty was austere less through its strict rule and more through its economic renunciation. Fourth, Dominican poverty served the preaching mission by establishing a harmony between the messenger and the message. In an age that looked to the poor Christ, the Dominican preachers sought credibility by striving for a concordance between their own life and the life of the poor Christ and his followers.

---

27. William A. Hinnebusch, "Poverty in the Order of Preachers," *Catholic Historical Review* 45 (1960): 436-53, here p. 449, cited in van den Eijnden, *Poverty on the Way to God*, p. 12.

The Practice of Poverty and Thomas's Alleged Change of Mind

Thomas displays his passion for following the poor Christ most clearly in the polemical treatises he wrote to defend mendicancy against those who considered it a scandalous novelty. But since his discussion in the *ST* appears more moderate, many have supposed that as he matured, his early fervor settled down. It is true that he wrote one of these polemical treatises, *Contra Retrahentes*, almost contemporaneously with the *ST* II-II.[28] But some have taken his earlier treatise, *Contra Impugnantes* (dated to 1256), to be more radical and to bear witness to a shift in Thomas's perspective over the years.[29] By examining the changing audiences and the fairly stable practice of poverty Thomas assumes in each text, I argue that Thomas's account of mendicancy has a consistent shape and that the polemical treatises help us appreciate the devotion to the poor Christ still evident in the *ST*.

The impression that Thomas changed his mind is created by prima facie differences between *CI* and the *ST*. One example of the apparent difference is the changing use Thomas makes of a quote from Gregory the Great. *CI* relates the story, borrowed from Gregory, of a certain holy monk named Isaac. When Isaac's disciples recommended that he accept the possessions offered to him for the use of the monastery, he sought to protect his poverty by saying, "A monk who seeks earthly possessions is not a monk at all." Thomas concludes from the story not only that renouncing common possessions is lawful, but that "it is a greater perfection and safety to lack common possessions than to have them."[30] Thomas apparently correlates degree of poverty and degree of perfection quite directly. How different is Thomas's use of the same quotation from Gregory in the *ST!* In II-II 188.7, Gregory's story about the monk Isaac appears as an objection to Thomas's point that common possessions do not diminish religious per-

---

28. Gilles Emery dates *CR* to 1271 and II-II to 1271-72. Gilles Emery, O.P., "Brief Catalogue of the Works of Saint Thomas Aquinas," in Jean-Pierre Torrell, ed., *Saint Thomas Aquinas*, vol. 1, *The Person and His Work*, trans. Robert Royal (Washington, DC: The Catholic University of America Press, 1996), pp. 330-61.

29. For an introduction to this work and its context, see Michel-Marie Dufeil, *Guillaume de Saint-Amour et la polémique universitaire parisienne, 1250-1259* (Paris: Picard, 1972), pp. 253-60.

30. "[M]aioris perfectionis et securitatis est possessionibus communibus carere quam eas habere." *CI*, chap. 6, § 4, 501-3.

fection. Thomas insists that poverty is merely instrumental to a perfection not defined by poverty, and that greater poverty does not mean greater perfection. Something has apparently changed.

This and similar shifts have led some modern scholars to propose that the wisdom that comes with years had cooled Thomas's earlier zeal, and that he had become a more moderate advocate of poverty.[31] But Ulrich Horst has shown that Thomas never identified poverty with perfection; even in *CI*, poverty is merely instrumental to it.[32] Horst argues that the change of language is due, not to a change of mind, but to the changing audience. In the polemical tracts, Thomas chooses language suitable for refuting opponents of mendicancy who allege that common dispossession is unlawful. In the *ST*, Thomas has an interest in guarding his fellow Dominicans against the emerging errors of the "spiritual" mendicants.[33]

The opponents of mendicancy primarily came from the secular clergy. The seculars' displeasure arose as the popularity of the mendicants began to divert income from the one to the other, to create a rivalry over liturgical functions, and to arouse the envy of the secular masters whose chairs at the university were being lost to the mendicants.[34] The campaign did not limit itself to defending traditional clergy privileges; it included all-out attacks on the mendicants' way of life, and especially on the new form of religious poverty that made that life possible. Opponents of the mendicants, such as William of St. Amour, argued that those in religious orders should be committed to manual labor, and that those new religious, like the old ones, should not only own common property but live on it and

---

31. Van den Eijnden gives the most comprehensive account of the issues and the scholarship. Van den Eijnden, *Poverty on the Way to God*, pp. 31-68. Cf. J. Bellemare, "Pour une théologie thomiste de la Pauvreté," *Revue de l'Université d'Ottawa* 26 (1956): 137-64; B. M. Dietsche, *Die Deutsche Thomasausgabe, Stände und Ständespflichten*, 2a-2ae, q. 183-89 (Regensburg, 1952); and S. di Mattia Spirito, "Il Problema della Povertà e della Perfezione Religiosa nell' ambito delle Polemiche tra Clero Secolare e Ordini Mendicanti," in *Tommaso d'Aquino nella Storia di Pensiero*, vol. 2, Dal Medievo ad Oggi, Atti del Congresso Internazionale (Naples, 1976), pp. 49-58.

32. Ulrich Horst, O.P., *Evangelische Armut und Kirche: Thomas von Aquin und die Armutskontroversen des 13. und beginnenden 14. Jahrhunderts* (Berlin: Akademie, 1992), p. 36. For another argument for continuity in Thomas's view, see Bellemare, "Pour une théologie thomiste de la Pauvreté."

33. Horst, *Evangelische Armut und Kirche*, p. 125.

34. D. L. Douie, *The Conflict Between the Seculars and the Mendicants at the University of Paris in the Thirteenth Century* (London: Blackfriars, 1954).

work it.[35] In response to such arguments, Thomas affirmed the legitimacy of renouncing property.

In the *ST*, on the other hand, Thomas writes primarily for his fellow Dominicans. The need to justify the order's existence against the protests of the seculars is not so much in view here. In fact, as Thomas writes in the *ST* II-II, he is aware of another threat, more recent and more internal: the tendencies of the "spirituals." The spiritual party among the Franciscans was yet to emerge with clarity, but the tendencies existed already, and it was important to clarify the Dominican position.[36] The mendicant orders had always had to balance their dedication to absolute poverty with the material demands of their preaching and teaching missions. The "spiritual" tendency is the name given to those who perceived that, in the pursuit of this balance, the practice of poverty was being compromised. These "spirituals" tended to see radical poverty as necessary to Christian perfection, and they resisted any apparent concessions to the need for some material goods.

The name "spirituals" was attached to these Franciscans, not only because they understood themselves as defending the spirit of St. Francis, but also because many of them shared a fondness for apocalyptic prophecies of a new age of the Spirit. Loosely based on the writings of Joachim of Fiore, such prophecies claimed that the age of the Old and New Testaments was ending and that the Franciscans themselves were the harbingers of a third age.[37] The apocalyptic note hardened them against any concern for the conditions necessary to sustain such poverty and deafened them to criticism that the church had never before allowed poverty to take precedence over evangelical and ecclesiastical concerns. Such tendencies were already evident as Thomas was writing the II-II.[38] Therefore, he makes a

---

35. Douie, *Conflict Between the Seculars and the Mendicants,* pp. 8-10. For a comprehensive treatment of William, see Dufeil, *Guillaume de Saint-Amour.*

36. For the conflict between the Spiritual and Conventual Franciscans, see M. D. Lambert, *Franciscan Poverty: The Doctrine of the Absolute Poverty of Christ and the Apostles in the Franciscan Order, 1210-1323* (London: S.P.C.K., 1961). David Burr has shown that the "spiritual" tendency was already there in the 1270s, although one should not imagine the existence of a coherent group. David Burr, "The *Correctorium* Controversy and the Origins of the *Usus Pauper* Controversy," *Speculum* 60 (1985): 331-42, and *The Spiritual Franciscans* (University Park: Pennsylvania State University Press, 2001).

37. Lambert, *Franciscan Poverty,* pp. 106-8.

38. Horst, *Evangelische Armut und Kirche,* p. 125.

point in 188.7 of offering an account of mendicant poverty that relativizes the importance of poverty, situating mendicancy within the broader framework of the ministry of the whole church, and affirming that all orders have some things in common.

Ulrich Horst emphasizes that Thomas was no more radical earlier than later. Horst's interest is to show that the parting of the ways that occurred after Thomas's death between Dominicans and Franciscans over issues of poverty was not due to a change in Thomas. Had the "spiritualists" been prevalent in the 1250s, Thomas would have had to oppose them just as he did in the 1270s, for his understanding of poverty was no different.

But asserting the continuity of Thomas's position cuts both ways. Not only is his earlier position no *more* radical than the later one; his position in the *ST* is also no *less* radical than his position in *CI*. Jan van den Eijnden has pressed this point: he has related Thomas's arguments in *CI* and the *ST* to the practice of Dominican poverty in Thomas's day in order to show that both texts are defending one and the same practice, even if the language appears contradictory.[39]

As we have seen, the Dominicans were not bereft of all things. Although each one individually gave away everything, and as a group they refused the accumulations of common wealth that were beginning to taint the reputations of some other monasteries, they did accept and hold in common such things as were necessary to sustain the life and mission of the order for the present. Hence, Thomas never claims that the friars lack what they need to eat or wear. Thomas's advocacy of common dispossession in *CI* accords with this fact of Dominican life: they are not bereft of basic needs.[40] Thomas's changing use of the example of the monk Isaac reflects not his changing his mind, but a focus on different aspects of the story. In *CI* the story illustrates that common dispossession is not illegitimate. In the *ST*, Thomas still affirms the point of the story, but notes that Isaac's refusal of possessions did not amount to a rejection of "such things as are commonly necessary for the upkeep of life."[41]

How does an order that practices common dispossession avoid being bereft of basic necessities? It continually receives those necessities from

39. Hence, Thomas's defense of renouncing collective property in *CI* and his defense of having certain things in common in the *ST* are in fact equivalent. Van den Eijnden, *Poverty on the Way to God*, pp. 31-68.

40. See *CI*, chap. 6, ad 6, ad 20.

41. *ST* II-II 188.7 ad 4.

others. Part of what made mendicant poverty possible was the existence of a social order in which the voluntary poor could be sustained through gifts. Van den Eijnden compares Thomas's comments on alms, begging, and manual labor in *CI* and the *ST* to show that Dominican income is conceived the same way in both. Furthermore, Thomas generally rehearses the same arguments, making the same points in reply. He consistently advances the same four points regarding mendicant income: (1) unlike monks, mendicants receive no income from vineyards or other landed properties; (2) mendicants' primary income derives from alms that are freely given, but alms that at the same time have a sense of obligation attached to them because friars provide spiritual benefits through preaching, teaching, and leading worship; (3) mendicants can engage in agricultural or craft labor, but such labor is not at all necessary as long as the alms received under point (2) are sufficient; and (4) begging is fully legitimate for the mendicants, especially when income from (2) and (3) is insufficient, or when they have little time for manual labor because of contemplation and teaching.[42]

It turned out that the mendicants were very popular objects of giving. In order to remain free from the burden of great possessions, they had to give away whatever they received beyond what was needed for their livelihood. But how much to retain? Dominic commanded them to take only what was needed for any given day. But the General Chapter of 1239 authorized stocking up a year's supply of food and drink.[43] We may presume that such provision, along with the material conditions for preaching and scholarship, is what Thomas has in mind when he speaks of retaining the necessities required for the present in both *CI* and the *ST*.

Despite Olivi's attack on Thomas, and despite the impression that Thomas's account of mendicancy relaxed over time, the *ST* presupposes the same practice of poverty as does *CI*, and is not more moderate in advocating it. Even II-II 188.7, where Thomas affirms having common things, does not betray a change of mind. The article avers that degrees of poverty do not translate into degrees of perfection, but Thomas complicates the picture by noting that the poorest orders should be the preaching orders, which the previous article affirms are "more excellent." And though Thomas counters excessive "spiritual" tendencies by saying that all orders

42. Van den Eijnden, *Poverty on the Way to God,* pp. 57-58.
43. Bedouelle, *Saint Dominic,* p. 153.

have some things in common, he shows his continuing concern for common dispossession by avoiding the term *possessiones* for the things friars have. He calls what the mixed orders keep *res communes*.[44] It is true that Thomas, in *CI*, includes money among those things that perfect men may relinquish, while in II-II, 188.7 he defends keeping some money. But the context in *CI* suggests quantities of money that would function as security beyond present needs.[45] In the *ST*, he defends keeping some money only as part of the limited supply of necessities. The shifts from *CI* to the *ST* are best explained as shifts of emphasis in light of changing audiences. In the *ST*, the account of mendicancy has not changed, but Thomas wards off those rigorists who would read the counsel of poverty so sternly that it would appear impossible to observe. Such rigorists were to cause quite a stir among the Franciscans within two decades of Thomas's death.[46]

Thomas's enthusiasm for Christ's poverty resounds through the polemical treatises, but that fervor is not confined to those treatises. We are not surprised to read in *CI* that Christ is the rationale for complete poverty. In chapter 6, objection 9, Thomas considers whether mendicancy misses the mean of liberality by giving away too much. He replies by appealing to Aristotle to show that the mean of a virtue is not a moderation of some quantity but whatever accords with right reason. Thus, an act that is prodigal in one situation may, by the addition of some circumstance, become a liberal act. The circumstance that makes mendicant poverty not "too much" is that mendicants undertake it "to fulfill the counsel of Christ" and "on account of Christ."[47] The same argument remains unchanged in the *Summa Contra Gentiles*. This poverty accords with right reason only because "right reason no longer takes its bearings from the standard of natural virtue; the standard is the transcendent end of union with God."[48]

44. The care Thomas takes here is obscured in the translation by the English Dominican Fathers, who translate *res communes* as "common property."

45. *CI*, chap. 6, ad 7.

46. Even the rigorist Peter Olivi was appalled at the audacity of some of them! See Burr, *Spiritual Franciscans*, pp. 69-71.

47. "Propter Christi consilium implendum"; "propter Christum." *CI*, chap. 6, ad 9, § 6, 744-45, 751.

48. Thomas S. Hibbs, *Dialectic and Narrative in Aquinas: An Interpretation of the Summa Contra Gentiles* (Notre Dame, IN: University of Notre Dame Press, 1995), p. 125. Cf. *ScG* III, 134.

Thomas makes the same argument in the *ST.* He may seem to have toned it down. In *CI,* before pointing to Christ, Thomas offers a more mundane example of how leaving everything could accord with right reason. One could give all his possessions to save his country from danger. The comparison between this reckless but praiseworthy act and Christian poverty highlights the radicality of the call of Christ. Thomas's mundane example in the *ST* is that a pagan philosopher might rightly "cast away *[abiicere]* riches in order to be free for the contemplation of wisdom."[49] The change of examples may appear to play down the recklessness of mendicant poverty. But Thomas emphasizes the excess of the mendicants by turning the example into an *a fortiori* argument: if circumstances can change prodigality to liberality for a pagan philosopher, how much more must it accord with right reason that "a man abandon *[relinquere]* all things in order perfectly to follow Christ."[50] Thomas evokes the evangelical and radical character of Christian mendicancy by concluding this reply with Jerome's reckless phrase: "Follow the naked Christ naked [*Nudum Christum nudus sequere*]."[51]

Mendicant Virtues

After discussing the evangelical and rigorous character of Thomas's consistent account of mendicancy, it remains to explore the shape of mendicancy more fully. The best way to do that is to display the virtues through which it is lived out, specifically humility and vulnerable, patient trust. As we will see, the logic of the cross of Christ draws these virtues toward ever-deeper expression.

As I have suggested, this Christlike humble vulnerability becomes a sort of *telos* for Thomas's economic teachings. We have seen how Thomas agrees with Aristotle that we are situated within a comprehensive order

---

49. "Divitias abiiciat ut contemplationi sapientiae vacet." *ST* II-II 186.3 ad 3.

50. "Homo omnia sua relinquat ad hoc quod Christum perfecte sequatur." The translation by the English Dominican Fathers downplays the difference by translating both *abiicere* and *relinquere* as "to renounce."

51. Fergus Kerr brings out Thomas's passion on this issue, but implies that the passion (and this phrase of Jerome's) is left out of the *ST.* Kerr points out that the phrase is absent from the III, but neglects to mention its occurrence here. Fergus Kerr, O.P., *After Aquinas: Versions of Thomism* (Oxford: Blackwell, 2002), p. 167.

that properly evokes deference and trusting dependence. But while Aristotle sets a higher threshold of security below which such receptive vulnerability should not fall, Thomas holds that threshold down, pushing toward a poverty that refuses to secure itself. Our proper deference and trusting dependence reach their perfect exemplification in the extreme humility and exposure of the poor Christ. The poverty of Christ refuses to limit its deference by the need to secure dignity and refuses to limit its dependence by the need to secure the future. It refuses to fortify the self against whatever may shame or degrade it, embracing instead the lowliest humility. It refuses to secure the future in the face of risks and dangers, accepting the abject vulnerability that goes with this lowliness.

As far as I know, Thomas never experienced a poverty that we would recognize as a real threat to his security. But on Thomas's account, the relatively stable provision of necessities his order received was due to God's care exercised through the gifts of God's people. It was an answer to the order's vulnerable trust. They continued to live out their humbly vulnerable poverty insofar as they refused to let those gifts become a guarantee of future security or a basis for living in a dignified manner. So this poverty had to be continually renewed. And what always called them to greater humility and greater trust was the unfathomable lowliness and insecurity of Christ on the cross.

The two aspects of Christ's insecurity, the humility and the vulnerability, are two sides of one coin. Each entails the other. The humble self-abasement jeopardizes one's access to necessities, and thus intensifies dependence; the status of vulnerable insufficiency is by its very nature humbling. Although they are inseparable, we can look at each in turn.

A Poverty of Cruciform Humility

The depth of Christ's poverty summons to an ever-deeper humility. This is clear enough in the article on begging in the *ST*. If Thomas had proposed a vaguely Aristotelian renunciation for the sake of contemplation, it could stop short of beggary. But whereas Aristotelian renunciation simply seeks freedom to contemplate and Aristotelian deference seeks only to avoid hubris, Thomas's mendicancy seeks the deepest humility possible. The begging article privileges a mendicant over a nonmendicant poverty on the grounds that the more abased one's practice of poverty is, the better it is.[52] The *sed contra* suggests on what grounds: "Christ was a mendicant, according to Psalm 39:18 — 'But I am a beggar and poor;' where a gloss says: 'Christ said this of Himself as bearing the 'form of a servant.'"

We can spell out more of the logic of this self-abasement by turning to Thomas's polemical texts against the seculars, where he discusses mendicancy more extensively. Thomas frequently begins his defense of poverty by appealing to Christ's example. Christ had nowhere to lay his head (Luke 9:58); he had no money to pay the tax (Matt. 17:24-27).[53] But how does Thomas know that this abject poverty is meant as a model for us? Many aspects of Christ's life are not exemplary for us, not least his refraining from writing.[54] Of course, Christ's teachings are important in this respect, most notably Matthew 19:21: "If you wish to be perfect, go, sell your possessions, and give the money to the poor, and you will have treasure in heaven; then come, follow me." Thomas uses this text, perhaps more than any other, to defend voluntary poverty.[55] But even this text does not explain Thomas's appeals beyond poverty to beggary. What is the basis for such a surprising degree of impoverishment?

The answer goes beyond the simple example of Christ's material poverty. What makes that example unquestionably relevant and also unfathomable is its connection to two other kinds of poverty associated with Christ: the relative poverty of the Incarnation and the existential poverty of suffering death on a cross. All three of these "poverties" come together in another of Thomas's favorite passages for explaining mendicancy. It is the text that serves as the epigraph for this book, 2 Corinthians 8:9: "For you know the grace of our Lord Jesus Christ, in that, although he was rich, for your sakes he became poor [*egenus factus est*], so that through his poverty you might be rich." Thomas uses this passage to show that the extent

---

52. *ST* II-II 187.5.

53. See, for example, *CI,* chap. 6, § 3, 270-89.

54. In commenting on the Lombard, Thomas enumerates several aspects of Christ's life that are not meant as examples for us. See the catalogue in Richard Schenk, O.P., "*Omnis Christi Actio Nostra Est Instructio:* The Deeds and Sayings of Jesus as Revelation in the View of Thomas Aquinas," in *La doctrine de la révélation divine de saint Thomas d'Aquin,* ed. Leo J. Elders (Vatican City: Libreria Editrice Vaticana, 1990), pp. 104-31, esp. p. 113.

55. It appears as the first testimony in *CI,* chap. 6 (§ 3, 272-74); it figures prominently in the meditation on poverty in *CR,* chap. 15; and Thomas uses it throughout the treatise on states of life in the *ST,* esp. II-II 186.3.

of abasement to which Christ calls takes its rationale from the degree of his own impoverishment from heavenly riches to death on a cross. While the text's reference to the poverty of the Incarnation and of the cross may be clear enough, it may appear that the text does not evoke Christ's material poverty. Presumably, that is why it does not appear among the proof-texts offered up in the early stages of the mendicant controversy to address the question of whether Jesus was factually poor.[56] But Thomas always interprets *egenus* here as actual material poverty.[57] That reading, we might note, fits Paul's rhetoric insofar as he is trying to elicit a response of monetary self-sacrifice. The connection Thomas makes among Christ's incarnational poverty, his material poverty, and the poverty of his death forms the core of the logic of self-abasement.

Therefore, the depth of material poverty to which Christ calls is not merely a positive command or example. Rather, material lowliness becomes an aspect of believers' participation in the saving act of Christ, in its downward movement from the riches of divinity through the Incarnation and death. Just as the human mind cannot traverse the distance covered by this downward movement into the utmost abasement, so Christ calls followers to an ever-deeper humility in conformity to Christ's saving poverty.

Thomas's most sustained account of the link between mendicancy and Jesus' saving acts is found in another polemical text, *Contra Retrahentes,* especially in chapter 15.[58] Thomas juxtaposes the heavenly riches and earthly poverty right from the beginning, in connection with 2 Corinthians 8:9. He quotes the *Gloss:* "For he assumed poverty and did not lose riches; rich inwardly, poor outwardly, hiding his Godhead with its wealth, showing his manhood in his poverty."[59] He draws the following lesson

---

56. Van den Eijnden, *Poverty on the Way to God,* p. 190.

57. We see this in *CI,* chap. 7, § 8, 762-70, in the commentary on 2 Corinthians, dating perhaps to 1265-68; in *CR,* chap. 15; and in *ST* III 40.3.

58. Many have seen in this chapter an echo of Thomas's youthful decision to follow the poor Dominicans. Torrell calls it the revelation of Thomas's "personal mysticism of attachment to the poor Christ." Torrell, *Saint Thomas Aquinas,* vol. 1, p. 89. Cf. the treatment of this chapter in Ulrich Horst, O.P., "Christ, *Exemplar Ordinis Fratrum Praedicantium,* According to Saint Thomas Aquinas," in *Christ Among the Medieval Dominicans,* ed. Kent Emery, Jr., and Joseph P. Wawrykow (Notre Dame, IN: University of Notre Dame Press, 1998), pp. 256-70, esp. pp. 259-61.

59. "Paupertatem enim assumpsit . . . et divitias non amisit, intus dives, foris pauper, latens Deus in divitiis, apparens homo in paupertate." *CR,* chap. 15, 8-12.

from one so willing to put on poverty from a position of such wealth: "Thus great dignity accrues to those who follow Christ's poverty."[60]

The movement from divine riches to material poverty is an unfathomable self-abasement that justifies the degree of humility sought by the mendicants. But the degree of lowliness involved only reaches its consummation in the cross. So Thomas points out that Jesus' material poverty is an example for us, but that "among all that Christ did and suffered in his mortal life, especially proposed for Christians to imitate is the example of the venerable cross."[61] It may seem that Christ's cross, his one-time death, cannot be imitated through a sustained practice like mendicant poverty. But Thomas finds a precedent in St. Paul to claim a continual adoption of cruciformity, appealing to Galatians 6:17: "I bear in my body the marks [stigmata] of the Lord." And poverty is a particularly fitting mode of such cruciformity, for "among all the remarkable aspects of the cross, evident in every way is its poverty, in which he was shorn of external things to the point of bodily nakedness."[62] Thomas's opponents, those who attack poverty, are revealed as enemies of the cross of Christ. The cross ultimately provides the logic for Thomas to propose a humble poverty aimed toward ever-deeper abasement.

1.2.4. A Poverty of Cruciform Vulnerability and Trust

Christ's poverty summons believers not only to refuse to secure the self against degradation and lowliness, but also to refuse to secure the future in the face of risk and danger. As I have suggested above, humility and vulnerability are, of course, two sides of the same coin. Those who embrace a state of humble beggary will have no other means of obtaining their livelihood apart from depending on others. But such dependence may soon turn into a new means of security — and will correspondingly conflict with their commitment to material humility — if they do not abandon whatever gifts they receive beyond what is needed for their

60. "Ex quo his qui Christi paupertatem sequuntur magna dignitas accrescit." *CR*, chap. 15, 12-13.

61. "Inter cetera vero quae Christus in mortali vita vel fecit vel passus est, praecipue christianis imitandum proponitur venerandae crucis exemplum." *CR*, chap. 15, 80-83.

62. "Inter alia vero cruces insignia apparet omnimoda paupertas, in quo exterioribus rebus privates est usque ad corporis nuditatem." *CR*, chap. 15, 89-92.

present livelihood. Commitment to following Christ in dependence means accepting an ever-renewed risk of future lack; sustaining one's radical humility depends on one's equally radical vulnerability. Hence, in his article on begging in the *ST*, Thomas appeals to Christ's beggary and points out that beggary involves radical dependence: it means being so needy that one must receive one's food from others.[63] When Thomas considers whether those in religious orders may live on alms, he affirms that those who give up all their possessions for the sake of Christ may live on the little *(modica)* they receive from others.[64] Furthermore, when he discusses the role of necessary goods among religious, he insists that they should not accumulate excess, but should keep only enough for their livelihood.[65]

It is, of course, the unfathomable exposure of Christ on the cross that summons us to this ever-renewed receptive vulnerability. But the earthly ministry of Christ and the apostles, and even the teaching of John the Baptist, help establish the pattern. Since the same God who calls to this renunciation is trustworthy to provide what is needed, we can have confidence to risk extreme vulnerability.

In the *ST*, Thomas emphasizes Christ's vulnerable trust as a model. During his ministry, Christ did not secure his future material sustenance, but entrusted himself to the care of God and of others. Christ's trust in God's care may seem compromised by the fact that he knew all things and thus the future was no mystery to him. But though the Son of God knew all things, even those yet to be,[66] the actualization of this knowledge conformed to Christ's historical development.[67] It can even be said that Christ hoped to receive necessities. True, Christ did not have the theological virtue of hope, for such hope relates to the unseen, while Christ enjoyed the beatific vision. But he did hope in the Lord for other things, short of beatitude, that concerned the perfection for which he was destined.[68] And his trust extended not only to the care of God, but to the care of others. Thus

63. *ST* II-II 187.5, resp.
64. *ST* II-II 187.4 ad 3.
65. *ST* II-II 188.7 ad 3.
66. *ST* III 10.2.
67. *ST* III 12.1-2. For a more extensive discussion of Christ's knowledge, see Matthew Levering, *Christ's Fulfillment of Torah and Temple: Salvation According to Thomas Aquinas* (Notre Dame, IN: University of Notre Dame Press, 2002), pp. 31-41.
68. *ST* III 7.4, resp. and ad 1.

we read in Luke 8 that Christ received alms from certain women, whose ministry enabled him to be fed and clothed.[69]

Thomas finds the gospel calling Christians to a degree of vulnerable dependence that at times appears scandalous. In *CI*, an objection attacks mendicancy on the grounds that it unnaturally refuses what is needed for the future. The objection refers to the Gloss on Luke 3:11: when John the Baptist advises the repentant sinner who has two tunics to give to whoever has none, the Gloss points out that John does not command someone with only one tunic to divide it, for then neither would be properly clothed, but "no one should render himself entirely destitute."[70] In reply, Thomas concedes the argument, but points out that it only refers to things like food and clothing for present needs. The occasion elicits Thomas's most extended description of his distinction between subsistence goods at the time they are to be used and wealth that could provide secure access to such goods for the future. The vulnerability involved in refusing the latter is justified by trust in divine providence. "I ought not to deprive myself entirely of other things, so that I am left naked or without food and drink when it is time to eat, and concerning such things the Gloss speaks. But there are certain temporal things kept back to provide the needs of the body in the future, such as money, possessions, and the like. And these things perfect men can give completely to others, since before they are needed they can be supplied in many ways by divine providence; and we are admonished in the Scriptures to have confidence that they will."[71] Similarly, to an objection that it is un-

---

69. *ST* III 40.3 ad 2; cf. *CI*, chap. 6, ad 14, § 6, 850-65.

70. "[N]on sibi unusquisque totum eripiat." *CI*, chap. 6, § 1, 62-63.

71. "[A]lias non debeo mihi totum eripere, ut scilicet nudus remaneam vel absque cibo et potu tempore comestionis, et de his loquitur Glosa. Quaedam autem sunt temporalia quae reservantur ad providendum necessitati corporis in futurum, sicut pecunia, possessiones et huiusmodi; et ista possunt a perfectis viris totaliter aliis dari, quia interim antequam necessitas immineat potest multipliciter per divinam providentiam subveniri, de qua fiduciam habere monemur in Scripturis." *CI*, chap. 6, ad 7, § 6, 673-83. The way Thomas uses the term "possessions" here is a good example of its symbolic function. The refusal of possessions does not mean that the mendicants have nothing to eat. Rather, "possessions" signify security, and that is what the mendicants reject. They refuse to secure themselves, not only in the sense that whatever they need they must depend on others to provide, but also in the sense that they do not convert the alms they receive into "possessions" by stockpiling them. The distinction works well to evoke mendicant vulnerability, but attempting to extend it so that in every case presently needed goods do not count as "possessions" runs counter to Thomas's intention. Of course, trying to extend it this way results in little sense,

lawful to expose oneself to starvation, Thomas replies, "He who leaves all things for Christ does not expose himself to starvation, because God will never abandon him to dying by hunger."[72] Thomas continues by suggesting how this confidence in God's providence repositions prudential foresight. A prudence patterned on Aristotelian virtues would oppose greed. What Aristotle calls *pleonexia* is a tendency to grasp too much, where "too much" is measured in terms of what foresight might legitimately hold onto to serve one's sustenance and the operation of virtue.[73] Thomas portrays mendicant dependence as a stronger antidote to the same tendency, which he calls being covetous *(cupidus)*. Thomas does not make natural prudence greedy, but he calls the reader to a more stalwart trust in God, hinting at a danger of covetousness hanging over foresight — if one is unwilling to expose oneself to depend on divine assistance.

In some texts Thomas even seems to see material insufficiency as a sort of goal. Another objection in *CI* appeals to Proverbs 30:8: "Give me neither beggary nor riches, but grant me only the necessities of life, lest perhaps being full (I deny you, or lest I be poor) and compelled by poverty to steal and foreswear the name of my God."[74] The objection identifies a state of sufficiency between poverty and wealth and faults mendicants for embracing a dangerous poverty that falls below sufficiency. Thomas does not reply that the objection fails because mendicants avoid such insufficiency. Rather, Thomas embraces the state of *mendicitas* proposed in Proverbs 30. The objection fails instead because the danger of vice associated with that state attends it only if it is not embraced willingly. The same pursuit of insufficiency is evident in another passage, where Thomas quotes from Chrysostom. To show that actual, and not merely habitual, poverty is required for religious perfection, Thomas praises the poverty of the apos-

---

and for this reason John D. Jones has trouble making sense of it. John D. Jones, "The Concept of Poverty in St. Thomas Aquinas's *Contra Impugnantes Dei Cultum et Religionem*," *The Thomist* 59 (1995): 409-39, here pp. 436-39.

72. "[I]lle qui dimittit omnia propter Christum non se exponit fami quae ipsum interimat, quia numquam a Deo ita deseritur quod fame moriatur." *CI,* chap. 6, ad 12, § 6, 814-17.

73. On *pleonexia* and its misconceptions, see Alasdair MacIntyre, *Whose Justice? Which Rationality?* (Notre Dame, IN: University of Notre Dame Press, 1988), pp. 111-12.

74. "Mendicitatem et divitias ne dederis mihi, tribue tantum victui meo necessaria ne forte satiatus . . . et egestate compulsus furer et periurer nomen Dei mei." *CI,* chap. 6, obj. 6, § 1, 12-15.

tles with Chrysostom's words: "Didn't they live in hunger and thirst and nakedness, and wasn't their glory great and magnificent on account of these things?"[75] Thomas derives the lesson that "actual poverty, which consists in the lack of things, pertains to apostolic perfection."[76]

The reader may wonder what happened to Aquinas's concern that friars get what they need to eat and drink. John D. Jones, in his inquiry into the meaning of poverty in *CI*, finds a tension here.[77] Jones claims that Thomas "gives two different accounts of actual poverty."[78] One account characterizes it as having no more than one's livelihood, and the other sees it as a more serious lack. The first is reflected in Thomas's penchant for referring to 1 Timothy 6:8: "But having food and something to wear, we are content with these."[79] But how does this square with the claim that apostolic poverty involves hunger and nakedness?

Jones concludes that Thomas is not at all clear about the poverty he is defending in *CI*. At times Thomas offers a "below subsistence" account of poverty, although he more often finds poverty compatible with the friars accepting their subsistence. For this and other reasons, Jones finds Thomas's account "unresolved."[80]

However, the tension between poverty as accepting one's sustenance and poverty as lacking it is not a confused muddle or a mystery. Rather, both conditions reflect the receptivity involved in this degree of dependence. Consider Christ. In his humble vulnerability, Christ refused to secure himself by, say, living off savings he had accumulated as a carpenter. On the one hand, this refusal does not mean he would not accept his sustenance when it was offered to him. On the other hand, this refusal reached its culmination in the vulnerable exposure of the cross, where Christ did lack even clothing. The nakedness he finally experienced on the cross was the culmination of his willingness to accept a receptive exposure.[81]

---

75. "Nonne in fame et siti et nuditate degebant, et pro his clari magni et magnifici habebantur." *CI*, chap. 6, § 3, 391-93.

76. "Actualis paupertas quae in penuria rerum consistit ad apostolicam perfectionem pertinet."

77. Jones, "Concept of Poverty."

78. Jones, "Concept of Poverty," p. 423.

79. "Habentes autem alimenta et quibus tegamur, his contenti simus." *CI*, chap. 6, ad 6, § 6, 663-64.

80. Jones, "Concept of Poverty," p. 439.

81. Thomas gives a vivid account of this receptivity in reply to an objection that

Furthermore, the more radical insufficiency of the cross functions as a kind of limit, summoning us to an ever-deeper humble vulnerability. How low one's humble vulnerability sinks depends in part on what one receives. In one sense, one's humility is measured by the extent of one's refusal of security against humiliation and want. Yet, in another sense, if that insecurity is met with rejection rather than support, the result is an even deeper humility. Therefore, the paradigm of Christ's humility is seen most fully on the cross. Christ did not leap onto a cross; yet he led a life of humility and vulnerability that did not secure itself against the cross.[82]

The cross summons Christians to follow Christ, and to imitate the hunger of the apostles, not by rejecting food when hungry but by leading a life of humble vulnerability that does not secure itself against hunger.[83] So mendicants follow the "naked Christ," who nonetheless did not refuse the meals that were set before him nor the clothes offered to him. Thomas refers to Jerome's famous invitation, *Nudum Christum nudus sequere* ("Follow the naked Christ naked"), but does not imply that Jesus never had clothes.[84] The phrase rather points to Christ's self-abasement and exposure, which come to their culmination in the cross. The summons Christ offers to an ever-deeper humble vulnerability draws its ultimate logic from the cross. The connection between that summons and the cross echoes from another of Jerome's exhortations used by Thomas: "Follow the naked and lonely cross with naked and lonely virtue."[85]

---

preachers who depend on alms must flatter. He asserts that they need not flatter if they are willing to do without. When preaching without flattery among the good, they may yet receive ample sustenance. But when they preach among the wicked and worldly, they sometimes have to suffer. Such swings are no hindrance to their mission, but rather conform them to the example of Christ, who at times had no roof and at other times was entertained by many, and of the apostles, who knew how to abound and how to suffer lack. *CI*, chap. 7, § 12, ad 1.

82. Thomas affirms that Christ's death was voluntary, but only in the sense that he did not prevent it. *ST* III 47.1.

83. The receptive character of this lowliness indicates that the cross does not summon Christians toward a self-immolation indicating contempt for God's creation. See the distinction between natural and unnatural asceticism made by Kallistos Ware, "The Way of the Ascetics: Negative or Affirmative," in *Asceticism*, ed. Vincent L. Wimbush and Richard Valantasis (New York: Oxford University Press, 1995), pp. 3-15.

84. *ST* II-II 186.3 ad 3; cf. *CI*, chap. 6, § 3, 344-45.

85. "Nudam solamque crucem virtute nuda sequaris et sola." *CI*, chap. 6, § 3, 297-98.

CHAPTER 5

Christ's Poverty
and the Completion of Nature

The argument of this book began on largely Aristotelian ground. It has now moved well out of Aristotle's territory, through the deeper lowliness of Christian ontological poverty and on toward the calling to ever-deeper humble vulnerability found in the cross of the poor Christ. I have sought to emphasize the similarities in order to challenge the proprietary imagination to consider the receptive, deferent dependence Aristotle and Thomas both defend, and in order to suggest how the same challenge is posed and deepened by the self-abandoning charity of the poor Christ. I hope the reader can begin to imagine the situation of human agency in such a way that the summons to "become poor" might herald its fulfillment.

If we can do that, we can see how the Aristotelian aspects of Thomas's economic thought do not set up an appreciation of nature that supplements or balances the calling of the poor Christ. Rather, they display how all human action involving wealth is directed toward its fulfillment in Christ, how the light of the poor Christ gives nature its utmost intelligibility. We understand our proper deference and trusting dependence best in view of our movement toward the deeper deference and more complete dependence of the poor Christ.

When we imagine ourselves as primordial proprietors, "becoming poor" portends the destruction of our nature. But even if we can imagine leaving the throne of proprietorship for something like the lowliness of Aristotelian receptive deference, wouldn't our descent have to stop somewhere? It may seem that the abased exposure of the poor Christ finally does upend nature, even the deferent accounting of what is natural in Aristotle. We have seen how Thomas invokes the instrumentality of poverty to draw a line against the unsustainable rigors advocated by some of the spiritual Franciscans. But Aristotle would complain that the line is misplaced. He would not recognize the fulfillment of human action involving external goods in the poverty of Christ. Indeed, from Aristotle's perspective, the mendicants, by pursuing the rags of beggary and the pangs of dependence, go beyond deference and acknowledged dependence toward a self-abnegation and self-destruction that means, finally, not the fulfillment of nature but its self-immolation.

In this chapter I take up in more detail the differences between Aristotle and Thomas in order to show why Aristotle would resist Thomas's degree of receptivity and how Thomas's theological convictions open up the possibility that a deeper receptivity could finally be supremely natural. The chapter proceeds in two parts. First, I suggest that Aristotle cannot countenance the degree of lowliness and vulnerability Thomas champions because of his greater aversion to suffering and his concern for human nobility. Second, I explore some of the ways in which, for Thomas, the integrity of nature is upheld even in the midst of the threat of suffering and the undermining of Aristotelian nobility. In short, the pattern of Christ finally upholds the integrity of the natural in Thomas's economic ethics: it defers to the God who intends to sustain our bodies and to raise up the poor, and even when our bodies are threatened, this pattern confirms the integrity of our nature by directing it to its eschatological fulfillment and by joining it to the Christian community's participation in Christ's sufferings, bringing it to participate in the self-surrendering love of the Trinity that is the pattern of all nature.

Aristotle and the Limits of Receptivity

Aristotle sets more stringent limits on how far receptivity should extend than does Thomas. To understand this difference, we have to grasp something more of the relationships among suffering, dependence, and security in both thinkers.

In this world of contingency, dependence means vulnerability: it means risk of suffering. In economic terms, the more dire one's lack of external goods, the more vulnerably dependent one is. And such a state of vulnerable dependence is construed in both Aristotle's and Thomas's societies as a sort of ignobility. This lowly dependence is ameliorated when one acquires external goods. However vulnerable a mendicant friar is, for example, when he receives alms, his power to secure himself against suffering is that far enhanced — at least for the present. At another point on the scale from risk to security is the possession of great wealth, a relative buffer against risk. The scale from vulnerability to security largely corresponds to the scale from poverty to wealth. Of course, wealth does not mean perfect insulation from risk. Aristotle points out that trying to protect excessive wealth carries its own risks; and no one, no matter how wealthy, is above the sometimes wild swings of fortune. For this reason, true stability is found not in wealth but in virtue. The virtuous person knows that the goods of the soul are superior to external goods, and hence is able to weather the storms of fortune with more constancy. But despite the desirability of virtue over wealth, the virtuous person will seek the relative security against risk that moderate wealth brings. There is a minimum threshold of security, of the insulation humans appropriately seek from the risk of suffering. Thomas acknowledges a similar threshold: we should not be so enamored of vulnerability that we embrace starvation or nakedness.

But Aristotle sets that minimum threshold of security markedly higher than Thomas does. His reason is twofold. First, Aristotle cannot tolerate the courting of suffering that Thomas countenances, because he cannot share Thomas's hope that such potential suffering could become part of the path to blessedness rather than the destruction of that path. Second, Aristotle understands the pursuit of the good life as in part a pursuit of the nobility appropriate to human nature. This nobility involves being more a principle of good action than a recipient of it. In order for our giving to outweigh our receiving in this way (or at least to achieve the illusion that it does), we must attain a social position of a certain degree of dignity and security. Beggary and abject dependence constitute an ignobility Aristotle could hardly comprehend.

Wealth and the Threat of Suffering

According to Aristotle, despite the general benevolence of the natural order that circumscribes us and intends our flourishing, many things can happen that threaten our flourishing, sometimes due to the vicissitudes of the natural order itself. There is, after all, a degree of chance in nature's workings.[1] Furthermore, what holds for the most part in nature sometimes goes otherwise, and nature at times makes mistakes.[2] Consider as well that our circumstances depend somewhat on the actions of many other human agents, and it will be evident why "fortunes revolve many times in one person's lifetime."[3]

Because of these risks and vulnerabilities, it is perfectly fitting for human beings to strive for some sort of stability amid the raging flux of contingency. In such a risky world, Aristotle affirms that "the good is a man's own possession which cannot easily be taken away from him."[4] This view he supposes he shares with most humans, who believe "that happiness has permanence and is not amenable to changes under any circumstances."[5] Understandably, one place people look for such stability is to the security that wealth provides against the risk of suffering.

Aristotle says that some degree of such security is required for the good life: "For it is impossible or at least not easy to perform noble actions if one lacks the wherewithal. . . . And there are some external goods the absence of which spoils supreme happiness."[6] That is why some have reckoned wealth as at least a crucial element in happiness. Moreover, even the noblest activity Aristotle names, contemplation, however worthy in itself, depends on other things, including external goods. After all, "our nature is not sufficient for engaging in study: our body must be healthy and we must have food and generally be cared for."[7]

Yet, while some temporal security is necessary, wealth does not provide the stability Aristotle seeks. For even the wealthy are subject to the winds of fortune that affect us all. But stability can be found in virtue. Virtuous activity can be sustained through drastic reversals in a person's temporal circumstances. Indeed, such changes themselves do not determine whether we are doing well or poorly, since fortune is merely an accessory to human life.[8] But the virtuous person is able to bear such vicissitudes in the

---

1. Jonathan Barnes, *Aristotle* (Oxford: Oxford University Press, 1982), p. 57.

2. Abraham Edel, *Aristotle and his Philosophy,* with new intro. (New Brunswick, NJ: Transaction Publishers, 1996), p. 63.

3. Aristotle, *NE,* I.10, 1100b3-4.

4. Aristotle, *NE,* I.5, 1095b26-27.

5. Aristotle, *NE,* I.10, 1100b1-3.

6. Aristotle, *NE,* I.8, 1099a32-1099b3.

7. Aristotle, *NE,* X.8, 1178b34-35.

8. Aristotle, *NE,* I.10, 1100b7-10.

right way and hence preserve her virtue. That is why "no function of man possesses as much stability as do activities in conformity with virtue."[9]

Not only does virtue provide the stability of character and the constancy of "faring well" that wealth cannot, but also to a certain degree it minimizes the need for wealth. The virtuous person realizes that he must subordinate his need for external goods to the nobler goods of the soul. Because he is self-controlled and moderate, he can do well with less than one might think, "for self-sufficiency and moral action do not consist in an excess of possessions."[10] Indeed, "private individuals evidently do not act less honorably but even more honorably than powerful rulers. It is enough to have moderate means at one's disposal, for the life of a man whose activity is guided by virtue will be happy."[11] In addition, for the sake of virtue it is not necessary to be preoccupied with securing oneself against ill fortune. Hence, Aristotle notes that certain sorts of risks are proper to the magnanimous man.[12] And he scorns those who excuse their miserliness by saying that they must keep what they have lest need compel them to do something base.[13]

Although Aristotle's virtuous man recognizes the limited importance of wealth, he still appropriately seeks to remain above a certain respectable threshold of security. First, the "moderate means" that virtue requires remains understood within a general context of privilege. Aristotle does not speak of the "moderate means" of the lower classes; the virtue he discusses is for the high-minded man who will not slavishly adjust his life

---

9. Aristotle, *NE*, I.10, 1100b12-13. Aristotle's search for stability amid contingency does not reflect a uniformly negative evaluation of vulnerability. Virtues in Aristotle's account can be described as the powers of acting well that enable us, in the midst of our necessary dependence and receptivity, to navigate the churning seas of fortune with the greatest degree of constancy and success. Thus the virtues equip us for living in a risky world; they do not seek to eliminate the risk. On the functional character of an Aristotelian account of virtue, see John Bowlin's helpful treatment of Aquinas's ethics: John Bowlin, *Contingency and Fortune in Aquinas's Ethics* (Cambridge, UK: Cambridge University Press, 1999). Indeed, as Martha Nussbaum has argued, the virtuous life not only suffers its dependence on receiving external goods, but also creates new vulnerable dependences through the cultivation of friendship. Martha Craven Nussbaum, *The Fragility of Goodness* (Cambridge, UK: Cambridge University Press, 1986).

10. Aristotle, *NE*, X.8, 1179a1-3.

11. Aristotle, *NE*, 1179a6-9.

12. Aristotle, *NE*, IV.3, 1124b7-9.

13. Aristotle, *NE*, IV.1, 1121b20-28.

to others (besides friends). People from the lower classes, on the contrary, are generally flatterers and therefore slavish.[14] Further, as we have seen, Aristotle points out that certain acts of virtue are inhibited in the absence of a certain amount of wealth. Although the importance of wealth is moderate, the threshold of security that Aristotle's virtuous man seeks to transcend is above anything that could be called "poverty." Aristotle rarely discusses poverty, but an instructive passage comes in his treatment of generosity. Aristotle tells of the vices opposed to generosity, namely stinginess and extravagance. He mentions that extravagance is the easier to correct, for the extravagant person easily exhausts his property and thereby learns a lesson. Therefore, "age and poverty easily cure him, and he can attain the median state."[15]

What explains Aristotle's higher threshold of security is that, though virtue enables us to bear misfortune nobly, there are some depths of suffering that destroy our chances for happiness. Aristotle says: "[F]requent reverses can crush and mar supreme happiness in that they inflict pain and thwart many activities."[16] That is why good fortune is required for true happiness. Even goodness is not by itself enough, for a person could have that while suffering the greatest misfortunes. "But those who assert that a man is happy even on the rack and even when great misfortunes befall him, provided that he is good, are talking nonsense, whether they know it or not."[17] If happiness can be destroyed in these ways, it is appropriate for the virtuous person to set a reasonable buffer of security against the likelihood of falling into suffering. Thomas can set the threshold lower because, for him, no suffering is irredeemable. Indeed, the way of redemption, the way blazed by Christ, the pioneer of the faith, is a way of vulnerability that is particularly devoid of the drive for security against suffering. On the other hand, for Aristotle such degrees of risk are to be avoided, because for him "there are a limited number of human circumstances or narrative sequences about which it makes sense for us to say that good can be found in them, or that the person who passes through them can reasonably be called happy."[18] Aristotle's aversion to suffering is one reason for us to hold our receptivity within bounds.

14. Aristotle, *NE*, IV.3, 1124b32-1125a3.
15. Aristotle, *NE*, IV.1, 1121a16-21.
16. Aristotle, *NE*, I.10, 1100b28-30.
17. Aristotle, *NE*, VII.13, 1153b19-21.
18. Stanley Hauerwas and Charles Pinches, *Christians Among the Virtues: Theological*

Wealth and Human Nobility

Avoiding suffering is important to Aristotle, but maintaining nobility is perhaps even more important. Even in the deepest suffering, something is salvaged if one bears it nobly. "Nobility shines through even in such circumstances, when a man bears many great misfortunes with good grace not because he is insensitive to pain but because he is noble and high-minded."[19] Aristotle's concern for what is *kalos* (noble) pervades the *Nichomachean Ethics.* Consider what it means to bear suffering nobly, which Aristotle describes in his discussion of friendship. One bears suffering best, he says, by striving to protect his friends from sharing in it. While nobility suggests that we eagerly invite our friends to share in our good fortunes, we should "be reluctant to ask our friend to share our misfortunes, since one should let others participate as little as possible in what is evil."[20] Interestingly, Aristotle's point is not that sufferers should be left in isolation. Rather, when considering the situation from the friend's perspective, Aristotle suggests that he should visit the unfortunate friend uninvited. And he concludes the chapter this way: "So we see that the presence of friends is desirable in all circumstances."[21]

It is noble for the suffering friend to keep his suffering to himself, and it is noble for the sympathetic friend to take the initiative and visit without being asked. The common factor, I think, is that nobility has to do with giving rather than receiving. The suffering friend has nothing to give but pain, and he remains noble by not seeking to receive when he cannot give. The other friend can give his presence, and is nobler for doing so on his own initiative, without needing to receive a summons to do a good turn.

Aristotle frequently praises action over reception. The virtuous man for Aristotle is a man of independent action, for "excellence consists in doing good, rather than in having good done to one."[22] Because the noble

---

Conversations with Ancient and Modern Ethics (Notre Dame, IN: University of Notre Dame Press, 1997), p. 48. Aquinas shows his more hopeful perspective on suffering also by considering endurance to be the greater part of courage. So for him, the primary model of courage is not the soldier but the martyr (*Christians Among the Virtues,* chap. 8).

19. Aristotle, *NE,* I.10, 1100b30-33.

20. Aristotle, *NE,* IX.11, 1171b16-18.

21. Aristotle, *NE,* 1171b27-28.

22. Aristotle, *NE,* IV.1, 1120a12-13.

person endeavors for his giving to exceed his receiving, even the suffering man refuses to ask for favors his giving could not outweigh. Of course, our necessarily dependent condition in some ways challenges the possibility of giving more than we receive. But the virtuous man prefers to think of himself as a giver; thus he either seeks to forget his receiving, or the tales of his receiving only provide a perpetual goading to further beneficence: "The high-minded also seem to remember the good turns they have done, but not those they have received. For the recipient is inferior to the benefactor, whereas a high-minded man wishes to be superior. They listen with pleasure to what good they have done, but with displeasure to what good they have received."[23]

Nobility has to do with being an initiating, active principle for good; it involves ensuring that one's freedom and initiative overshadow one's receptivity and dependence. And it requires one to be a certain degree along on the scale from vulnerability to security: it requires one to maintain a social position that reflects and enables that nobility and that dignity.[24]

In contrast, for Thomas, the most virtuous human action is found not in human initiative but in action in which the agent has first suffered the initiative of God. Therefore, a social position conducive to noble independence (or at least the illusion of independence) is not a requirement for the highest virtue.[25] Rather, the life Thomas most praises is one that seeks out lowliness. On the other hand, Aristotle's concern for nobility and his aversion to suffering come together to demand a higher threshold of security.[26]

---

23. Aristotle, *NE,* IV.3, 1124b12-15.

24. This point is corroborated in an interesting essay on generosity by T. H. Irwin. Irwin argues that, though Aristotle appeals to the exercise of the virtue of generosity as a reason for the institution of property, he is not concerned with whether generous use of property provides for human need better than communal ownership. Rather, the exercise of generosity is worthwhile on its own, exactly because it manifests human freedom and initiative. Human nobility seems to be the fundamental concern, not human interdependence. T. H. Irwin, "Generosity and Property in Aristotle's *Politics,*" *Social Philosophy and Policy* 4 (1987): 37-54.

25. Alasdair MacIntyre applauds Thomas in this respect, and suggests that Aristotle's position reflects "an illusion of self-sufficiency, an illusion . . . that is all too characteristic of the rich and powerful in many times and places." Alasdair MacIntyre, *Dependent Rational Animals: Why Human Beings Need the Virtues* (Chicago: Open Court, 1999), p. 127.

26. Some light is shed on Aristotle's aversion to suffering and his concern for human nobility by the suggestion that all ancient Greek accounts of virtue depend on the theme of

The Pattern of Christ as the Completion of Nature

Thomas's theological convictions show why, for him, a greater risk of suffering and a disregard for pursuing Aristotelian nobility do not portend the destruction of nature. The God revealed in the poor Christ gives nature hope in the midst of suffering and intends for nature to receive its flourishing rather than "nobly" securing it. The humble vulnerability Thomas extols even conduces to such flourishing, he suggests, because such self-surrendering receptivity properly defers to God's providence and so duly trusts that sustenance will be forthcoming. Still, this promise of sustenance is no assurance of ease or of insulation from suffering. Rather, following Christ is likely to lead to hardship and difficulty of just the kind that Aristotle seeks to avoid as antithetical to human flourishing.

However, Thomas claims that holding on to this salutary, self-surrendering receptivity even in the face of suffering is no embrace of self-destruction. Instead, such a practice both directs nature to its eschatological fulfillment and offers a participation in that divine charity that is the pattern and final cause of all nature. The humble and vulnerable charity of the cross is ultimately an invitation to Trinitarian communion. By participating in such charity, the lowly suffering of the voluntary poor outshines the nobility Aristotle sought to protect. It is because the longing for such communion with God is at the heart of nature that Thomas can see this humble and vulnerable charity as the truth of our nature toward which Aristotle groped inchoately. Rather than undermining the integrity of nature, the pattern of Christ's poverty brings nature to its completion.

The instrumentality of poverty plays an important role here, and it means a couple of things. First, poverty is not to be equated with perfection; it is only an instrument. Contrary to the tendencies Thomas saw in some of his contemporaries, he perceived that poverty is not good in itself. Insufficiency is not what God finally intends for us. Nature's provision is

---

mastery. John Milbank has argued that Greek virtue derives its meaning from its relationship to the heroic struggle to secure the city. Although the specifically martial contexts fade in the philosophers as opposed to the epic poets, areteic excellence remains a matter of conquering, whether of city over city, reason over appetite, or master over slave. Though Milbank makes perhaps more of Aristotle's doctrine of the mean than is fair to Aristotle, his point that Aristotle's virtue is fundamentally about mastery against the backdrop of an assumed conflict seems on target. John Milbank, *Theology and Social Theory: Beyond Secular Reason* (Oxford: Blackwell, 1990), pp. 332-36.

meant to reach those for whom God intends it, that is, those who need it, and the call to become poor is not aimed at the destitution of either the voluntary poor or the involuntary poor. Second, the instrumentality of poverty means that although poverty is not perfection, it does point the way. Though poverty is not good in itself, evangelical poverty helps to specify the direction of the charity toward which the pattern of the cross summons.

Poverty Is Not Good in Itself

God's intentions for creation are not lack, but sustenance directed to flourishing, not death, but life. In *Summa contra Gentiles*, Thomas invokes an Aristotelian claim that marks Thomas's thought throughout his life. He says that whereas virtue is good in itself, external things "are good to the extent that they contribute to virtue, but not in themselves."[27] The statement applies equally to the abundance or the want of external things, to riches or to poverty. Therefore, some do well to have riches, for they use them in the practice of virtue, while others are thrown off the path of virtue by wealth, and in that case riches can be considered as evils. Similarly, insofar as poverty conduces to virtue, it is good, while it is bad if and when it frustrates virtue. Both riches and poverty are considered instruments or means in this way. However, neither riches nor poverty is completely indifferent, that is, an unpredisposed instrument that can be used well or badly no matter what its degree. Too great a poverty cannot be used well; in fact, riches rather than poverty are required up to a point. Without some riches, there could be no virtue, for some external things are needed to support the body and to give assistance to others. Poverty that keeps us from helping others may yet not be an evil if the lack of temporal help is compensated for by some greater good, such as a freer devotion to divine matters. "But the good of supporting oneself is so necessary that it can be compensated for by no other good, since no man should take away from himself the support of life, under the pretext of obtaining another good."[28]

This concern for sustenance applies to both voluntary and involun-

---

27. *ScG* III, 133.

28. *ScG* III, 133, cited from the translation of Book III by Vernon J. Bourke, 2 vols. (Notre Dame, IN: University of Notre Dame Press, 1975), vol. 2, p. 178.

tary poor. In the case of voluntary poor, it suggests that their self-divestment should attend to what they can duly hope in the Lord to receive from others. And friars should accept the necessities of daily living, as well as keeping what is required for their specific religious apostolate.

In the case of involuntary poor, Thomas's concern may not be so apparent. Van den Eijnden rightly notes that Thomas does not make much of evangelical poverty as a judgment on the injustices suffered by the involuntary poor.[29] Thomas focuses much more on how evangelical poverty helps direct one's attention away from external things and toward spiritual things. Furthermore, he sometimes seems to suggest that the involuntary poor are likewise spiritually better off for being poor and that they should be satisfied with what they have.

In *Contra Doctrinam Retrahentium et Religionem*, Thomas advocates poverty in a way that seems to commend involuntary as well as voluntary poverty. Thomas urges from Scripture and tradition that material possessions can hinder a proper response to the gospel. He appeals to the parable of the supper, in which those who were called are too busy to attend and finally the host summons the poor and feeble. Thomas quotes Ambrose's comment on this text: "[H]e who lacks the enticement of sin offends more rarely, and he is more quickly converted to God who does not have worldly delights."[30] He concludes that "not having possessions and any riches whatsoever inclines more toward evangelical perfection."[31] It could appear that spiritual benefit renders involuntary poverty a blessing.

Furthermore, at times Thomas suggests that if involuntary poverty leads to temptation rather than blessing, the trouble is in the willingness of the poor to accept their poverty. In the *ST*, Thomas addresses an objection that had long been leveled against the mendicants: by giving away all, do

---

29. Jan van den Eijnden, O.F.M., *Poverty on the Way to God: Thomas Aquinas on Evangelical Poverty* (Leuven: Peeters, 1994), p. 30. Samuel Fleischacker suggests that adequate provision of material goods to the needy was not generally seen as a matter of distributive justice until the Enlightenment. Nevertheless, many ancient writers, including Aquinas, did see some sort of injustice in the excessively wealthy failing to succor the poor. Samuel Fleischacker, *A Short History of Distributive Justice,* new ed. (Cambridge, MA: Harvard University Press, 2005).

30. "[R]arius delinquit cui deest illecebra peccandi, et citius ad Deum convertitur qui non habet in mundo unde delectetur." *CR,* chap. 15, 386-89.

31. "[P]ossessiones et quascumque divitias omnino non habere, magis ad evangelicam perfectionem pertineat." *CR,* chap. 15, 389-91.

they not expose themselves to the dangers and temptations that the book of Proverbs suggests accompany the state of poverty? Thomas replies that the corporal dangers are negated by trust in divine providence, and that the spiritual dangers follow from poverty only when it is involuntary, "because those who are unwillingly poor, through the desire of money-getting, fall into many sins."[32] The only trouble with involuntary poverty in this view is that the poor greedily seek to get more. In *CI*, to the objection that "poverty diminishes friendship," Thomas replies that the saying refers to involuntary poverty, since it necessarily involves covetousness, which is opposed to friendship.[33] The aphorism does not apply to those who are satisfied with a little. It seems that the involuntary poor should remedy their situation by altering the "involuntary" character of their poverty.

But to use Thomas's arguments to justify the poverty of those who have not chosen poverty is an abuse of his texts. Each of the texts cited above is part of an argument to defend voluntary poverty against those who claim it is unlawful. Their intent does not go beyond defending voluntary poverty. Thomas equates the poverty in the Proverbs text with a covetous involuntary poverty in order to show its inapplicability to the case of the voluntary poor, not to suggest that all the involuntary poor sin if they have any desire for better sustenance. To be assured of this point, one need only consider that the involuntary poor may be so destitute that their potential for virtuous action is crippled. To desire what is necessary for virtue is no sin.

It may seem that the theological virtues qualify the requirement that life be sustained for the exercise of virtue, since they direct us to an end beyond this life. But it is this life that affords the crucial opportunity for advancing toward that end. Thus our very ordering even to a supernatural end requires that life be sustained.

Thomas's comments about the virtues of almsgiving and liberality show the importance of channeling goods to those in need, for "one man cannot overabound in external riches, without another man lacking them."[34] Thomas's sensibilities on these issues are formed by Scripture. In Deuteronomy 15:4, the Lord commands that there should be no poor man nor beggar among the people. In *CI*, Thomas considers this text as a po-

---

32. *ST* II-II 186.3 ad 2.
33. *CI*, chap. 6, ad 5.
34. *ST* II-II 118.1 ad 2.

tential objection against voluntary mendicancy. He points out in reply that the text forbids not voluntary poverty, but that other men abandon someone to fall into such a state that he must beg out of necessity.[35] Further, the very command to love our neighbor as ourselves aligns us against involuntary poverty. For all seek to procure good things for themselves and to keep adversity away. Thus, if we truly love others as ourselves, we will seek to be fruitful and effective in procuring benefits for them.[36] Thomas's defense of voluntary poverty cannot be read as a justification of involuntary poverty except by doing violence to Thomas's texts. Poverty is good in itself for neither voluntary nor involuntary poor.

Evangelical Poverty and God's Providential Care

Poverty cannot be more than an instrument of perfection, because poverty is not the end toward which we are directed. And yet, evangelical poverty remains an instrument and not something less, because the pattern of Christ it instantiates does mark out the character of the end. It even conduces to our sustenance, since it sets us in a stance of dependent trust that God is faithful to answer.

The reality of God's providence was a topic that exercised Thomas to a significant degree, especially while he was writing the *ScG* and his profound meditation on the problem of providence in light of the suffering of the just in his commentary on Job.[37] But it was not only Averroistic denials of providence or age-old questions of divine justice that drove Thomas's concern about this question; it was also the importance of divine providence for justifying the insecurity of the mendicants.

Providence most broadly considered involves God's knowledge and

---

35. "[N]on ita derelinquatur ab aliis ut in talem statum incidat in quo eum oporteat ex necessitate mendicare." *CI*, chap. 7, § 11, ad 1, 1252-54.

36. *DP*, chap. 14.

37. See the English translation in *The Literal Exposition on Job: A Scriptural Commentary Concerning Providence,* trans. Anthony Damico (Atlanta: Scholars Press, 1989). For the setting of these reflections and their connection with *ScG,* see Jean-Pierre Torrell, O.P., *Saint Thomas Aquinas,* vol. 1, *The Person and His Work,* trans. Robert Royal (Washington, DC: The Catholic University of America Press, 1996), pp. 101-16, 120-21. Cf. Marie-Dominique Chenu, O.P., *Toward Understanding St. Thomas,* trans. A. M. Landry, O.P., and D. Hughes, O.P. (Chicago: Henry Regnery, 1964), p. 246.

execution of the ordering of things to their end.[38] It is true that the ultimate end for human beings does not consist in material things, but in order for them to progress toward their true end, they must be sustained in existence, for which they do require material goods. God's provision for creatures' sustenance is parallel to God's initial gift of existence. In the *ST,* Thomas says that it is only fitting for the supreme goodness, having produced things, also to bring them to their end.[39] Or, as he puts it in the *ScG,* "on the things on which He has lavished being He must also lavish preservation and guide them toward perfection in their ultimate end."[40]

God can be counted on to provide sustenance. Indeed, when dependence on providence takes on the special meaning it has for the mendicants, their trust in it can become a part of their hope for beatitude. The theological virtue of hope expects to be brought to beatitude by God's help, and the object of that hope can be both the end hoped for and the means of attaining it.[41] Mendicants hope to reach the goal of union with God, and part of the means they hope for from God is their material sustenance: "So the hope of the voluntary poor for God helping in the solicitudes of daily life is a kind of expectation of being united with God in arriving at the final end, for which unification man needs to be preserved in his goodness in spite of the necessities of life caused by voluntary Poverty."[42] Furthermore, the counsels themselves are part of the means by which God brings them to their end. Those who have heeded God's advice and thus been brought so far through God's efforts to bring them to their final end can expect God to be faithful in providing the sustenance required. In this way the very trusting vulnerability of evangelical poverty conduces to sustenance. Voluntary poverty, far from tending toward self-destruction, especially fits the order of nature's sustenance by its receptive trust in divine providence.

This point sheds a unique light on the so-called "Thomist axiom": "Grace does not destroy nature, but perfects it."[43] A common understand-

---

38. *ST* I 22.1.

39. *ST* I 103.1.

40. *ScG* III, 94. See the Bourke translation, vol. 2, p. 53; cf. *Lectura super Matthaeum,* chap. 6.

41. *ST* II-II 17.1-2.

42. Van den Eijnden, *Poverty on the Way to God,* p. 178.

43. Of the vast literature on this axiom, some texts that have stood the test of time include J. B. Beumer, "Gratia supponit naturam: Zur Geschichte eines theologischen Prinzips,"

ing of this axiom would suggest that the practices proposed in the state of grace do not challenge what we might have known apart from *sacra doctrina*. But Thomas proposes a quite different interpretation with regard to this issue of trusting for our sustenance. In *CI*, one objection to mendicancy claims that it is unreasonable and thus contrary to Romans 12:1. Thomas replies with perhaps his first appeal to this "axiom": "Grace is the perfection of nature, whence nothing that pertains to grace destroys nature."[44] But here he puts the supposed "Thomist axiom" to a most revealing use. Thomas gives two reasons why mendicancy does not destroy nature. First, things such as food and sleep, which are immediately required to preserve nature, must not be completely abandoned. Sustenance is necessary; cruciformity is not self-destruction. This is not too surprising, but note how modest the point is. Thomas does not say that mendicancy is an extra discipline on top of a lifestyle of sufficiency, but only that the friars must not starve themselves. Want, neediness, and exposure are not vicious and against reason; but depriving oneself "beyond what nature can sustain" is so.[45]

The second reason confounds expectations and also exegetes the first. Nature can be preserved, Thomas says, without the *dominium* of earthly possessions if we hope that God will help us in many ways. For this reason, no matter how much one gives up, it will not be superfluous if it is done for God's sake.[46] The need to avoid starving does not mean mendi-

---

Gregorianum 20 (1939): 381-406, 535-52; B. Stoeckle, *"Gratia supponit naturam": Geschichte und Analyse eines theologischen Axioms* (Rome, 1962); Bernard Quelquejeu, "Naturalia manent integra," *Revue des Sciences Philosophiques et Théologiques* 94 (1965): 640-55. See also Servais Pinckaers, O.P., *The Pinckaers Reader: Renewing Thomistic Moral Theology*, ed. John Berkman and Craig Steven Titus (Washington, DC: The Catholic University of America Press, 2005), pp. 366-67.

44. "[G]ratia est perfectio naturae, unde nihil quod ad gratiam attinet naturam interimit." *CI*, chap. 6, ad 10, § 6, 755-57. Fergus Kerr suggests that the first instance is in the commentary on Boethius's *De Trinitate*, dated to 1257-58. Fergus Kerr, O.P., *After Aquinas: Versions of Thomism* (Oxford: Blackwell, 2002), p. 138. *CI* dates from 1256.

45. "[S]i in istis aliquid sibi subtrahat ultra id quod natura sustinere potest, rationis modum excedit et vitiosus est." *CI*, chap. 6, ad 10, § 6, 761-63.

46. "[P]otest enim sine dominio possessionum terrenarum natura conservari cum spe divini auxilii multis modis, unde quantumcumque ei subtrahatur non erit superfluum si propter Deum fiat." *CI*, chap. 6, ad 10, § 6, 777-81. Thomas's use of *dominium* here is slightly different from *ST* II-II 66. This is another example of a changing vocabulary in light of changing audiences.

cants must have a reasonably stable and secure means of livelihood, but that they must trust that the God who called them to poverty will not abandon them to destruction. Thomas uses the "grace does not destroy nature" axiom not to calibrate the calling of grace to the prior demands of nature, but to affirm that the God who proposes the evangelical counsels is trustworthy to keep them from destroying those who follow them, though the risks may seem inordinate.

If one shares Thomas's theological convictions, one can see, as Aristotle could not, that the self-surrendering receptivity of mendicant poverty is not opposed to our sustenance. Rather, such receptivity draws human action involving external goods not to its demise but to the culmination of its dependence on the God who wills our sustenance. In Aristotle's economic thought, Thomas recognized a glimpse of the proper deference and receptivity that fits us to nature's circuit of nourishment. But Thomas's account of mendicant poverty suggests that the receptivity to which we are called is much deeper than that countenanced by Aristotle. Aristotle's virtuous man is deferent enough to keep his *chrematistike* ordered toward use values, but he is loath to accept the inferior position of a recipient or to risk too much suffering. From Thomas's perspective, that noble deference perhaps still betrays a hint of presumption standing in the way of God's provision reaching those for whom it is intended. On the other hand, the exposure to which the pattern of the cross summons trains us to acknowledge the true depth of our dependence. By fostering trust in God, it guards us from a presumptive blindness unable to acknowledge the debt of gratitude we owe according to nature.[47] Far from warping or corroding nature, the poverty of Christ most fully rejects the presumption that truly warps and fractures nature.

Evangelical Poverty and the Completion of Nature

The call of the poverty of Christ invites us to accept a risky receptivity that fits us to the truth about the natural order. But accepting such risk evokes our fear of suffering, a fear that is quite natural. In this world corrupted by sin, God's providence is no guarantee of insulation from suffering. Embodying the receptivity of the cross can leave one, if not bereft of suste-

47. *ST* II-II 106.3; 107.2.

nance, at least having to endure degradation, and in some cases the voluntarily poor may even join the apostles in suffering hunger.

Mendicant poverty particularly seems to court such suffering. Thomas does not hide the fact that such difficulties, as well as the fastings and watchings and so forth, make mendicancy a hard life. In *CR*, Thomas considers the objection that young men should not be led to a vow of religion, since the harshness of the life is likely to dispose them to unfaithfulness. Thomas replies that such young men are not deceived, for in mendicant recruiting the "rather weighty burdens of religion" (*graviora religionis onera*) and its "severities" (*asperitates*) are not hidden.[48]

Finding confidence to keep trusting in God and heeding the summons of the cross amid such hardship depends, for Thomas, on the fortitude that comes with the theological virtue of hope, which moderates our legitimate fear. In such confidence, we can avoid retreating toward a presumptive protection from the dependence of giving and receiving. Thomas's theological convictions underwrite this confidence in at least two ways. First, the same cross that teaches us to trust so radically in God's providence teaches that no degree of poverty, suffering, or even death can keep God from faithfully leading nature to its eschatological perfection. Second, bearing such suffering becomes an expression of the Christian community's participation in the suffering of Christ, conforming us even now to the very exemplar of nature, the bottomless charity of God's own life.

Accepting the sufferings that mendicancy seems to court is not against nature, first of all, because the divine drama of redemption swallows up such sufferings and draws them into the glory of resurrection. Thus, in addition to contending that mendicant recruiting is truthful, Thomas adds an even better reason why such recruiting is not dangerous to young men's faith: because, as Augustine says, despite the hardships, the Holy Spirit "in the abundance of the delights of God and in the hope of future beatitude wipes away all present harshness."[49]

In the *ST*, Thomas, in his treatment of Christ's Transfiguration, explores the relationship between Christian suffering *in via* and victory *in patria*. It was important that the Transfiguration, a kind of anticipatory revelation of the glorious end, follow quickly on Jesus' teaching that the

---

48. *CR*, chap. 13, 137-40.

49. "[I]n affluentia deliciarum Dei, in spe futurae beatitudinis omnia praesentia deliniret aspera." *CR*, chap. 13, 153-54.

disciples would participate in his sufferings. For those sufferings are the road to a certain goal, but one cannot travel such a road well without having the goal in sight. This is especially so "when hard and rough is the road, heavy the going, but delightful the end."[50] Christ was thus fittingly transfigured, to show his followers the glory to which he would configure those who "follow the footsteps of His Passion."

This eschatological reserve shows that the call to embrace the sufferings that may attend mendicancy does not simply invert our normal grammar of good and evil. Poverty and destitution do not become good in themselves, any more than the cross acquires a goodness that could be ascribed to it independently of the resurrection. Death remains death and suffering remains suffering. The final goal remains specifiable only in terms of goods nature recognizes as good: life, riches, glory. It is such goods that render the cruciformity of mendicancy intelligible, as when suffering the ignobility of asking for help anticipates eschatological splendor.

In his discussion of the resurrection, Thomas affirms that the negation of nature that might be suggested in the cross does not merely label good what was formerly thought to be evil. One objection he considers suggests that perhaps the resurrection was unnecessary, since the cross had already achieved our salvation. Perhaps, in other words, death could have been Jesus' ultimate, instead of merely penultimate, goal. But in the body of the article, Thomas insists that the work of salvation was not complete without the resurrection. "Just as for [our salvation] did He endure evil things in dying that He might deliver us from evil, so was He glorified in rising again in order to advance us towards good things."[51] Christ indeed showed us the depths of divine charity in enduring evils for our sake, but that display of charity was only complete when those evils were swallowed up in the triumph of the good. So the suffering to which those who follow Christ are subject conduces to the good of our nature because it joins us to Christ, who is the way to the glory for which nature is destined.

The second reason mendicant sufferings are not against nature is because they become part of an ecclesial participation in the sufferings of Christ, uniting the voluntary poor with the self-donating charity of the Trinity that is at the heart of nature.

50. *ST* III 45.1.
51. *ST* III 53.1.

We have explored in earlier chapters the directedness of human life toward charity. Thomas makes clear that this directedness accords with nature. In *ScG*, he says that the perfection of everything is to become like God, to "attain to divine goodness."[52] We become like God by moving toward God, and as intellectual creatures we do that by loving God. Love not only begins in a certain likeness to the thing loved, but also effects a greater likeness.[53] We become like what we love. We become like the self-giving God by giving ourselves in a love that loves God ahead of self.[54]

The love to which nature is ordered, then, involves a sort of self-offering, but the charity revealed in the cross of Christ unveils the true depths of this self-offering. Still, this self-abandoning love is no rejection of nature. For the cross demonstrates the self-donating love among the persons of the Trinity, a love that is the exemplar and goal of nature. Here mistakes about Thomas's theology of the Trinity can get in the way of our seeing how the communion that characterizes the life of the Trinity is woven into the fabric of the world of creatures. It is commonly supposed that Thomas provides a speculative investigation of the inner workings of the Trinity in a way that keeps Trinitarian theology at arm's length from the economy of salvation.[55] As Gilles Emery has shown, however, Thomas does not ground his accounts of God's creating and saving acts in some lonely monad, while reducing the Trinity to the arcane distinctions produced by this monad's self-reflection. On the contrary, Thomas grounds God's creating and saving acts in the procession of the persons of the Word and Holy Spirit.[56] Further, scholarly readings often suggest that Thomas's account downplays the distinction of the persons, so that the intercommunion within the Trinity looks like God's navel-gazing. In that case, it is hard to see what the self-offering love of the cross has to do with the love that is proper to God's own life or with the love for which nature was cre-

52. *ScG* III, 19.

53. *ST* I-II 28.1 ad 2; cf. Paul J. Wadell, C.P., *The Primacy of Love: An Introduction to the Ethics of Thomas Aquinas* (Mahwah, NJ: Paulist Press, 1992), pp. 74-78.

54. This is true even of the "proportionate" love of God that falls short of charity. *ST* I-II 109.3 ad 1; cf. I 60.5.

55. Perhaps most influentially, Karl Rahner, "Remarks on the Dogmatic Treatise 'De Trinitate,'" in *Theological Investigations*, vol. 4, trans. Kevin Smyth (New York: Crossroad, 1982), pp. 79-102.

56. Gilles Emery, O.P., *Trinity in Aquinas* (Ypsilanti, MI: Sapientia Press, 2003), pp. 171-75 and *passim*.

ated. As Rowan Williams has argued, however, the divine life as Thomas understands it is constituted by dynamic and incalculable self-bestowal. The distinction of the triune persons is irreducible here, even if there are no persons *prior to* the relationship or to the shared divine life.[57]

A full-scale explication of Thomas's teaching on the Trinity is beyond the scope of this book. But a reading of Thomas's Trinitarian theology that is attentive to the lessons of recent scholarship can see in the self-offering embodied in the lowly love of the cross a revelation in the world of the charity that characterizes the divine life. Nor is this self-offering an isolated and unrequited service; rather, it is the deepest charity both stemming from and calling forth the deepest communion. Just as, among the divine persons, the "self-emptying" movement does not begin or end in emptiness but in an interpenetrating fullness-in-difference, so the charity exemplified on the cross reflects and invites the perfect communion of the divine life.[58]

We should not be shocked, then, to find that following the cruciform charity of the poor Christ is the path to the completion and perfection of our nature. Christ suffered and died in the nakedness of the cross, granting us an example of the highest charity. If it were opposed to our nature, it could not attract us.[59] The reason this example compels us, the reason we desire to follow it, is because it impresses on us with unprecedented beauty the depths of God's love.[60] Thomas contends that God could have saved us

---

57. Rowan Williams, "What does love know? St Thomas on the Trinity," *New Blackfriars* 82 (2001): 260-72. For another important account of Thomas on the Trinity that emphasizes the "impulsion" and "enjoyment" within the divine life while strongly rejecting any tritheism, see Herbert McCabe, O.P., "Aquinas on the Trinity," *New Blackfriars* 80 (1999): 268-83.

58. Williams, "What does love know?" p. 271.

59. This is the flip side of a point Thomas Hibbs expresses with felicity: "Theology sustains a dialectical engagement of the natural order. If we were to claim that human nature is entirely bereft of the capacity for good, then we would be left with no means, except by way of negative critique, to link up the Christian life with human experience or reason, which would uproot the moral life from a framework within which the passage from one way of life to another might be spoken of intelligibly." Thomas S. Hibbs, *Virtue's Splendor: Wisdom, Prudence, and the Human Good* (New York: Fordham University Press, 2001), p. 185.

60. For a recent discussion of the aesthetic elements in Thomas's reasoning, see Gilbert Narcisse, O.P., *Les Raisons de Dieu: Argument de convenance et Esthétique théologique selon saint Thomas d'Aquin et Hans Urs von Balthasar* (Fribourg: Éditions Universitaires, 1997).

in some other way.[61] But Christ's suffering and death represented the most suitable way, and the first reason of its fittingness is that "man knows thereby how much God loves him, and is thereby stirred to love Him in return, and herein lies the perfection of human salvation."[62]

I can clarify the relationship between Christ's self-offering and the perfection of our nature by comparing what Thomas says about the shape of all love and what in his view the cross teaches us about the shape of God's charity. In the commentary on Romans, Thomas discerns three ways in which the cross teaches us the immensity *(immensitas)* of God's love.[63] The cross shows charity's incredible gratuitousness, the length to which God goes to show it, and its willingness to bear evils out of love. These three aspects of God's charity form a suitable map through the comparison.

First, charity's gratuity is unfathomable. God's love simply in creating is gratuitous. Love in general is based on likeness: like loves like.[64] However, God's love is different from ours in that, while the goodness of things calls forth our love, God's love is the cause of goodness.[65] Whatever goodness we have is already the result of God's unelicited love for us. We might expect God's love to end there, for insofar as we lack goodness, that is, insofar as we are sinners, God does not love, but hates us — for God hates sin.[66] But if we leave it there, the depths of God's love are not plumbed, for the same unelicited and creative love of God that brings humans into being and sustains them is found on the cross to be an unelicited, *re*-creative love that reaches across the chasm of sin and pays a great price to call people into an unmerited salvation. Thus Thomas invokes Gregory the Great: "O the incalculable love of your charity! To redeem slaves you delivered up your Son."[67]

Second, the cross teaches us the immensity of God's charity, not only in its gratuity, but also by the length to which God goes in sending Christ. All love offers itself to the beloved, seeking union and mutual in-

---

61. *ST* III 46.2.

62. *ST* III 46.3.

63. *In Roman.,* chap. 5, lect. 2.

64. *ST* I-II 27.3.

65. *ST* I 20.2.

66. *ST* I 20.2 ad 4; III 49.4 ad 1.

67. *Commentary on Ephesians,* chap. 2, lect. 2; see the translation by Matthew L. Lamb, *Commentary on Saint Paul's Epistle to the Ephesians* (Albany, NY: Magi Books, 1966), p. 90.

dwelling with the beloved by way of ecstasy.[68] The immensity of God's charity is seen in the distance across which God offers Christ for our sakes. Recall the coordination of Christ's incarnational poverty, his material poverty, and the poverty of his death on the cross. The distance is already incalculable in the Incarnation. For humanity and divinity are infinitely diverse, yet uniting them was a fitting act for God by reason of God's infinite goodness.[69] Therefore, "[h]ow beautiful to say that He *emptied himself*," for the fullness of divinity assumed for our sakes the emptiness of humanity.[70] That incalculable distance is rendered, if possible, even more unfathomable in that the life Christ led was one of abject poverty. Hence, his poverty becomes a sign of the immensity of his love. Thomas palpably expresses his wonder at that immensity in his eulogy to the poor Christ in *CR*. There he evokes the paradox of the great treasure of divinity dwelling in the most abased poverty. The rhetorical pitch intensifies as he recalls more and more examples of Christ's poverty — his poor mother, his modest clothes, his birth in a lowly manger — until the passage climaxes in this memorable line: "Therefore let the enemies of poverty hold their tongues, while its glory shines with splendor in the very cradle of Christ."[71] Thomas then goes further to glory in that distance as underscored by Christ's cross.

Third, the cross teaches us the immensity of God's charity in its willingness to bear evils out of love. Love in general is divided into love of concupiscence and love of friendship, but the latter is most simply called love, because it loves the other simply for herself, as if it were another self, while the former loves something instrumentally.[72] Thus does the love of friendship go outside itself most simply, seeking the good of the other for her own sake. Nevertheless, in willing the good of the other, the lover does not will her friend's good more than her own.[73] But for the sake of something greater than herself, such as the common good or the love of God, one may

---

68. *ST* I-II 28.1-3.

69. *ST* III 1.1 ad 2.

70. *Commentary on Philippians*, chap. 2, lect. 3. See the translation by F. R. Larcher and Michael Duffy, *Commentary on Saint Paul's First Letter to the Thessalonians and the Letter to the Philippians* (Albany, NY: Magi Books, 1969), p. 80.

71. "Confundantur igitur paupertatis detractores, cuius gloria in ipsis Christi cunabulis praeclare refulget." *CR*, chap. 15, 32-34.

72. *ST* I-II 26.4.

73. *ST* I-II 28.3 ad 3.

expose oneself to harm for the sake of the greater good.[74] We see the immensity of God's charity in the degree to which Christ is willing to face exposure to harm for the sake of our salvation, a good that is neither prior to nor greater than God's love, but rather is created by it. Thus is the "exceeding charity" of Christ evident in "the extent of the Passion, and the greatness of the grief endured."[75] Christ shows the depths of God's love by offering himself so completely as to bear such sufferings for our sake.

We cannot act in utter gratuity, nor can we condescend from a heavenly throne and suffer such pain as only the God-man could suffer. But we can participate in this highest charity by joining ourselves with Christ through the church. Through the Holy Spirit, who brings us to such membership, God creates charity in us that "draws human beings up into the community of his blessed life, and gives them that character and dignity that altogether and alone enable a friendship with him."[76] We then find ourselves progressing toward greater charity, toward a charity that approaches the humble and exposed charity of Christ on the cross, a charity whose self-forgetfulness, vulnerability, and willingness to bear suffering reflects the immensity of the divine charity even as it participates in it.

Just as Christ's self-offering act on the cross is no self-immolation but a participation in and anticipation of divine communion, so our acts of parting with possessions and humbly receiving our daily bread conduce to charitable community. True, Christ accepted his passion and death even though they "were repugnant to the natural will."[77] And mendicants practice an analogous renunciation: "Now self-denial, according to Basil, is total forgetfulness of past things and retreat from our own will; so it is clear that in this self-denial is meant also getting rid of the riches possessed of one's own will."[78] But this immense degree of self-abandonment and bear-

---

74. *ST* I 60.5. Such exposure is not an "altruistic" sacrifice, but a positive act of love that both presupposes and preserves a common love. See David Matzko McCarthy, *Sex and Love in the Home: A Theology of the Household* (London: SCM Press, 2001), chap. 7.

75. *ST* III 48.2.

76. Eberhard Schockenhoff, "The Theological Virtue of Charity (IIa IIae, qq. 23-46)," in *The Ethics of Aquinas,* ed. Stephen J. Pope (Washington, DC: Georgetown University Press, 2002), pp. 244-58, here p. 248.

77. *ST* III 47.2 ad 2; cf. *Commentary on Philippians,* chap. 2, lect. 2.

78. "Abnegatio autem sui ipsius, secundum Basilium, est totalis praeteritorum oblivio et recessus a propriis voluntatibus: et sic patet quod in hac negatione sui ipsius intelligitur etiam depositio divitiarum quae per voluntatem propriam possidentur." *CR,* chap. 9, 143-48.

ing of suffering could not have its term within the self or in the annihilation of the self. Thomas appeals to Dionysius the Areopagite: "[D]ivine love makes one ecstatic, i.e., it places a man outside himself, not suffering him to belong to himself but to that which is loved."[79] Thomas concludes from this that love relinquishes and denies itself. Therefore, "the more dearly a thing is loved according to nature, the more perfect it is to despise it, for the sake of Christ."

The degree of humbly vulnerable self-offering to which the cross of Christ summons sheds new light on the dependent readiness for communion in which we are created. Aristotle already knew that what is "natural" for us involves embracing our properly deferent limitedness as rational animals dependent on a trustworthy natural order whose contours antecedently shape and condition us. What Aristotle did not know is the much greater degree of lowliness, even the gratitude, that is appropriate to us as creatures. And he did not know that our position of deferent dependence reflects our being created for communion. Acknowledging that truth can help us avoid the illusion of self-sufficiency to which Aristotle was prone. Thomas knows not only that we are created for communion, but that a greater communion than we could have anticipated has been achieved for us through the grace of Christ. And the measure of that grace conditions Thomas's grasp of our created lowliness. For the degree of our ontological poverty before our Creator corresponds to the distance we learn to acknowledge that Christ traversed to lift us to the heights of divinity. From Thomas's perspective, it turns out that Aristotelian deference is a sort of groping toward the lowly dependence of charitable self-offering, a self-offering brought to its fulfillment in the cross of Christ. Far from destroying nature, mendicant sufferings participate in the charity that brings nature to its completion. It is not that nature demands our suffering, but that the self-offering charity at the heart of nature bears such suffering rather than seeking security against it. Therefore, it offers itself — to God, to neighbor, to the other — on the basis of and in anticipation of the fullness of communion for which nature was intended.

---

79. "[D]ivinus amor est extasim faciens, id est hominem extra se ipsum ponens, non sinens hominem sui ipsius esse, sed eius quod amatur." *DP,* chap. 11, 7-10.

Humble Vulnerability and Market Society

I have in these pages searched Thomas's economic teachings and found there a logic that seeks to organize human action involving wealth toward a sort of lowliness. This lowliness has a number of aspects. In it we recognize our created ontological poverty, a sign of our need for communion and of our membership in and dependence on a web of interrelationships both physical and spiritual that conditions our agency and its potential for flourishing. The lowly nakedness of Christ on the cross summons this created lowliness toward ever-deeper expression, with the promise of fulfillment through graced communion with God and with others.

This Thomistic economic logic hinges on seeing the correspondence between our created lowliness and the lowliness of the cross. What most keeps us from grasping that correspondence, and from reading Thomas's economic teachings well, are the economic practices that pattern our lives, forming in us habits of imagining ourselves as proprietors — as primordial owners. Alienated from our constitutional lowliness, we perceive that the cross either threatens our nature or offers a kind of Manichaean good news, a redemption through the destruction of nature.

Hearing Thomas's economic teachings anew is an urgent project for us, those who have been formed by modern market society. Not only do we need something like the lowliness they promote in order to find rest from the economic and technological imperatives that impel us to secure ourselves; we also need it to recover our ability to apprehend the beauty of the beatitude toward which Christ summons. That is, Thomas's economic teachings could be one tool for helping us imagine ourselves leaving our proprietorship and answering the summons to "become poor."

When we recognize the correspondence between our created lowliness and the lowliness of the cross, we also gain insight into how to appreciate Thomas's agreements with Aristotle. They both reject economic practices that raise the specter of an unconditioned or autonomous claim to security from nature's goods, a claim not antecedently shaped by the limitations that a prior membership in a natural or created order imposes. The created lowliness Thomas tries to protect and promote bears significant analogies to the receptive deference Aristotle defends with similar economic teachings. At the same time, Thomas's use of Aristotelian-sounding arguments should not be read as counterbalancing the devotion to the cross he expresses elsewhere. Rather, Thomas places those arguments in the context of Christian living on the way toward perfection in conformity to Christ. Arguments for an Aristotelian-sounding receptivity become in Thomas's hands signposts directing human action toward a greater degree of dependent trust. Aristotle's concern to limit the desire for security is transformed in Thomas, as the cross of Christ summons human action toward a more complete self-abandonment. These transformations of Aristotle suggest that the humbly vulnerable charity that promises our fulfillment is the completion-by-elevation of a nature that is made to defer and to depend.

But can this lowliness be recovered? The applicability of Thomas's economic teachings is obscure for us, because the logic of exchange value that dominates market society appears both comprehensive and inevitable. Market forces seem gradually to convert more and more of human life and of the world into commodities governed by the laws of the circulation of exchange value. The steady spread of the logic of exchange value seems to demonstrate the futility of Thomas's nay-saying to some of the basic practices of market society (assuming that an agreed-upon price is a just price, contracting a price for the use of money, and so forth).

Despite the appearance that all economic action falls under the sway of exchange value, exchange value remains a human convention (and a rather metaphysically dubious one at that). The "laws" of the circulation of exchange value cannot circumscribe the wider natural order that exceeds and encompasses them. When we act as though they do, we only give those "laws" a legitimacy that hides the dispossessions, injustices, and presumptions enacted under their auspices. The apparently exhaustive circuit defined by those "laws" offers a truncated account of human economic activity, neglecting or distorting the comprehensive circuit of nature that could only be acknowledged in deference and in trust.

At stake is not only good action with our wealth, but also our ability to entrust ourselves to an order suffused with divine purpose and intention. Thomas understood that, by resisting some practices of a developing profit economy, he was defending the very notion that reality is penetrated by divine reason. Joel Kaye illuminates these issues in his *Economy and Nature in the Fourteenth Century*. Kaye's thesis is that scholastic thinkers of the fourteenth-century naturalistic revival were willing to reconceptualize nature in more mathematical terms, terms that would lay the groundwork for the future growth of science, partly due to their attention to emerging market realities. As they sought to understand changing economic realities, scholastics gradually learned to accept approximation, relative measurement, and the quantification of qualities in place of an older conception of nature characterized by fixed and absolute values and stable essences and perfections. Intensified monetization made it difficult to avoid the conclusion that relative prices produced by a social equilibrium of shifting individual calculations was producing order and equality. The same thinkers who most clearly saw into the workings of that apparently self-equalizing system of exchange were also the ones who made the most notable contributions to the new natural philosophy of the fourteenth century, applying some of the same notions of approximation, relativity, and geometrical equalization.[1]

The idea that order might arise out of such an impersonal, mechanical process was hard for some scholastic thinkers to swallow, Thomas among them. For Thomas, order always involves some active intelligence doing the ordering, and to accept order as a sort of accident of the market would undermine both the sufficiency and necessity of that divine rationality in nature and the dependence of justice on the just intentions of particular agents.[2] Kaye rightly recognizes that Thomas's just-price teach-

---

1. Joel Kaye, *Economy and Nature in the Fourteenth Century: Money, Market Exchange, and the Emergence of Scientific Thought* (Cambridge, UK: Cambridge University Press, 1998), p. 11. Interestingly, one of the key figures here is Peter Olivi. The connections between his apocalyptic idealization of poverty and his role in developing a type of economic thought sensitive to "market realities" remain largely unexplored.

2. Thomas is quite far from Adam Smith's promotion of an arrangement in which an individual would be "led by an invisible hand to promote an end which was no part of his

ing cannot be equated with simple market price. According to Kaye, Thomas refuses to make that equation because of the serious ethical and metaphysical implications of accepting justice in terms of an impersonal logic. In short, it would undermine his entire theological understanding of nature as producing an order imbued with the very rationale of the divine, an order with which humans can and should harmonize, aligning their own reason with the divine reason.[3] Kaye is surely right in this. Yet Kaye leaves readers with the impression that Thomas's defense of an antiquated notion of the rationality of the cosmos was an unwinnable battle, that recognizing the rationality of markets was inevitable.

Kaye's account of Thomas's position, though illuminating, is incomplete because he fails to recognize that any order that the logic of exchange value produces, if taken to be adequate on its own, comes at the cost of recognizing not only the divine reason at work, but also the rationality of the wider comprehensive natural circuit within which human economic activity is inscribed. For both Aristotle and Thomas, the logic of exchange value cannot be exhaustive; rather, it is parasitic on a wider, inexhaustible, uncircumscribable order. A proper deference to the limits of this order involves entrusting ourselves to it, and both Aristotle and Thomas correspondingly acknowledge that this order is imbued with the rationality of an active one who orders. This order is more than the measurements of exchange value can convey. Accounts of economic activity that begin and end in exchange value fail to notice the embedding of economic activity in this wider order aiming at use values.

If this wider order is the final basis and context for any human eco-

---

intention." Adam Smith, *An Inquiry into the Nature and Causes of the Wealth of Nations* (1776), ed. R. H. Campbell, A. S. Skinner, and W. B. Todd (Oxford: Oxford University Press, 1976), p. 25. I argue that a conception like Smith's not only distorts what our economic responsibilities are, but does so exactly because it prescinds from the kind of wondrous attention to an antecedent natural order that we have been investigating, assuming something much more like the proprietary, Lockean self. Samuel Fleischacker has argued that Smith does not have Locke's excessive preoccupation with self-interest, but Smith's more "common sense" perspective still presupposes a fundamental isolation of the self reflecting its unconditioned character. For a reading of the Smithian self as encompassed in a sympathetic hall of mirrors that amounts to isolation, see Kelly S. Johnson, *The Fear of Beggars: Stewardship and Poverty in Christian Ethics* (Grand Rapids: Eerdmans, 2007), pp. 102-14; cf. Samuel Fleischacker, *On Adam Smith's* Wealth of Nations (Princeton, NJ: Princeton University Press, 2004), p. 84.

3. Kaye, *Economy and Nature*, p. 98.

nomic activity, then, although such economic activity can be arranged so as to obscure the fact, we can never be bereft of the possibility of recovering economic practices that escape the logic of a dominating exchange value.[4]

A recent work by Alasdair MacIntyre sheds light on how the truth about our situation in the world, though it can be neglected or obscured, always provides a basis from which practices that distort human action can be resisted. In *Dependent Rational Animals,* MacIntyre proposes to join certain feminists and others in noting the significance of the basic facts of human vulnerability and animality for describing human flourishing, the required virtues and their development, and the political structures that would foster those virtues. The book marks an important revision of MacIntyre's posture in *After Virtue.* There his post-Hegelian polarization between the biological/natural and the social/historical held sway, so that he attempted to derive an account of the virtues simply from an account of social practices, apparently in order not to have to venture a necessarily historically contingent and culturally determined account of human nature. *Dependent Rational Animals* is still in some ways a development of the project begun in *After Virtue,* and yet he confesses that he erred in supposing "an ethics independent of biology to be possible."[5]

The biological characteristics to which MacIntyre appeals to correct his earlier blind spot are largely ones that humans share with other intelligent animal species, especially a bodily comportment in the world that pursues certain goods but is so vulnerable (more or less at various times) to dangers that threaten the attainment of those goods that flourishing is possible only through a remarkable degree of dependence on others. MacIntyre insists that if we recognize that *we* are dependent in these ways (have been, are in certain ways now, and are likely to be in the future), rather than thinking of the disabled and the dependent always as those "others" who

---

4. This point resonates with the traditional "Platonic conception of the predatory dependence of human vice on virtue." Oliver O'Donovan and Joan Lockwood O'Donovan, *Bonds of Imperfection: Christian Politics, Past and Present* (Grand Rapids: Eerdmans, 2004), p. 5. It also relates to the complaints of Herman Daly and John Cobb that *homo economicus* is an inadequate intellectual construct since it abstracts too far from the many ways in which actual flesh-and-blood human beings are interrelated and interdependent. Herman E. Daly and John B. Cobb, Jr., *For the Common Good: Redirecting the Economy toward Community, the Environment, and a Sustainable Future,* 2nd ed. (Boston: Beacon, 1994), p. 86.

5. Alasdair MacIntyre, *Dependent Rational Animals: Why Human Beings Need the Virtues* (Chicago: Open Court, 1999), p. x.

call forth our self-sufficient beneficence, we will have to acknowledge the central importance for our flourishing of virtues that are otherwise easily neglected. He calls these the "virtues of acknowledged dependence," and they are the defining virtues of what he calls "networks of relationships of giving and receiving." Perhaps the most telling of these virtues is something MacIntyre calls "just generosity."[6] This virtue is more than justice because, rather than seeking a fair balance, it gives uncalculatingly, acknowledging the incalculable debts incurred by being nourished in networks of giving and receiving. At the same time, it is not more than justice, because offering such uncalculating giving is precisely what is owed.

Such virtues, MacIntyre claims, have been extremely marginal if not completely neglected in much of the history of Western moral philosophy. MacIntyre does not try to summarize all the reasons for this neglect, but various relevant factors emerge throughout the book. The individualism of much modern moral theorizing assumes that I can only be held accountable for a debt when I have voluntarily entered the relationship in question. Debts incurred before we could choose our creditors cannot be held against us. Such assumptions cannot accommodate the virtues of acknowledged dependence.[7] Further, MacIntyre perceives a sense of superiority even in Aristotle's *megalopsychos*, which has worked to obscure the extent of our dependence, though Aristotle is at the same time a prime example for understanding the animality of human beings.[8]

A further factor in this neglect is particularly relevant to the present argument. MacIntyre suggests that an economic practice that allows the logic of the market to subordinate all other considerations stands in opposition to the cultivation of the virtues of acknowledged dependence. Adam Smith's thought is a case in point. The flip side of Smith's affirmation of the egoism of the market is his altruistic theory of moral sentiments; but the whole edifice of his thought works together to obscure networks of giving and receiving that would acknowledge a common good in place of the contrast between what is good for you but not for me and what is good

6. MacIntyre, *Dependent Rational Animals,* pp. 120-22.

7. MacIntyre, *Dependent Rational Animals,* pp. 113-15.

8. MacIntyre, *Dependent Rational Animals,* pp. 5-7, 127. MacIntyre thus offers a critique of Aristotle that undermines what I have called his emphasis on "nobility," but MacIntyre undermines it from the standpoint of our natural dependence rather than in view of God's providence or of eschatology. I take my presentation of Thomas's and MacIntyre's critiques of Aristotle to be complementary on this point.

for me but not for you.[9] When a market logic suppresses the importance of these networks of giving and receiving, the possibilities for human flourishing are compromised. Therefore, when considering the political structures required in order to foster flourishing, MacIntyre details some of the requisite economic considerations. Since these networks of giving and receiving can only be embodied in local communities, such communities will "require some significant degree of insulation from and protection from the forces generated by outside markets."[10]

In an illuminating review of *Dependent Rational Animals,* Joseph Dunne expresses sympathy with MacIntyre's project, but remains uncertain whether this "local protectionism" can actually offer a meaningful alternative to market logic. "MacIntyre is surely right to see unrestrained market-forces as inimical to the kind of politics he espouses. But these forces are no respecter of borders, national *or* local, and it is hard to see how they can ever be properly checked without political institutions whose scope is coterminous with themselves."[11] Dunne's point is compelling, for the history of the forward march of market society has been a history of local protections proving insufficient against the greater economic and often military power of those who want local communities to "open their markets."[12] But Dunne's suggestion fails to recognize that, from MacIntyre's perspective, an international political body, which would necessarily be impersonal and bureaucratic, whatever its intentions, would be

9. MacIntyre, *Dependent Rational Animals,* p. 119.

10. MacIntyre, *Dependent Rational Animals,* p. 145. Similarly, in his new introduction to *Marxism and Christianity,* MacIntyre points out that, given the worldwide dominance of capitalism, "what is most urgently needed is a politics of self-defence for all those local societies that aspire to achieve some relatively self-sufficient and independent form of participatory practice-based community and that therefore need to protect themselves from the corrosive effects of capitalism and the depradations of state power." Alasdair MacIntyre, *Marxism and Christianity,* 2nd ed. (London: Duckworth, 1995), p. xxvi. Note the similarity to Thomas's suggestion that the socially corrupting activities of merchants must be kept marginal to social organization.

11. Joseph Dunne, "Ethics Revised: Flourishing as Vulnerable and Dependent," *International Journal of Philosophical Studies* 10 (2002): 339-63, here p. 353.

12. As Wendell Berry has argued, the bonds of community break down in modern times due most often to aggression from outside the community, and that aggression has typically been economic. Thus, "the destruction of the community begins when its economy is made — not *dependent* (for no community has ever been entirely independent) — but *subject* to a larger external economy." Wendell Berry, *Sex, Economy, Freedom and Community* (New York and San Francisco: Pantheon, 1993), p. 126.

more, not less likely than local communities to be co-opted toward the service of the ends of exchange value. More significantly, Dunne's implication that local communities, however important, provide little traction for resisting the market misses one of the crucial points of MacIntyre's argument. By rooting his account of flourishing in human animality, MacIntyre hopes not only to remind us of our vulnerability and dependence, but also to sketch an ethics that is truly *natural.* In other words, because we are the kinds of animals we are, we cannot flourish — or even grow to maturity — other than through networks of giving and receiving. So our lives already depend on such networks, even if our economic practices work against them, tending to break them down into collections of competing individuals. Thus, even as MacIntyre notes the corrosive effects of market forces, he insists that market relationships themselves already presuppose "norms of giving and receiving . . . to some large degree."[13]

Those networks of giving and receiving, on which we depend whether we acknowledge it or not, constantly regenerate the possibility of resisting their demise at the hands of a corrosive economic practice. MacIntyre highlights the opposition between the virtues of acknowledged dependence and the goals of a consumer society. But in spite of the apparent ubiquity of consumerism, he does not suggest that those who defend these virtues are without a basis from which to fight back. On the contrary, he hardly mentions the conflict before he points out "the extent to which these norms (of networks of giving and receiving) are to some extent already accepted in a variety of those settings — households, workplaces, schools, parishes — in which resistance to the goals and norms of a consumer society is recurrently generated."[14] These networks of giving and receiving may be easily obscured and may be constantly threatened by a variety of modern practices that deny their significance. But they are necessary for us, just as they are for dolphins, and so they always provide, for those who attend to them and champion them, both a space for resistance and even a leverage for providing the moral education that will encourage people to find their flourishing in them and to resist the breakdowns to which they are always vulnerable.[15]

13. MacIntyre, *Dependent Rational Animals,* p. 117.
14. MacIntyre, *Dependent Rational Animals,* p. 145.
15. Since Dunne misses MacIntyre's interest in showing the naturalness of the virtues of acknowledged dependence, he cannot see why the first six chapters, on the character of

Thomas's economic teachings fit well with MacIntyre's arguments. Just as MacIntyre sees under the obfuscations produced by market rationality a set of networks of giving and receiving on which we truly depend, so Thomas resists the logic of the market by defending our natural deference to a deeper natural network of nourishment that encompasses and sustains us. Also, just as MacIntyre's networks of giving and receiving bring forth uncalculating giving and grateful acknowledgment of dependence, Thomas's encompassing antecedent order and the call of Christ that completes it summon humble self-offering and trusting receptivity.

Both MacIntyre and Thomas suggest that when we neglect these underlying networks, we lose touch with some of what is natural to us. These reflections help us lay a finger on one of the deep wounds of our age. When our habits of thought and action train us to imagine ourselves as primordial proprietors, we become rebels against our own nature. Our unconditioned, proprietary desires find the most constitutive truths about our lives to be distasteful constraints on our freedom. What Pinckaers calls our "freedom of indifference" sees nature not as presupposition but as an option to be obeyed, rejected, or scientifically reconstructed.[16] We ask, Did I choose this desire and this goal? Did I choose to be subject to these principles of nourishment, when I would rather choose ones that allow me to pursue unending growth, such as with a cancer, yet without becoming diseased or malignant? Did I choose to be a member of a larger social body and a larger ecological body for which I must be patient of the limits and reciprocal duties imposed by my place?

So we resent our nature, and we resent nature in general. We struggle against it, and we seek ways to triumph over it through technology. Ours is

---

the animality that humans and certain intelligent nonhuman species share, are crucial to his argument. Dunne, "Ethics Revised," p. 348.

16. Servais Pinckaers sees evidence of our resentment in our discomfort with Thomas's notion of spiritual instincts. Calling the gifts of the Spirit "instincts" sounds heteronomous, as if they make us act apart from our freedom. But interior principles of action, whether natural or spiritual, are presuppositions of freedom rather than alternatives to it. "We could compare it to the plant's instinct, which directs it toward the sun, which makes the sap rise in spring and lets it flow until the fruit ripens." Today, when we sense such principles of movement within us, pushing us toward our flourishing, we wonder whether we are truly free. It is no wonder that in our day we often find it difficult to imagine being free where God acts. Servais Pinckaers, O.P., *The Pinckaers Reader: Renewing Thomistic Moral Theology*, ed. John Berkman and Craig Steven Titus (Washington, DC: The Catholic University of America Press, 2005), p. 391.

a pathological ingratitude, but an especially desperate sort of ingratitude, because it amounts to being resentful of who we are. Sometimes it expresses itself in our self-hatred. Equally, it is manifested in our hatred of God. This resentment is a sign of how urgently we need to learn the trust, the receptivity, the humility promoted by Thomas's economic teachings. Our very ability to live well in our own skin depends on recovering the lowliness that can rejoice in the news that "he became poor."

Thomas's economic teachings also suggest possibilities for resistance to the distortions of the market that supplement MacIntyre. The dependence MacIntyre discusses is exclusively a matter of human beings' dependence on one another. That dependence is not to be underplayed, particularly not by Thomas, as MacIntyre would point out. But Thomas's economic teachings prompt us to consider what virtues are required by our dependence — a dependence not only on one another, but also on a natural order that exceeds us, provides our sustenance, and intends our flourishing. If MacIntyre asks how our practices foster or fail to foster the just generosity that fits our networks of giving and receiving, what questions must we ask to also foster that trusting receptivity that fits us to a wondrous and encompassing natural network of nourishment?

Some questions will be ones MacIntyre asks. For example, since trade tends to expand the logic of exchange value, is the practice of trade suitably restrained? Others will push toward a more explicit acknowledgment of our dependence on nature's circuit of nourishment. They might include: Do our exchanges yield to natural order by taking use values ordered to human need as their end? Or do they aim at the increase of exchange value? Do our exchanges refuse the presumption that would secure a claim on nature's goods that is guaranteed in advance of the unfolding of nature's provision? Or do we use increases produced by the conventions of exchange value to secure our future? Is the logic we use in our economic activity patient of its dependence, and even open to the summons of the self-divesting refusal of security seen in the poor Christ?

By asking such questions, and by turning to instances of local community that provide alternatives to the logic of market society, we can imagine a meaningful recovery of Thomas's economic teachings. In such contexts the proprietary approach to nature fostered by a market society could fade, displaced by the lowliness, the trusting receptivity and humble dependence, that characterizes Thomas's economic teachings from beginning to end.

Bibliography

Anscombe, G. E. M. "Modern Moral Philosophy." *Philosophy* 33 (1958): 1-19.

Aquinas, Thomas. *An Apology for the Religious Orders.* Translated from *Contra Impugnantes* and *Contra Retrahentes* by John Proctor, O.P. London: Sands & Co., 1902.

———. *The Catechetical Instructions of St. Thomas Aquinas.* Translated by Joseph B. Collins. New York: Joseph F. Wagner, 1939.

———. *Commentary on Aristotle's* Nichomachean Ethics. Translated by C. I. Litzinger, O.P. Revised with foreword by Ralph McInerny. Notre Dame, IN: Dumb Ox Books, 1993.

———. *Commentary on Aristotle's* Politics. Translated by Richard J. Regan. Indianapolis: Hackett, 2007.

———. *Commentary on Saint Paul's Epistle to the Ephesians.* Translated by Matthew L. Lamb. Albany, NY: Magi Books, 1966.

———. *Commentary on Saint Paul's First Letter to the Thessalonians and the Letter to the Philippians.* Translated by F. R. Larcher and Michael Duffy. Albany, NY: Magi Books, 1969.

———. *The Literal Exposition on Job: A Scriptural Commentary Concerning Providence.* Translated by Anthony Damico. Atlanta: Scholars Press, 1989.

———. "On Buying and Selling on Credit." Translated by Alfred O'Rahilly. *The Irish Ecclesiastical Record* 31 (1928): 159-68.

———. *On Evil.* Translated by Jean Oesterle. Notre Dame, IN: University of Notre Dame Press, 1995.

———. *On Kingship to the King of Cyprus.* Translated by Gerald B. Phelan. Revised by I. Th. Eschmann, O.P. Toronto: Pontifical Institute of Mediaeval Studies, 1949.

———. *The Religious State, the Episcopate, and the Priestly Office.* Translated from

De Perfectione Spiritualis Vitae by John Proctor, O.P. Westminster, MD: The Newman Press, 1950.

———. *Sancti Thomae Aquinatis Doctoris angelici ordinis predicatorum Opera Omnia secundum impressionem Petri Fiaccadori.* 25 vols. Parma, 1852-73. Reprint, New York: Musurgia, 1948-50.

———. *Sancti Thomae de Aquino Opera Omnia iussu Leonis XIII.* Rome, 1882-.

———. *Summa Contra Gentiles,* Book III. Translated by Vernon J. Bourke. 2 vols. Notre Dame, IN: University of Notre Dame Press, 1975.

———. *Summa Theologica.* 3 vols. Translated by the Fathers of the English Dominican Province. New York: Benziger Brothers, 1947.

———. *Thomas Aquinas: The Gifts of the Spirit.* Translated by Matthew Rzeczkowski, O.P. Edited by Benedict M. Ashley, O.P. New York: New City Press, 1995.

Aristotle. *Nichomachean Ethics.* Translated by Martin Ostwald. New York: Macmillan, 1962.

———. *Politics.* Translated by H. Rackham. Loeb Classical Library. London: William Heinemann, 1932.

Ashley, W. J. "Just Price." In *Dictionary of Political Economy,* ed. R. H. I. Palgrave, 2: 500. 3 vols. London: Macmillan, 1896.

Augustine. *The City of God against the Pagans.* Edited and translated by R. W. Dyson. Cambridge Texts in the History of Political Thought. Cambridge, UK: Cambridge University Press, 1998.

Backhouse, Roger E. *The Ordinary Business of Life: A History of Economics from the Ancient World to the Twenty-First Century.* Princeton, NJ: Princeton University Press, 2002.

Baldwin, John W. *The Medieval Theories of the Just Price: Romanists, Canonists, and Theologians in the Twelfth and Thirteenth Centuries.* Philadelphia: American Philosophical Society, 1959.

Barnes, Jonathan. *Aristotle.* Oxford: Oxford University Press, 1982.

Bedouelle, Guy, O.P. *Saint Dominic: The Grace of the Word.* Translated by Mary Thomas Noble, O.P. San Francisco: Ignatius Press, 1987.

Bellemare, J. "Pour une théologie thomiste de la Pauvreté." *Revue de l'Université d'Ottawa* 26 (1956): 137-64.

Berry, Wendell. *Home Economics.* New York: North Point Press, 1987.

———. *Sex, Economy, Freedom and Community.* New York and San Francisco: Pantheon, 1993.

Beumer, J. B. "Gratia supponit naturam. Zur Geschichte eines theologischen Prinzips." *Gregorianum* 20 (1939): 381-406, 535-52.

Bloch, Marc. *Feudal Society.* Translated by L. A. Manyon. 2nd ed. New York: Routledge, 1962.

Bonino, Serge-Thomas, O.P. "Charisms, Forms, and States of Life (IIa IIae, qq. 171-

189)." In *The Ethics of Aquinas,* edited by Stephen J. Pope, pp. 340-52. Washington, DC: Georgetown University Press, 2002.

Bowlin, John. *Contingency and Fortune in Aquinas's Ethics.* Cambridge, UK: Cambridge University Press, 1999.

Boyle, Leonard, O.P. *The Setting of the Summa Theologiae of Saint Thomas.* Toronto: Pontifical Institute of Medieval Studies, 1982.

Bradley, Denis J. M. *Aquinas on the Twofold Human Good: Reason and Human Happiness in Aquinas's Moral Science.* Washington, DC: The Catholic University of America Press, 1997.

Burr, David. "The Correctorium Controversy and the Origins of the Usus Pauper Controversy." *Speculum* 60 (1985): 331-42.

———. *The Persecution of Peter Olivi.* Philadelphia: American Philosophical Society, 1976.

———. *The Spiritual Franciscans.* University Park, PA: Pennsylvania State University Press, 2001.

Burrell, David B., C.S.C. "Analogy, Creation, and Theological Language." In *The Theology of Thomas Aquinas,* edited by Rik Van Nieuwenhove and Joseph Wawrykow, pp. 77-98. Notre Dame, IN: University of Notre Dame Press, 2005.

———. *Aquinas: God and Action.* Notre Dame, IN: University of Notre Dame Press, 1979.

Cantalamessa, Raniero, O.F.M. Cap. *Poverty.* Translated by Charles Serignat. New York: Alba House, 1997.

Cessario, Romanus, O.P. *Christian Faith and the Theological Life.* Washington, DC: The Catholic University of America Press, 1996.

———. *The Virtues, or the Examined Life.* New York: Continuum, 2002.

Chenu, Marie-Dominique, O.P. *Toward Understanding St. Thomas.* Translated by A. M. Landry, O.P., and D. Hughes, O.P. Chicago: Henry Regnery, 1964.

Claassens, L. Juliana M. *The God Who Provides: Biblical Images of Divine Nourishment.* Nashville: Abingdon Press, 2004.

Crisp, Roger, and Michael Slote, eds. *Virtue Ethics.* Oxford: Oxford University Press, 1997.

Daly, Herman E., and John B. Cobb, Jr. *For the Common Good: Redirecting the Economy toward Community, the Environment, and a Sustainable Future.* 2nd ed. Boston: Beacon, 1994.

De Lubac, Henri, S.J. *The Mystery of the Supernatural.* Translated by Rosemary Sheed. London: Geoffrey Chapman, 1967.

———. *Surnaturel: Etudes historiques.* Paris: Aubier, 1946.

Dempsey, Bernard W. *The Functional Economy: The Bases of Economic Organization.* Englewood Cliffs, NJ: Prentice-Hall, 1958.

De Roover, Raymond. "The Concept of the Just Price: Theory and Economic Policy." *Journal of Economic History* 18 (1958): 418-34.

Bibliography

Dietsche, B. M. *Die Deutsche Thomasausgabe, Stände und Ständespflichten.* 2a-2ae, q. 183-89. Regensburg, 1952.

Douie, D. L. *The Conflict Between the Seculars and the Mendicants at the University of Paris in the Thirteenth Century.* London: Blackfriars, 1954.

Dufeil, Michel-Marie. *Guillaume de Saint-Amour et la polémique universitaire parisienne, 1250-1259.* Paris: Picard, 1972.

Dunne, Joseph. "Ethics Revised: Flourishing as Vulnerable and Dependent." *International Journal of Philosophical Studies* 10 (2002): 339-63.

d'Urso, G. "S. Tommaso d'Aquino e la povertà religiosa." *Rivista di Ascetica e Mistica* 54 (1985): 283-95.

Edel, Abraham. *Aristotle and His Philosophy,* with new introduction. New Brunswick, NJ: Transaction Publishers, 1996.

Eijnden, Jan G. J. van den, O.F.M. *Poverty on the Way to God: Thomas Aquinas on Evangelical Poverty.* Leuven: Peeters, 1994.

Emery, Gilles, O.P. *Trinity in Aquinas.* Ypsilanti, MI: Sapientia Press, 2003.

Feingold, Lawrence. *The Natural Desire to See God According to St. Thomas Aquinas and His Interpreters.* Rome: Apollinare studi, 2001.

Finley, M. I. *The Ancient Economy.* Berkeley: University of California Press, 1973.

Fleischacker, Samuel. *On Adam Smith's* Wealth of Nations. Princeton, NJ: Princeton University Press, 2004.

———. *A Short History of Distributive Justice.* New edition. Cambridge, MA: Harvard University Press, 2005.

Funkenstein, Amos. *Theology and the Scientific Imagination from the Middle Ages to the Seventeenth Century.* Princeton, NJ: Princeton University Press, 1986.

González, Justo L. *Faith and Wealth: A History of Early Christian Ideas on the Origin, Significance, and Use of Money.* San Francisco: Harper and Row, 1990.

Gordon, Barry. "Aristotle and the Development of Value Theory." *Quarterly Journal of Economics* 78 (1964): 115-28.

———. *Economic Analysis before Adam Smith: Hesiod to Lessius.* New York: Barnes and Noble, 1975.

Grundmann, Herbert. *Religious Movements in the Middle Ages.* Translated by Steven Rowan. Notre Dame, IN: University of Notre Dame Press, 1995.

Gutiérrez, Gustavo. *A Theology of Liberation.* 15th anniversary edition. Translated by Caridad Inda and John Eagleson. Maryknoll, NY: Orbis Press, 1988.

Hagenauer, Selma. *Das "Justum Pretium" bei Thomas von Aquino: ein Beitrag zur Geschichte der objectiven Werttheorie.* Stuttgart: W. Kohlhammer, 1931.

Hall, Pamela M. *Narrative and the Natural Law: An Interpretation of Thomistic Ethics.* Notre Dame, IN: University of Notre Dame Press, 1994.

Hauerwas, Stanley, and Charles Pinches. *Christians Among the Virtues: Theological Conversations with Ancient and Modern Ethics.* Notre Dame, IN: University of Notre Dame Press, 1997.

Heilbroner, Robert L. *The Nature and Logic of Capitalism.* New York: W. W. Norton, 1985.

———. *The Worldly Philosophers: The Lives, Times, and Ideas of the Great Economic Thinkers.* 6th ed. New York: Touchstone, 1986.

Hibbs, Thomas S. *Dialectic and Narrative in Aquinas: An Interpretation of the Summa Contra Gentiles.* Notre Dame, IN: University of Notre Dame Press, 1995.

———. "Imitatio Christi and the foundation of Aquinas's ethics." *Communio* 18 (1991): 556-73.

———. *Virtue's Splendor: Wisdom, Prudence, and the Human Good.* New York: Fordham University Press, 2001.

Hill, William J., O.P. *Hope: Summa Theologiae IIa IIae. 17-22.* Blackfriars edition, edited by Thomas Gilby et al. Vol. 33. New York: McGraw-Hill, 1966.

Hinnebush, William A., O.P. *The Dominicans: A Short History.* New York: Alba House, 1975.

Hinze, Christine Firer. "What Is Enough? Catholic Social Thought, Consumption, and Material Sufficiency." In *Having: Property and Possession in Religious and Social Life,* edited by William Schweiker and Charles Mathewes, pp. 162-88. Grand Rapids: Eerdmans, 2004.

Hirschfeld, Mary. "Standard of Living and Economic Virtue: Forging a Link between St. Thomas Aquinas and the Twenty-First Century." *Journal of the Society of Christian Ethics* 26 (2006): 61-78.

Hollander, Samuel. "On the Interpretation of the Just Price." *Kyklos* 18 (1965): 615-34.

Hoppe, Leslie J., O.F.M. *There Shall Be No Poor Among You: Poverty in the Bible.* Nashville: Abingdon, 2004.

Horst, Ulrich, O.P. "Christ, *Exemplar Ordinis Fratrum Praedicantium,* According to Saint Thomas Aquinas." In *Christ Among the Medieval Dominicans,* edited by Kent Emery, Jr., and Joseph P. Wawrykow, pp. 256-70. Notre Dame, IN: University of Notre Dame Press, 1998.

———. *Evangelische Armut und Kirche: Thomas von Aquin und die Armutskontroversen des 13. und beginnenden 14. Jahrhunderts.* Berlin: Akademie, 1992.

Irwin, T. H. "Generosity and Property in Aristotle's Politics." *Social Philosophy and Policy* 4 (1987): 37-54.

James, William. *The Varieties of Religious Experience: A Study in Human Nature.* New York: Penguin, 1985.

Johnson, Kelly S. *The Fear of Beggars: Stewardship and Poverty in Christian Ethics.* Eerdmans Ekklesia Series, edited by Michael L. Budde and Stephen E. Fowl. Grand Rapids: Eerdmans, 2007.

———. "Praying: Poverty." In *The Blackwell Companion to Christian Ethics,* edited by Stanley Hauerwas and Samuel Wells, pp. 225-36. Oxford: Blackwell, 2004.

Jones, John D. "The Concept of Poverty in St. Thomas Aquinas's *Contra Impugnantes Dei Cultum et Religionem.*" *The Thomist* 59 (1995): 409-39.

Jordan, Mark D. *The Alleged Aristotelianism of Thomas Aquinas.* The Etienne Gilson Series, 15. Toronto: Pontifical Institute of Mediaeval Studies, 1992.

Kavanaugh, John F. *Following Christ in a Consumer Society: The Spirituality of Cultural Resistance.* 25th anniversary edition. Maryknoll, NY: Orbis Press, 2006.

Kaye, Joel. *Economy and Nature in the Fourteenth Century: Money, Market Exchange, and the Emergence of Scientific Thought.* Cambridge, UK: Cambridge University Press, 1998.

Keenan, James F., S.J. *Goodness and Rightness in Thomas Aquinas's* Summa Theologiae. Washington, DC: Georgetown University Press, 1992.

Kennedy, Margrit. *Interest and Inflation Free Money: Creating an Exchange Medium That Works for Everybody and Protects the Earth.* Revised and expanded edition. Philadelphia: New Society Publishers, 1995.

Kerr, Fergus, O.P. *After Aquinas: Versions of Thomism.* Oxford: Blackwell, 2002.

———. *Immortal Longings: Versions of Transcending Humanity.* Notre Dame, IN: University of Notre Dame Press, 1997.

Lambert, M. D. *Franciscan Poverty: The Doctrine of the Absolute Poverty of Christ and the Apostles in the Franciscan Order, 1210-1323.* London: S.P.C.K., 1961.

Langholm, Odd. *Economics in the Medieval Schools: Wealth, Exchange, Value, Money and Usury according to the Paris Theological Tradition, 1200-1350.* Leiden: E. J. Brill, 1992.

Levering, Matthew. *Christ's Fulfillment of Torah and Temple: Salvation According to Thomas Aquinas.* Notre Dame, IN: University of Notre Dame Press, 2002.

———. *Scripture and Metaphysics: Aquinas and the Renewal of Trinitarian Theology.* Challenges in Contemporary Theology, edited by Gareth Jones and Lewis Ayres. Oxford: Blackwell, 2004.

Little, Lester. *Religious Poverty and the Profit Economy in Medieval Europe.* Ithaca, NY: Cornell University Press, 1978.

Lloyd, G. E. R. "The idea of nature in the Politics." In *Aristotelian Explorations,* pp. 184-204. Cambridge, UK: Cambridge University Press, 1996.

Locke, John. *First Treatise of Government.* In *Two Treatises of Government,* edited by Peter Laslett. New York: Cambridge University Press, 1963.

———. *The Second Treatise of Government.* Edited by Thomas P. Peardon. New York: Macmillan, 1986.

Long, D. Stephen. *Divine Economy: Theology and the Market.* Radical Orthodoxy, edited by John Milbank, Catherine Pickstock, and Graham Ward. New York: Routledge, 2000.

Long, D. Stephen, and Tripp York. "Remembering: Offering Our Gifts." In *The Blackwell Companion to Christian Ethics,* edited by Stanley Hauerwas and Samuel Wells, pp. 332-45. Oxford: Blackwell, 2004.

Long, Steven A. "On the Possibility of a Purely Natural End for Man." *The Thomist* 64 (2000): 211-37.

Lowry, S. Todd. "Economic and Jurisprudential Ideas of the Greeks." In *Ancient and Medieval Economic Ideas and Concepts of Social Justice*, edited by S. Todd Lowry and Barry Gordon, pp. 11-37. Leiden: E. J. Brill, 1998.

Lustig, B. Andrew. "Natural Law, Property, and Justice: The General Justification of Property in John Locke." *Journal of Religious Ethics* 19 (1991): 119-48.

MacIntyre, Alasdair. *After Virtue: A Study in Moral Theory.* 2nd edition. Notre Dame, IN: University of Notre Dame Press, 1984.

————. *Dependent Rational Animals: Why Human Beings Need the Virtues.* Chicago: Open Court, 1999.

————. *Marxism and Christianity.* 2nd edition. London: Duckworth, 1995.

————. *Whose Justice? Which Rationality?* Notre Dame, IN: University of Notre Dame Press, 1988.

Macpherson, C. B. *The Political Theory of Possessive Individualism: Hobbes to Locke.* Oxford: Oxford University Press, 1962.

Madigan, Kevin. "Aquinas and Olivi on Evangelical Poverty: A Medieval Debate and Its Modern Significance." *The Thomist* 61 (1997): 567-86.

Mäkinen, Virpi. *Property Rights in the Late Medieval Discussion on Franciscan Poverty.* Recherches de Théologie et Philosophie médiévales, Bibliotheca, 3. Leuven: Peeters, 2001.

Mathewes, Charles. "On Using the World." In *Having: Property and Possessions in Religious and Social Life*, edited by William Schweiker and Charles Mathewes, pp. 189-221. Grand Rapids: Eerdmans, 2004.

Mattia Spirito, S. di. "Il Problema della Povertà e della Perfezione Religiosa nell' ambito delle Polemiche tra Clero Seculare e Ordini Mendicanti." In *Tommaso d'Aquino nella Storia di Pensiero*, vol. 2, Dal Medievo ad Oggi, Atti del Congresso Internazionale, pp. 49-58. Naples, 1976.

McCabe, Herbert, O.P. "Aquinas on the Trinity." *New Blackfriars* 80 (1999): 268-83.

McCarthy, David Matzko. *Sex and Love in the Home: A Theology of the Household.* London: SCM Press, 2001.

McCool, Gerald A., S.J. *Catholic Theology in the Nineteenth Century: The Quest for a Unitary Method.* New York: Seabury Press, 1977.

————. *From Unity to Pluralism: The Internal Evolution of Thomism.* New York: Fordham University Press, 1989.

McDonald, William J. *The Social Value of Property according to St. Thomas Aquinas.* Washington, DC: The Catholic University of America Press, 1939.

Meeks, M. Douglas. *God the Economist: The Doctrine of God and Political Economy.* Minneapolis: Fortress Press, 1989.

Meikle, Scott. *Aristotle's Economic Thought.* Oxford: Clarendon Press, 1995.

Milbank, John. "Can a Gift Be Given?" *Modern Theology* 11 (1995): 119-61.

————. *Theology and Social Theory: Beyond Secular Reason.* Oxford: Blackwell, 1990.

————. *The Word Made Strange: Theology, Language, Culture.* Oxford: Blackwell, 1997.

Mollat, Michel. *The Poor in the Middle Ages.* Translated by Arthur Goldhammer. New Haven: Yale University Press, 1986.

Narcisse, Gilbert, O.P. *Les Raisons de Dieu: Argument de convenance et Esthétique théologique selon saint Thomas d'Aquin et Hans Urs von Balthasar.* Fribourg: Éditions Universitaires, 1997.

Noonan, John T., Jr. *The Scholastic Analysis of Usury.* Cambridge, MA: Harvard University Press, 1957.

Norberg-Hodge, Helena. "The Pressure to Modernize and Globalize." In *The Case Against the Global Economy and for a Turn toward the Local,* edited by Jerry Mander and Edward Goldsmith, pp. 33-46. San Francisco: Sierra Club, 1992.

Nussbaum, Martha Craven. *The Fragility of Goodness.* Cambridge, UK: Cambridge University Press, 1986.

Nygren, Anders. *Agape and Eros.* Translated by Philip S. Watson. New York: Harper and Row, 1969.

O'Donovan, Joan Lockwood. "Historical Prolegomena to a Theological Review of 'Human Rights.'" *Studies in Christian Ethics* 9 (1996): 52-65.

O'Donovan, Oliver, and Joan Lockwood O'Donovan. *Bonds of Imperfection: Christian Politics, Past and Present.* Grand Rapids: Eerdmans, 2004.

Outka, Gene. *Agape: An Ethical Analysis.* New Haven: Yale University Press, 1972.

Parel, Anthony. "Aquinas's Theory of Property." In *Theories of Property: Aristotle to the Present,* edited by Anthony Parel and Thomas Flanagan, pp. 88-111. Waterloo, ON: Wilfrid Laurier Press, 1979.

Pieper, Josef. *Faith, Hope, Love.* Translated by Richard and Clara Winston and Sister Mary Frances McCarthy, S.N.D. San Francisco: Ignatius Press, 1997.

————. *The Four Cardinal Virtues: Prudence, Justice, Fortitude, Temperance.* New York: Harcourt, Brace, and World, 1965.

————. *Introduction to Thomas Aquinas.* Translated by Richard and Clara Winston. London: Faber and Faber, 1962.

Pinches, Charles R. *Theology and Action: After Theory in Christian Ethics.* Grand Rapids: Eerdmans, 2002.

Pinckaers, Servais, O.P. *The Pinckaers Reader: Renewing Thomistic Moral Theology.* Edited by John Berkman and Craig Steven Titus. Washington, DC: The Catholic University of America Press, 2005.

————. *The Sources of Christian Ethics.* Translated by Mary Thomas Noble, O.P. Washington, DC: The Catholic University of America Press, 1995.

Placher, William C. *The Domestication of Transcendence: How Modern Thinking about God Went Wrong.* Louisville: Westminster John Knox, 1996.

Polanyi, Karl. *The Great Transformation: The Political and Economic Origins of Our Time.* Boston: Beacon, 2001.

Porter, Jean. *Nature as Reason: A Thomistic Theory of the Natural Law.* Grand Rapids: Eerdmans, 2005.

Post, Stephen. *A Theory of Agape.* Lewisburg, PA: Bucknell University Press, 1990.

Pounds, N. J. G. *An Economic History of Medieval Europe.* 2nd edition. New York: Longman, 1994.

Pourrat, P. "Commençants." In *Dictionnaire de spiritualité.* Vol. 2, col. 1143-56. Paris, 1953.

Quash, Ben. "Offering: Treasuring the Creation." In *The Blackwell Companion to Christian Ethics,* edited by Stanley Hauerwas and Samuel Wells, pp. 305-18. Oxford: Blackwell, 2004.

Quelquejeu, Bernard. "Naturalia manent integra." *Revue des Sciences Philosophiques et Théologiques* 94 (1965): 640-55.

Rahner, Karl. "Remarks on the Dogmatic Treatise 'De Trinitate.'" In *Theological Investigations.* Vol. 4. Translated by Kevin Smyth. New York: Crossroad, 1982.

Rhonheimer, Martin. *Natural Law and Practical Reason: A Thomist View of Moral Autonomy.* Translated by Gerald Malsbary. New York: Fordham University Press, 2000.

————. "Sins Against Justice (IIa IIae, qq. 59-78)." Translated by Frederick G. Lawrence. In *The Ethics of Aquinas,* edited by Stephen J. Pope, pp. 287-303. Washington, DC: Georgetown University Press, 2002.

Rogers, Eugene F., Jr. *Thomas Aquinas and Karl Barth: Sacred Knowledge and the Natural Knowledge of God.* Notre Dame, IN: University of Notre Dame Press, 1995.

Ross, W. D. *Aristotle.* 5th edition. London: Methuen and Co., reprint, 1953.

Schenk, Richard, O.P. "*Omnis Christi Actio Nostra Est Instructio:* The Deeds and Sayings of Jesus as Revelation in the View of Thomas Aquinas." In *La doctrine de la révélation divine de saint Thomas d'Aquin,* edited by Leo J. Elders, pp. 104-31. Vatican City: Libreria Editrice Vaticana, 1990.

Schockenhoff, Eberhard. "The Theological Virtue of Charity (IIa IIae, qq. 23-46)." In *The Ethics of Aquinas,* edited by Stephen J. Pope, pp. 244-58. Washington, DC: Georgetown University Press, 2002.

Sherwin, Michael S., O.P. *By Knowledge and By Love: Charity and Knowledge in the Moral Theology of St. Thomas Aquinas.* Washington, DC: The Catholic University of America Press, 2005.

Smith, Adam. *An Inquiry into the Nature and Causes of the Wealth of Nations* (1776). Edited by R. H. Campbell, A. S. Skinner, and W. B. Todd. Oxford: Oxford University Press, 1976.

Sokolowski, Robert. *The God of Faith and Reason: Foundations of Christian Theology.* Notre Dame, IN: University of Notre Dame Press, 1982.

Somme, Luc-Thomas. *Fils adoptifs de Dieu par Jésus Christ: La filiation divine par adoption dans la théologie de saint Thomas d'Aquin.* Paris: Vrin, 1997.

Stackhouse, Max. "Business, economics, and Christian ethics." In *The Cambridge Companion to Christian Ethics,* edited by Robin Gill, pp. 228-42. Cambridge, UK: Cambridge University Press, 2001.

Staley, Kevin M. "Happiness: The Natural End of Man?" *The Thomist* 53 (1989): 215-34.

Stoeckle, B. *"Gratia supponit naturam": Geschichte und Analyse eines theologischen Axioms.* Rome, 1962.

Tanner, Kathryn. *Economy of Grace.* Minneapolis: Fortress, 2005.

Tawney, R. H. *Religion and the Rise of Capitalism: A Historical Study.* London: John Murray, 1926.

Taylor, Charles. *Sources of the Self: The Making of Modern Identity.* Cambridge, MA: Harvard University Press, 1989.

Tierney, Brian. *The Idea of Natural Rights: Studies on Natural Rights, Natural Law, and Church Law, 1150-1625.* Emory Studies in Law and Religion, edited by John Witte, Jr. Grand Rapids: Eerdmans, 1997.

Torrell, Jean-Pierre, O.P. *Saint Thomas Aquinas.* 2 vols. Translated by Robert Royal. Washington, DC: The Catholic University of America Press, 1996-2003.

Tuck, Richard. *Natural Rights Theories: Their Origin and Development.* Cambridge, UK: Cambridge University Press, 1979.

Von Mises, Ludwig. *The Theory of Money and Credit.* Translated by H. E. Batson. New Haven: Yale University Press, 1953.

Wadell, Paul J., C.P. *Friends of God: Virtues and Gifts in Aquinas.* New York: Peter Lang, 1991.

———. *The Primacy of Love: An Introduction to the Ethics of Thomas Aquinas.* Mahwah, NJ: Paulist Press, 1992.

Ware, Kallistos. "The Way of the Ascetics: Negative or Affirmative." In *Asceticism,* edited by Vincent L. Wimbush and Richard Valantasis, pp. 3-15. New York: Oxford University Press, 1995.

Weithman, Paul J. *Justice, Charity, and Property: The Centrality of Sin to the Political Thought of Thomas Aquinas.* Ph.D. diss., Harvard University, 1988.

———. "Natural Law, Property, and Redistribution." *Journal of Religious Ethics* 21 (1993): 165-80.

Wheeler, Sondra Ely. *Wealth as Peril and Obligation: The New Testament on Possessions.* Grand Rapids: Eerdmans, 1995.

Williams, A. N. *The Ground of Union: Deification in Aquinas and Palamas.* New York: Oxford University Press, 1999.

Williams, Bernard. *Ethics and the Limits of Philosophy.* Cambridge, MA: Harvard University Press, 1985.

Williams, Rowan. "What does love know? St Thomas on the Trinity." *New Blackfriars* 82 (2001): 260-72.

Wood, Neal. *John Locke and Agrarian Capitalism*. Berkeley: University of California Press, 1984.

Worland, S. T. *Scholasticism and Welfare Economics*. Notre Dame, IN: University of Notre Dame Press, 1967.

Yearley, Lee H. "The Ascetic Grounds of Goodness: William James's Case for the Virtue of Voluntary Poverty." *Journal of Religious Ethics* 26 (1998): 105-35.

———. *Mencius and Aquinas: Theories of Virtue and Conceptions of Courage*. Albany: State University of New York Press, 1990.

Index

Anscombe, G. E. M., 94n.68

Aquinas, Saint Thomas: Aristotle, agreements with, 2, 4, 5, 8, 21, 30, 32, 35, 120, 183; on the church, 127-28, 130n.93, 145, 175, 180; economic teachings in modern scholarship, 1-2, 6, 35, 61-63, 68-76, 84-92; evangelical character of his thought, 2, 7, 8, 23, 26, 27, 29-31, 32, 107-8, 121n.60, 122, 132, 133-35, 142-48; modern economic analysis, anticipation of, 61-63, 68, 75, 89, 104; works: *Contra Impugnantes*, 142, 143, 145-48, 154-56, 169; *Contra Retrahentes*, 124, 126-27, 142, 151, 168, 174, 179; *De Malo*, 72, 74, 75; *De Regno*, 102; "On Buying and Selling on Credit," 92; *Summa contra Gentiles*, 129n.90, 147, 167, 170, 171, 176; *Summa Theologiae*, 11, 12, 56, 62, 72, 74, 75, 97, 99-101, 124-25, 133, 142, 143, 144, 145, 146, 148, 149, 153, 168, 171, 174

Aristotle, 18, 21, 86, 106, 148-49, 158-65, 166, 173, 185; and deferent dependence, 3-7, 8, 16, 18, 21, 28, 31, 32, 33, 35-37, 45-46, 49, 53, 66, 68, 71, 76, 111-12, 158, 159; modern economic analy-sis, anticipation of, 45n.37; works: *Metaphysics*, 45, 46; *Nichomachean Ethics*, 38, 39, 44, 46, 47, 51, 72, 85, 88, 164; *Politics*, 38, 39, 42, 44, 62, 97

Augustine, Saint, 57, 99, 113, 115, 118, 174

Backhouse, Roger, 50, 79, 91

Barter, 36, 38, 39, 47. *See also* Exchange

Beatitude, 8, 12, 15, 17, 106n.3, 122, 129, 160, 171, 174, 182

Begging, 140, 146, 149-50, 153, 155, 159, 160, 170

Berry, Wendell, 4-5, 16, 188n.12

Boyle, Leonard, 11

Cantalamessa, Raniero, 13n. 32

Capitalism, 1n.2, 27, 28, 48n.49, 55, 84, 188n.10

Cessario, Romanus, 109n.7

Charity, 2, 7-8, 13, 14, 29, 31, 33, 58n.81, 130-31, 134, 181, 183; Christ's, 9, 15n.36, 24, 30, 31, 120, 175-80; and filial fear, 109, 111; God's, 12, 15, 16, 53, 129, 166, 174, 175-80; order of, 115-20; as poor relief, 64-65, 80n.28; stages of, 123-29; as *telos* of human action, 18, 23, 30, 105, 122

Index

Franciscans, 9, 10, 14, 57-59, 130n.93, 133, 140; spiritual, 143-47, 159

Gerard of Abbeville, 126
Gregory the Great, 142, 178

Heilbroner, Robert L., 48n.49
Hibbs, Thomas S., 11-12, 177n.59
Hill, William, 110, 114
Hirschfeld, Mary, 40n.18, 43n.26
Hollander, Samuel, 89-90, 102
Hope, 2, 13, 106, 108, 111, 166; Christ's, 153; friars', 168, 171, 172, 174
Horst, Ulrich, 130n.93, 143, 145
Human nature, 8, 19, 24n.57, 24n.59, 113, 118, 161, 186; modern accounts of, 6, 10, 21-22, 27. See also Proprietary self
Humility, 2, 7, 8, 14, 58n.81, 110, 112, 113, 141, 149-53, 157, 191. See also Lowliness; Vulnerability

Irwin, T. H., 165n.24
Ius necessitatis (right of necessity), 63-66

James, William, 6n.8
Jerome, 114, 148, 157
Joachim of Fiore, 57, 130n.93, 144
Johnson, Kelly S., 14, 58n.81, 184n.2
Jones, John D., 154n.71, 156
Justice, 13, 14, 27, 29, 30, 32, 33, 49, 67, 73, 76-77, 78, 83, 84, 86, 92-93, 96-99, 102, 103, 105-7, 120, 168, 170, 183-85, 187; in exchange, 2, 8, 39, 53, 85, 97, 104. See also Just price; Usury
Just price, 1, 3, 28, 32, 67, 69, 71, 73, 82n.33, 84-104, 183, 184-85

Kaye, Joel, 60n.88, 184-85
Keenan, James F., 10n.19
Kerr, Fergus, 12, 148n.51, 172n.44

Ladakh, 25
Langholm, Odd, 62, 63, 64n.98, 68-69, 71, 75-79, 90-91, 97
Leo XIII, 1n.2
Liberality, 15, 64, 119, 147-48, 169
Little, Lester, 59, 137-38
Lloyd, G. E. R., 42n.23
Locke, John, 31, 35, 37, 53-67, 184n.2
Long, D. Stephen, 29n.69
Lowliness, 2, 3-16, 17, 25, 31, 110-13, 149, 151, 152, 157n.83, 165, 181-83, 191. See also Humility
Lowry, S. Todd, 45n.37

MacIntyre, Alasdair, 1n.2, 7n.12, 94n.68, 165n.25, 186-91
Macpherson, C. B., 52n.59, 53n.61, 54n.67
Market society, 3, 28n.68, 31, 49, 51, 52, 182, 183, 188; history of emergence, 6, 54-55, 59, 69, 135-41; and nature, 36, 53, 67; and nonmarket society contrasted, 32, 35, 37, 38, 41-42, 47, 50, 68; possibility of resistance to, 189, 191; and utility concept, 94. See also Exchange; Exchange value; Money
Marx, Karl, 27, 84, 85, 87, 88
Meeks, M. Douglas, 28n.68
Meikle, Scott, 39-40
Mendicancy, 9-16, 32, 108, 130n.93, 132-35, 140-51, 154, 170, 172, 174, 175
Milbank, John, 15n.36, 165n.26
Monasteries, role in economic changes, 136-38
Money, 29, 33, 60n.88, 97, 119, 136-37, 169, 183; Aquinas on, 70, 71, 72-73, 75, 76, 77-79; Aquinas on titles to interest from, 80-83; Aquinas on traders and, 100, 102; Aristotle on, 38-39, 41, 47-49, 86; as credit, 71, 76, 78, 79n.27; economy based on, 4, 14, 26, 137-38, 141; relinquished by mendicants, 139, 140, 141, 147, 150, 154. See also Exchange